Disagreements about justice are not simply academic matters. They create problems for practice and for policy-making. In a morally fragmented society in which 'nobody knows what justice is' issues such as wages policy, punishment and poverty become particularly difficult to handle. People striving to act justly are often uncertain how this might be done. Secular theories such as those of Rawls, Hayek, Habermas and modern feminist theorists, examined here, give some guidance for problems of justice that arise on the ground, but have serious limitations. This book argues that Christian theology, although it can no longer claim to provide a comprehensive theory of justice, can provide insights into justice – 'theological fragments' – which give illumination, challenge some aspects of the conventional wisdom, and contribute to the building of just communities in which people may flourish in mutuality and hope.

CAMBRIDGE STUDIES IN
IDEOLOGY AND RELIGION IO

CHRISTIAN JUSTICE AND PUBLIC POLICY

CAMBRIDGE STUDIES IN IDEOLOGY AND RELIGION

General Editors: DUNCAN FORRESTER *and* ALISTAIR KEE

Editorial Board: JOSÉ MÍGUEZ BONINO, REBECCA S. CHOPP,
JOHN DE GRUCHY, GRAHAM HOWES, YEOW CHOO LAK,
DAVID MCLELLAN, KENNETH MEDHURST, RAYMOND PLANT,
CHRISTOPHER ROWLAND, ELISABETH SCHÜSSLER-FIORENZA,
CHARLES VILLA-VICENCIO, HADDON WILLMER

Religion increasingly is seen as a renewed force, and is recognised as
an important factor in the modern world in all aspects of life –
cultural, economic, and political. It is no longer a matter of surprise
to find religious factors at work in areas and situations of political
tension. However, our information about these situations has tended
to come from two main sources. The news-gathering agencies are well
placed to convey information, but are hampered by the fact that their
representatives are not equipped to provide analysis of the religious
forces involved. Alternatively, the movements generate their own
accounts, which understandably seem less than objective to outside
observers. There is no lack of information or factual material, but a
real need for sound academic analysis. Cambridge Studies in Ideology
and Religion attempts to meet this need. It gives an objective,
balanced, and programmatic coverage to issues which – while of wide
potential interest – have been largely neglected by analytical investi-
gation, apart from the appearance of sporadic individual studies.
Intended to enable debate to proceed at a higher level, the series
should lead to a new phase in our understanding of the relationship
between ideology and religion.

A list of titles already published in the series is given at the end of the
book.

CHRISTIAN JUSTICE
AND PUBLIC POLICY

DUNCAN B. FORRESTER

New College, University of Edinburgh

CAMBRIDGE
UNIVERSITY PRESS

PUBLISHED BY THE PRESS SYNDICATE OF THE UNIVERSITY OF CAMBRIDGE
The Pitt Building, Trumpington Street, Cambridge CB2 1RP, United Kingdom

CAMBRIDGE UNIVERSITY PRESS
The Edinburgh Building, Cambridge CB2 2RU, United Kingdom
40 West 20th Street, New York, NY 10011–4211, USA
10 Stamford Road, Oakleigh, Melbourne 3166, Australia

First published 1997

Printed in the United Kingdom at the University Press, Cambridge

Typeset in Baskerville 11/12½ pt

A catalogue record for this book is available from the British Library

Library of Congress cataloguing in publication data

Forrester, Duncan B., 1933–
Christian justice and public policy / Duncan B. Forrester.
p.   cm. – (Cambridge studies in ideology and religion; 10)
Includes bibliographical references and index.
ISBN 0 521 55431 4 (hardback)   ISBN 0 521 55611 2 (paperback)
1. Christianity and justice. 2. Church and social problems.
3. Christianity and politics. 4. Political planning.
I. Title. II. Series.
BR115.J8F67   1997
261.8–dc21   96–48229 CIP

ISBN 0 521 55431 4 hardback
ISBN 0 521 55611 2 paperback

He has told you, O mortal, what is good;
and what does the Lord require of you
but to do justice, and to love kindness,
and to walk humbly with your God?

Micah 6.8 (New Revised Standard Version)

Contents

General editors' preface

Only twenty years ago it was widely assumed that religion had lost its previous place in Western culture and that this pattern would spread throughout the world. Since then religion has become a renewed force, recognised as an important factor in the modern world in all aspects of life, cultural, economic and political. This is true not only of the Third World, but in Europe and North America. At this moment surprisingly and unpredictably it is the case in the UK. It is no longer unusual to find a religious dimension present in areas of political tension.

Religion and ideology form a mixture which can be of interest to the observer, but which is in practice dangerous and explosive. Our information about such matters comes for the most part from three types of sources. The first is the media which understandably tend to concentrate on newsworthy events, without taking the time to deal with the underlying issues of which they are but symptoms. The second source comprises studies by social scientists who often adopt a func-tionalist and reductionist view of the faith and beliefs which motivate those directly involved in such situations. Finally, there are the statements and writings of those committed to the religious or ideological movements themselves. We seldom lack information but there is a need – often an urgent need – for sound objective analysis which can make use of the best contemporary approaches to both politics and religion. Cam-bridge Studies in Ideology and Religion is designed to meet this need.

The subject matter is global and this is reflected in the choice of both topics and authors. The initial volumes have been concerned primarily with movements involving the Christian religion, but it is intended that movements involving other world religions will be subjected to the same objective critical analysis. In all cases it is our intention that an accurate and sensitive account of religion should be informed by an objective and sophisticated application of perspectives from the social sciences.

The present volume explores the possibility that theology might have, even in a pluralist, secular society, a constructive and questioning contribution to make both to the theoretical discussions which undergird policy and to policy-making itself. In this huge field attention is focused on the central and much debated issue of justice. Specific theological insights emerge in chapters dealing with two major issues of concern in contemporary society, poverty and penal policy. Religion no longer occupies the place it did in western societies as an institution, but that does not mean it must be restricted to the private, domestic or leisure spheres of life. As this book goes to press politicians in the UK, as in the USA, are claiming that their policies are based on Christian values. Duncan Forrester, a social scientist as well as a professor of theology, makes a timely contribution to a new public theology.

DUNCAN FORRESTER AND ALISTAIR KEE
New College, University of Edinburgh

Preface

This book has been some time in gestation. As will be obvious to the reader it has been much influenced by the attempts of the Centre for Theology and Public Issues (CTPI) in the University of Edinburgh to relate theology and some specific questions on the public agenda. I am immensely indebted to a wide range of people from diverse specialities and life experiences who have contributed to the work of the Centre, and have challenged and stimulated my own thinking. It would not have seen the light of day had I not twice had the privilege of escaping for a time from my regular duties to the congenial and stimulating context of the Center of Theological Inquiry at Princeton. I am grateful to friends and colleagues at the Center and in the Divinity Faculty of Edinburgh University, who patiently read and commented on my drafts, particularly James Buckley, David Dawson, Nick Adams, George Newlands, Ian McDonald, Michael Northcott, Ruth Jonathan and Marcella Althaus-Reid. A very special debt of gratitude is due to my friend and former doctoral student, Dr Graham Blount, who gave me invaluable research assistance and from whose scholarship I have benefited a great deal. And the encouragement and stimulus of students and friends has meant a great deal to me. In this project, as in everything I do, I constantly learn afresh from my wife, Margaret, and from our children, Donald and Catriona, that the love which moves the sun and the other stars is the clue to the heart of what justice is.

Versions of parts of this book were given as the F. D. Maurice Lectures in King's College, London, in 1995 and as the Bishop Butler Lecture in the University of Bristol in 1996. I am grateful to Professor Colin Gunton and Professor Ursula King and their colleagues for the warmth of their welcome and the incisiveness of their constructive comments.

Introduction

This is a book about the practice of justice. The Christian position from which I write assumes that both knowing what justice is and doing justice are inherently and deeply problematic. Human beings have an in-built propensity to distort ideas of justice and manipulate them so that they are compatible with our interests and desires, and, at the extreme, disguise our selfishness and exploitation as morally acceptable. And even when we believe we know what justice is in a particular situation, and its demands are recognised as having a claim on us, we frequently fail to act justly. This is the perennial human predicament recognised by Paul when he wrote, 'The good which I want to do, I fail to do; but what I do is the wrong which is against my will.'[1] There is in us a deep in-built resistance to acting justly, and a reluctance to recognise justice. These are reinforced by the powerful forces of collective selfishness and by the human reluctance to face the realities of our motivation.

These constant elements in the human condition have been complicated in modern times by profound uncertainties about what justice is, which add to the difficulties facing those who try conscientiously to act justly. Because understandings of justice are so varied, volatile and confusing, administering justice and attempting to frame and apply policies that are just become perplexing and systematically confusing operations. In many areas of life, as I attempt to show, the problems for people on the ground who feel a calling to act justly and dispense justice

[1] Rom. 7.19.

I

are acute. Different and sometimes incompatible ideas of justice are presented to them as having claims on their allegiance, and in a situation where 'nobody knows what justice is', often enough it is the self-interest of the powerful that prevails because the trumpet-call for justice makes an uncertain sound.

The recent renaissance of grand theories of justice has resulted in much clarification and significant insights. There is no doubt that practitioners and policy-makers find some of these insights from modern theorists illuminating and helpful. But there are remaining problems which circumscribe the practical usefulness of contemporary theories of justice. Although many theorists appeal to some kind of consensus, there remain fundamental and irreducible incompatibilities between the various accounts of justice which are offered, and no generally acceptable criterion or procedure for resolving these differences is in sight. What is in dispute may be made increasingly clear in the course of discussion but, in the absence of some agreed standard, the choice between differing positions appears to be largely arbitrary. Only very rarely is an account of justice presented as resting on an ontology, or the nature of things, or as being in some sense 'true'.

A second problem affecting almost all the influential contemporary theories of justice is this: unlike pre-modern social theory, religious and theological factors, insights and narratives are systematically excluded as a matter of principle. It is not hard to see why this should be so. In western societies, at least, it is commonly assumed that religious believers are a declining minority of the population. Theological notions are assumed to be no more than the in-house discourse of religious communities; they have no general relevance, and cannot be presented either as public truth or as the nucleus of a consensus. Since the seventeenth century religion has been seen increasingly as divisive and arbitrary. And it is only fair to add that religious discourse has often been discredited by the way religious believers present it. People of integrity and intelligence who watch American TV evangelists, for instance, and derive from this their understanding of the Christian faith must find it impossible to regard religion and theology as serious contributors to public debate or to the common good. Believers, and theologians too, have made no small contribution to the discrediting of theology, and sometimes they have themselves willingly evacuated the public square, lacking confidence that they have anything to offer there.

It is the argument of this book that the gulf that has opened up between theology and theories of justice has impoverished both. I particularly want to argue that theories of justice which on principle eschew theology tend to end up narrow and thin, incapable of playing adequately the central role in society that justice should. They have quite specific problems in fulfilling the classical role of most accounts of justice in constraining the constant tendency to individual and group selfishness and disregard for the claims of the other. They need the kind of enrichment that theology – and perhaps one should add, tradition in general – can provide. But I am not proposing 'a [even less *the*] Christian theory of justice'. I doubt whether this would be possible or desirable in the present situation. And I am not convinced by attempts in the recent or more distant past to derive a comprehensive theory of justice from the Bible or the theological corpus. Rather I see theology's task as to offer 'fragments' – insights, convictions, questions, qualifications – some of which may be identified as true and as necessary complements or modifications or enlargements of conventional and commonly accepted accounts of justice. Hence the last section of the book is concerned with theological *fragments* rather than with some elaborate theory. Fragments, as I attempt to show, often have sharp edges, and it is often illuminating to know the quarry from which a fragment comes, for theological fragments come from a coherent view of reality and are related to one another. I do not apologise for this approach. Whatever the weaknesses in my own presentation, the procedure itself seems to me to have theological integrity and also to be specially appropriate in the conditions of postmodernity.

Perhaps I can illustrate the importance and the practical usefulness of the kind of broad, rich and tradition-related account of justice which I advocate in terms of the present process of reconciliation and nation-building which is taking place in South Africa. After a war or a revolutionary social change it is customary and natural for people to seek justice, meaning primarily redress and retribution. After the Second World War, for instance, the Nuremberg Trials and countless other legal processes against the perpetrators of atrocities took place. Justice demanded that they be brought to book. There is no doubt of that. But on the whole the offences of the victors were not noticed or dealt with. Justice was understood as the infliction of their just deserts upon the perpetrators of atrocities on the defeated side, and this was seen as having little to do with reconciliation, forgiveness, the healing of memories and the restoration of relationships. After the First World War the post-war settlement visited a punishment which was presumably believed to be just upon the whole defeated populace. The bitterness and recrimination which resulted fuelled the disputes which culminated in the Second World War. In neither post-war situation was the process of justice seen as restorative, as oriented to the future, as concerned with healing relationships, rather than settling past accounts. In neither case was the past dealt with adequately. And these instances represent the common response to offence, which in fact does not enable an escape from the cycle of recrimination and is rooted in a very partial account of justice which sometimes encourages retaliation and even vengeance.

In South Africa they are today attempting an alternative approach to their apartheid past, with all its atrocities and wounds and bitterness. They are using 'a different kind of justice',[2] which is restorative, and sees justice as 'indispensable in the initial formation of political associations' with forgiveness as 'an essential servant of justice'.[3] The issues of guilt and of retribution are not avoided or disguised, but put within a broader frame and a fuller understanding of justice and its end;

---

[2] The phrase is taken from an unpublished paper by the theologian Charles Villa-Vicencio who is at present serving as Director of Research in the South African Truth and Reconciliation Commission.

[3] Donald W. Shriver, *An Ethic for Enemies: Forgiveness in Politics*. New York: Oxford University Press, 1995, p. 6.

the truth must be faced and moral responsibility accepted; and the attitudes of the victims towards the perpetrators must be taken into account, for reconciliation is the ultimate aim. Perpetrators as well as victims need rehabilitation and healing. Justice and reconciliation rest on truth-telling which is in itself often healing. Villa-Vicencio explains the work of the Truth and Reconciliation Commission:

Our task is to explain and to understand, making every effort to enter the mind of even the worst perpetrators – without allowing those who violate the norms of decency to escape the censure of society. Guilt rests not only with those who pull the trigger, but also with those who wink as it happens. It does, however, rest decidedly more with those who kill. The one who plots and designs death may well be more guilty than the person who pulls the trigger. The person, too terrified or even too indifferent to restrain the killer, is at the same time surely less guilty than the killer who may simply have followed orders. An appeal to superior orders or to due obedience is insufficient ground for claiming immunity – and the concern of the T[ruth and] R[econciliation] C[ommission] focuses clearly on those who gave the command to kill and those who did the killing – not on fearful bystanders or 'passive collaborators'. It would at the same time be a betrayal of history to suggest that they alone supported the evils of apartheid and its crimes. To fail to identify the extent of the evasion of moral responsibility for the failures of the past is to undermine the possibility of there emerging a moral fabric capable of sustaining a society within which the atrocities of the past shall never again occur.[4]

The Commission holds hearings throughout the country under the slogans 'Revealing is Healing' and 'Truth the Road to Reconciliation', inviting people to tell their stories and listen to the stories of others for the healing of memories, for the redress of offences, for the overcoming of animosities and the lies that hostility engenders and, above all, quite consciously for the doing of justice.

An old woman has told of the disappearance of her fifteen-year-old son years before. She had heard he had been tortured and killed. She wanted to know what had happened, who had killed her son, and where. The only redress she asked for was to

4 Villa-Vicencio, Unpublished paper, p. 10.

know that they were sorry.[5] Then she could forgive and turn to the future.

Top generals of the old Special Branch and Army have approached the Commission to enquire whether, if they accepted responsibility for a list of atrocities, killings and illegalities, there was a possibility of amnesty: a tricky question, because cheap forgiveness is no forgiveness at all, and outrages the memory of the victims. But the Commission is entrusted with the power to grant amnesty where clear penitence is expressed in a willingness to make restitution, even if largely symbolic (the dead cannot be brought back to life), and where amnesty serves for the just healing of the nation.

The former President, F. W. de Klerk, has declared before the Commission: 'The National Party is prepared to admit its many mistakes of the past and is genuinely repentant . . . and we have gone on our knees before God Almighty to pray for his forgiveness.'[6] And when President Nelson Mandela visited a hearing of the Commission in Johannesburg the subject on which evidence was being given was atrocities committed by the African National Congress upon suspected dissidents in exile in Lusaka. The offences of the victors too need to be taken to the bar of justice and brought into the open, if healing and reconciliation are to be possible.

Where did this broad understanding of justice as something that is healing, relational, restorative come from? Informed commentators are quite clear: it is derived directly from the depths of the Judaeo-Christian tradition, and finds significant affinities and resonances within African traditional culture and society.

It is this kind of rich and profound understanding and practice of justice that this book seeks to examine and commend.

---

[5] 'The public hearings of the Truth and Reconciliation Commission (TRC) to date, indeed, show that the majority of victims and their relatives want little more than this basic knowledge': Villa-Vicencio, p. 6.

[6] *The Scotsman*, 22 August 1996.

PART I

Justice in dispute

CHAPTER I

Theology and public policy yesterday and today

What kind of Christian voice is appropriate in the public realm in relation to debates about public policy, and how might it be most appropriately articulated today? This question has a history which presents us with warnings, constraints and possibilities, some of which are certainly relevant to the present situation. Yet in many respects it is not only theology but also political theory and public policy-making, which face an unprecedented situation in the post-modern world, where many of the signposts and guidelines of the past seem to have lost their relevance and cogency. Together they are venturing into unknown territory. Has theology anything to offer in this venture?

The place of Christian theology in the public sphere is now increasingly believed to be problematic, and there is widespread suspicion that theology can no longer claim to be dealing with public truth rather than articulating the beliefs of a minority of 'cognitive deviants' in the population. There has also been a widespread failure of nerve among theologians, many of whom are content to walk away from the public square and devote themselves to the minutiae of technical scholarship with little conviction that theology might have something important and distinctive to offer to public debate. Having long since, and for good reason, abandoned its claim to be 'Queen of the Sciences', theology is often regarded as one of the less relevant humanities, or as having forfeited any right to a place in the liberal academy. Nor does theology have a recognised standing in the public arena; it has to earn the right to be heard by the relevance and cogency of what it has to say. 'The time is past',

writes Jeffrey Stout, 'when theology can reign as queen of the
sciences, putting each other voice in the conversation in its
place and articulating, with a conviction approaching certainty,
the presuppositions all share . . . [It] must take its place among
the other voices, as often to be corrected as to correct.'[1] Of
those who believe that theology should remain in the public
sphere, some hold that in order to do so it must speak the
'world's language'; others stress the need for a distinctive
Christian voice, speaking from the riches of the Christian
tradition.[2]

It is not only theology that faces major uncertainties today.
The public forum itself also has serious difficulties. The lack of
any widely acceptable overarching theory or ideology often
makes policy-making volatile and uncertain. There is increasing confusion and uncertainty about the bases for public
policy. Some argue for a pragmatic ad-hoc approach; others
seek a popular consensus around some theoretical core; others
again appear to support any policy they believe likely to win
votes. A variety of incompatible theories is on offer, and policy
often swings erratically as the favoured theory changes. Post-
modernists sustain a serious critique of the whole project of
developing universalising theories, regarding them as inherently oppressive.

A brief glance at some moments in the history of the relation
of theology and the political realm should prove helpful in
distinguishing what is perennial and what is specifically modern
in the situation that we face. And the record of the past may
provide some illumination for our present perplexities and even
perhaps some neglected resources for dealing with them responsibly and well.

THEOLOGY AND POLITICS IN THE PRE-MODERN WEST

In the past a theological approach, or at least an explicitly
theological dimension to the discussion, was almost universal in

[1] Jeffrey Stout, *Ethics after Babel*. Boston: Beacon, 1988, p. 164.
[2] For a fuller discussion of this, see my *Beliefs, Values and Policies*. Oxford: Clarendon,
1989, pp. 81–6, and later in the present chapter.

western political thought. Most major theologians as a matter of course wrote extensively on political themes, interpreting the structures, processes and choices of the political sphere within the horizon of the Christian narrative. Augustine of Hippo's political thought was – and is – immensely influential. He saw 'political theory as public confession'[3] – the presentation of a Christian perspective on the political process and on historical development which was in a real sense the proclamation of the gospel. Aquinas drew analogies between the one God's rule over the universe and the authority of pope and emperor over a society the hierarchical ordering of which reflected the divinely instituted structure of things. Luther developed Augustine's model of the two cities, the *civitas Dei* and the earthly city, into a full-blown doctrine of two kingdoms following different principles and fulfilling different functions, but both in their varying ways expressions of God's love and justice. Calvin provided a sophisticated doctrine of power and of sovereignty, out of which came a recognition of the need for checks and balances on the exercise of power by fallen human beings. These, and almost all major theologians as well, gave political advice, engaged with the current theoretical accounts of political life and sought to relate the gospel to the public realm. They saw addressing such issues as an unavoidable dimension of the theologian's vocation. The political significance of theology was almost universally assumed.[4]

This was, of course, not unrelated to the fact that the Christian church was such an immensely influential social – and political – institution. The church was itself a major power centre and a political community which was chronically in tension with the 'secular' authorities. During the so-called Dark Ages the churches developed and preserved patterns of

---

[3] This is the title of a fine book on Augustine's political thought: Peter D. Bathory, *Political Theory as Public Confession: The Social and Political Thought of St Augustine of Hippo.* New Brunswick: Transaction Books, 1981. See also Jean B. Elshtain, *Augustine and the Limits of Politics.* Notre Dame: Notre Dame University Press, 1995.

[4] For an example, see Gerald R. McDermott, 'Jonathan Edwards and the Culture Wars: A New Resource for Public Theology', *Pro Ecclesia,* 4:3 (1995), 268–80 and his book *One Holy and Happy Society: The Public Theology of Jonathan Edwards.* Pennsylvania State University Press, 1992.

fellowship and civility which provided templates for the development of social and political structures; some of these were inherited from the Roman Empire and the Constantinian settlement; others were more clearly rooted in the Judaeo-Christian heritage and the specifics of Christian faith.[5] In the struggles between pope and emperor, in the disputes between papalists and conciliarists about the proper decision-making structure of the church and in the efforts to relate the Christian tradition to the truths to be found in other systems, such as that of Aristotle, the main elements in future controversies in the West about society and the political order were forged. Even the most secular (if one may use that term without anachronism) of medieval theorists had to take account of Christian theology and of the Christian church. And theology learned to address the issues of society and of politics with increasing sophistication and seriousness. Policy and authority, it was almost universally assumed, were to be legitimated, authorised and shaped by Christian belief, and political theory was often seen as little more than a satellite of theology. That faith had to do with the shaping and guidance of society was assumed almost as universally as it is today in Islamic societies.

There were, however, distinctive tensions, problems and possibilities in Christianity fulfilling its political role quite in the way many people expected arising from the nature of the Christian narrative. Christianity resists, with more or less effectiveness, operating according to theories of the political function of religion which suggest that it should sacralise the political order and teach subjects to be obedient. It is interesting, for example, that when Aquinas wishes to draw analogies between divine and earthly power which are intended to shape and legitimate earthly authority he operates with a

---

[5] Sheldon Wolin argues that the early Christian communities were a major source for the revitalisation of political thought (*Politics and Vision: Continuity and Innovation in Western Political Thought*. London: Allen & Unwin, 1961, pp. 96–7). A similar argument is presented by Michael Mann in *The Sources of Social Power*. vol. 1, *A History of Power from the Beginning to AD 1760*. Cambridge: Cambridge University Press, 1986, ch. 10. Alasdair MacIntyre takes this as a precedent for the proper response to the new 'Dark Ages' which he believes are engulfing us today in his famous conclusion to *After Virtue: A Study in Moral Theeory*. London: Duckworth, 1981, pp. 144–5.

monotheistic rather than a trinitarian understanding of God. Trinitarianism, it has been suggested, would hardly have served his purpose, for it is more congruent with a communitarian, participative and loving understanding of power rather than a monolithic and top-down one. Again, the central narrative of Jesus, represented in every church by the ikon of the one unjustly crucified by the legitimate authorities who sacrificed justice to expediency, presented obstacles for any Christian theology of politics which gave an easy blessing to the existing political order. And eschatology – the expectation that all earthly orders were to be superseded – allied with the pervasive fear of idolatry tended to relativise the pretensions of any ambitious ruler to make absolute his position or ascribe eternity to his rule. No temporal order or earthly authority could be ascribed permanence or divine status; all stood under the authority of God and of God's law.

THE DAWN OF MODERNITY

It was not so much the Reformation as the ensuing Wars of Religion which signified the break-up of Christendom and which brought with them a new fragmentation which was social and political as much as it was ecclesiastical, theological and intellectual. For a time under the slogan of *cuius regio eius religio* efforts were made to maintain within states microcosms of Christendom. But uniformity was hard to retain internally, and the religious wars indicated how difficult it was for states to tolerate the existence of neighbours who followed another confession. The Wars of Religion led to a mounting despair of the capacity of religion to provide the basis for people to live together in peace. But still most people on both sides continued to believe that the state stood under God, that its policies must reflect Christian convictions, and that the exercise of power could best be legitimated with reference to the biblical narrative.[6]

---

[6] William Cavanagh argues that 'to call these conflicts "Wars of Religion" is an anachronism, for what was at issue in these wars was the very creation of religion as a set of privately held beliefs without direct political relevance'. But surely at the

This was clearly true also of legal systems. The law of Scotland, according to Viscount Stair's definitive *The Institutions of the Law of Scotland* (1681), was founded upon fundamental rational principles which were theologically validated as the law of God. These principles include: the conviction that 'God is to be adored and obeyed'; not only is the foundation of the law theological but also there are divine sanctions behind its observance; and the fundamental obligation on human beings is to obey God and his law which is expressed, if imperfectly as yet, in the law of Scotland and other legal codes.[7] Blackstone's classical *Commentaries on the Law of England* (1765) expresses a different understanding of law, but one that is no less theologically grounded. The law of England is rooted in the natural law which is confirmed and supported by God's revelation, but over time this law has unfolded in the experience of the English people under some kind of divine guidance. Other jurists affirmed in a general way that Christianity is written into the law of England.[8] Alasdair MacIntyre argues that despite the importance that Blackstone allocates to theology in his understanding of law, 'with the assertion that the foundation of ethics and law resides in the precept "that man should pursue his own true and substantial happiness", the theology becomes redundant, at most reinforcement, at least decoration, for what is asserted and argued for on entirely non-theological grounds'. MacIntyre sees the start of the secularisation of law in Blackstone. 'But in Stair's *Institutions* the theology cannot be excised without irreparable damage to the whole.'[9] Harold J. Berman has forcefully argued that in the past two generations the entire western legal tradition has been transformed by separating it from its ancient religious foundations. He quotes Justice W. O.

---

time they were seen as conflicts between rival forms of public religion, and the development of pietist and private forms of Christianity was largely in the aftermath of these wars? See ' "A Fire Strong Enough to Consume the House": The Wars of Religion and the Rise of the State', *Modern Theology*, 11:4 (1995), 397–420.

[7] *Institutions* I.1.1, cited in Alasdair MacIntyre, *Whose Justice? Which Rationality?* London: Duckworth, 1988, p. 227.

[8] Harry Potter, *Hanging in Judgement: Religion and the Death Penalty in England*. London, CSM, 1993, p. 10: 'Since the days of the jurist, Sir Matthew Hale, the dictum of the judges had been that "Christianity is part and parcel of the law of England".'

[9] MacIntyre, *Whose Justice?*, pp. 230–31.

Douglas saying, on behalf of the majority of the US Supreme Court as recently as 1951: 'We are a religious people, whose institutions presuppose a Supreme Being.' But no longer, Berman argues, are western legal systems and political institutions generally believed to be derived from the Bible, the Christian faith, or what the American Declaration of Independence called 'the Laws of Nature and of Nature's God'.[10]

Seeds of a new approach can be discerned early. Grotius (1583–1645) has aptly been used to mark a turning point, with his assertion that thought about politics and political action must proceed *etsi Deus non daretur*. Political commitments are now to be bracketed off from one's religious convictions; they belong in the private sphere; and public life must now be shaped by something other than the varying and often conflicting particularities of religious belief. Yet we must not give too simple a picture of a development which was slow and never more than patchy in its impact. It was easier to speak about two autonomous realms than to define them precisely; and it was almost impossible to control, let alone prohibit, traffic between them. We tend to read back too easy an account of the cumulative triumph of the secular.

It is true that Hobbes and Locke borrowed and reshaped in their very different ways medieval ideas of covenant and contract which enabled them to suggest that all rational beings, no matter what their religious persuasion, would agree to enter into a contract in order to provide peace and prosperity for all. But Hobbes devoted two substantial parts of *Leviathan* to detailed theological discussion: 'Of a Christian Commonwealth' and 'Of the Kingdom of Darkness'. These are rarely read by students today, but Hobbes scholars still debate vigorously whether Hobbes was in fact a religious believer and the influence of his theology on his political writings.[11] At the very

---

[10] H. J. Berman, *Law and Revolution: The Formation of the Western Legal Tradition*. Cambridge, Mass.: Harvard University Press, 1983, and 'Religious Foundations of Law in the West: An Historical Perspective', *Journal of Law and Religion*, 1:3 (1983), 3–43 (3–4).

[11] On this see particularly F. C. Hood, *The Divine Politics of Thomas Hobbes: An Interpretation of 'Leviathan'*. Oxford: Clarendon, 1964, and A. P. Martinich, *The Two Gods of 'Leviathan': Thomas Hobbes on Religion and Politics*. Cambridge: Cambridge University Press, 1992.

least he had an understanding of sovereignty which appears to
be a mirror image of Calvin's doctrine of the sovereignty of
God, and he was more than a little intrigued by theological
controversies, which he obviously considered important. Locke,
likewise, devoted much of his considerable intellectual energies
to theology, and the most impressive modern interpreter of his
political writings believes that they cannot be understood apart
from his theology.[12] Dunn writes: 'The entire framework of his
thinking was "theocentric" and the key commitment of his
intellectual life as a whole was the epistemological vindication
of this framework.'[13]

Kant and Rousseau saw duties as derived from the structure
of the moral law. But the roots of Kant's thought in his
Lutheran pietistic ethos are crucial and, for all his Enlightenment emphasis on the need to dare to think, he would have
been amazed to be regarded as someone who was moving
beyond and away from the Christian tradition into a new
secularism, hostile to or detached from religion.

Rousseau, like Machiavelli before him, shows little trace of
personal religious convictions, but both are obsessed with the
necessity for a civil religion. Christianity, Machiavelli teaches, is
a thoroughly bad civil religion. We would be better off – or the
ruler would be in a better position – were we to restore the old
religion of Rome. But as it is, we should probably strive to
adapt Christianity to serve political purposes as best it may. At
most what is happening here is a tentative and gradual
politically motivated endeavour to loosen political thought
from its embeddedness within biblical narrative, seeking to
locate it within a more universal and a less theistic story.[14]

Yet, having argued that the political thinkers of the seven-

---

[12] John Dunn, *The Political Thought of John Locke*. Cambridge: Cambridge University
Press, 1969. See also John Marshall, *John Locke: Resistance, Religion and Responsibility*.
Cambridge: Cambridge University Press, 1994.

[13] John Dunn, 'From Applied Theology to Social Analysis: The Break between John
Locke and the Scottish Enlightenment' in Istvan Hont and Michael Ignatieff (eds.),
Wealth and Virtue: The Shaping of Political Economy in the Scottish Enlightenment. Cambridge:
Cambridge University Press, 1983, pp. 119–36 (119).

[14] These issues have been addressed very creatively by Joshua Mitchell in his *Not By
Reason Alone: Religion, History and Identity in Early Modern Political Thought*. Chicago:
University of Chicago Press, 1993.

teenth and eighteenth centuries were not on the whole as 'secular' as many of their modern interpreters suggest, it is still true that these centuries marked a decisive turning point, a partly successful effort to transcend the divisive and particular-istic aspects of religion and to ground public policy on some sort of universalising reason. Gradually the initially pragmatic assumption that one should not have recourse to theological considerations because of the bitterness of theological divisions and the pervasive *odium theologicum* became a matter of prin-ciple. An independent universalising reason was to be the new criterion, arbitrator and motive. Enlightened people should no longer rely on the divisive and arcane particularities of theology because a better light was now available to illumine their path.

It is important, however, not to exaggerate the impact of the Enlightenment in 'emancipating' the secular from theological scrutiny and in privatising theology and religion. The Enlight-enment meant different things in different contexts; but in most situations theologians were welcome to continue to operate in the public sphere and in the academy, and they themselves made little, if any, effort to evacuate the public square. Alasdair MacIntyre is surely right in seeing Hume's scepticism as a subversion of the basically Christian thrust of the Scottish Enlightenment.[15]

R. H. Tawney has argued that with the rise of modern capitalism theology showed itself incapable of relating construc-tively to modern economic problems:

> In an age of impersonal finance, world markets and a capitalist organization of industry, [the church's] traditional social doctrines had no specific to offer, and were merely repeated when, in order to be effective, they should have been thought out from the beginning and formulated in new and living terms . . . Faced with the problems of a wage-earning proletariat, it could do no more than repeat, with meaningless iteration, its traditional lore as to the duties of master to servant and servant to master.[16]

---

[15] MacIntyre, *Whose Justice?*, ch. XV, pp. 281–99.
[16] R. H. Tawney, *Religion and the Rise of Capitalism*. London: Allen & Unwin, 1926, pp. 184–5.

Accordingly, Tawney suggested, Christian social thought took refuge, with relief, in a realm of inwardness and of feeling, believing that 'it is in the heart of the individual that religion has its throne, and to externalize it in rules and institutions is to tarnish its purity and to degrade its appeal'.[17] Tawney's view has now been shown by Waterman to be a serious misinterpretation, for in the eighteenth and nineteenth centuries theologians such as Malthus and Chalmers, Paley and Sumner were taken very seriously indeed by economists and policy-makers, and even up to Keynes some leading economists continued to be attentive to what theologians and church leaders had to say.[18] And in a quite different field – criminal justice – Timothy Gorringe has now shown that theologians' work on the atonement had significant impact on penal policy and practice well into the twentieth century.[19]

This quick and necessarily superficial historical review does not, of course, demonstrate the continuing necessity of a theological dimension in the discussion of policy-making and of public affairs. I simply want to show that in the past such a theological element has been present almost always, for good or ill. If there is today a strong effort to exclude theology from public debate, and an inclination on the part of some theologians to evacuate the public square, we are indeed in a new ball-game where the rules, procedures and resources are uncertain.

THE PUBLIC AND THE PRIVATE

The boundaries and the relationships between the private and the public spheres have been enduring questions for modern political theory. A central issue of post-Enlightenment political

[17] R. H. Tawney, *Religion*, p. 280. Waterman has shown the continuing importance of theologians in economics: A. M. C. Waterman, *Revolution, Economics and Religion: Christian Political Economy, 1798–1833*. Cambridge: Cambridge University Press, 1991.
[18] Note for example J. M. Keynes's detailed and positive response to William Temple's *Christianity and the Social Order*, cited in my *Christianity and the Future of Welfare*. London: Epworth, 1985, p. 35.
[19] See Timothy Gorringe, *God's Just Vengeance: Crime, Violence and the Rhetoric of Salvation*. Cambridge Studies in Ideology and Religion, Cambridge: Cambridge University Press, 1996.

thought has been how to hold together a society in which there is a diversity of world-views, where people have different and often conflicting convictions and commitments. In such a situation, where the forces of intellectual fragmentation are so strong, how is it possible to formulate and defend policies? Diversity and pluralism could not simply be wished away by the enlightened reason, at least in the short run, and there was an increasing tendency to see them as good in themselves. Perhaps, it was felt, a society in which there were many different understandings of the *good* might be healthy and dynamic if there was an adequate area of public agreement about the *right*. Was it conceivable that if religion were separated from the state and moved out of the public sphere that even its integrity might be more obvious and it might flourish more creatively? Perhaps autonomous politics and economics in the public sphere might provide more social goods than if their operations were tightly monitored by metaphysics or theology. The public sphere required a degree of consensus, contract and obligation if it were to operate effectively; but diversity in the private sphere could vitalise the whole society. Accordingly strenuous efforts were made to distinguish the public from the private sphere and to allocate as much as possible of persistent diversity to the latter.

The public and the private spheres were distinguished in various ways, but typically religion was allocated firmly to the private sphere as its proper locale, since religion was assumed to be concerned with feeling, subjectivity and domestic life, and to be arbitrary or intuitive so that it could not claim to be public truth or to pass the scrutiny of the dispassionate reason. The early theorists of civil society saw the dialectic between the public and the private as constitutive of civil society and believed this to be a healthier and more progressive social form than a society dominated by any monolithic orthodoxy, whether theological or political.[20] Yet, according to Seligman, 'civil society, as originally articulated in the Scottish

---

[20] On civil society see Adam Seligman, *The Idea of Civil Society*. New York: Free Press, 1992, and Jean L. Cohen and Andrew Arato, *Civil Society and Political Theory*. Cambridge, Mass.: MIT, 1992.

Enlightenment . . . owed . . . as much to Revelation as to Reason'. The 'unique, fragile and historically contingent balance between them' gave the original notion of civil society 'its overwhelming saliency'. But today this balance is, Seligman believes, irrecoverable.[21]

The Enlightenment reconceptualisation of the relation between the public and the private raises a number of problems. The first has been articulated recently most effectively by Seyla Benhabib. She argues that the public sphere has been defined in characteristically male terms, so that the forms of rationality which are operative and acceptable there rest on the male experience, and women and the female experience are disfranchised in the public realm and confined to the private and the domestic.[22] Experience which is in fact that of a particular group is privileged in the public sphere and declared to be universal. The autonomous self, which is the ideal, is disembodied and disembedded; this self belongs to no community and has no history. Virtues such as impartiality are stressed, and the self is seen as having no particular attachments or responsibilities. This, Benhabib argues, constitutes a massive impoverishment of the public sphere by evacuating it of values of care, generosity, altruism and sacrifice. These 'feminine virtues' are regarded as having a continuing place in the private and domestic sphere of face-to-face relations, but do not belong in the public sphere which is the locus of impartiality, justice and the universalising reason. I will return to this important line of argument later as it has great significance for the way we construe justice today. Meanwhile, Seyla Benhabib reminds us of the powerful feminist critique of the now customary distinction between the public and the private which continues to be hugely influential in social and political theory.

The second kind of unease with the common modern way of distinguishing the public and the private spheres has to do with

---

[21] Seligman, *Idea of Civil Society*, p. 6.

[22] Seyla Benhabib, *Situating the Self: Gender, Community and Postmodernism in Contemporary Ethics.* New York: Routledge, 1992, pp. 108–9. See also Jean Bethke Elshtain, *Public Man, Private Woman: Women in Social and Political Thought.* Princeton: Princeton University Press, 1981, and Susan Moller Okin, *Women in Western Political Thought.* Princeton: Princeton University Press, 1979.

the place of religion. It is presented in its sharpest form by political theologians indebted to the Marxist tradition, but it has important similarities with the feminist criticism. By being relegated to the private and domestic realm, it is argued, religion is confined to a sphere where it is no longer expected to contribute to public debate except on matters of the family and personal morality. It has been domesticated and deprived of public relevance and is no longer capable of feeding into public discussion disturbing memories or distinctive insights into the human condition. It is, according to the German political theologian, Johann Baptist Metz:

an extremely privatized religion that has been, as it were, specially prepared for the domestic use of the propertied middle class citizen. It is above all a religion of inner feeling. It does not protest against or oppose in any way the definitions of reality, meaning and truth, for example, that are accepted by the middle class society of exchange and success. It gives greater height and depth to what already applies even without it.[23]

Content, more or less, in its domestic captivity, religion passively legitimates the social and economic order to which it has capitulated. Metz argues that this privatisation and domestication of religion involves a serious distortion of the Christian religion, and deprives the public realm of the challenges and contributions which religion might and should offer.

A third problem with the customary distinction between the private and the public spheres is that it tends to make absolute secular pluralism and disfranchise any serious questioning of this order. Bruce Ackerman makes explicit a widely shared view. For the public realm to operate effectively, he suggests, it must be generally or universally accepted that no one conception of the good is better than another; 'while everybody has an opinion about the good life, none can be known to be superior to any other'.[24] This principle – virtually a dogma – of neutrality is the condition of profitable discourse about the best

[23] Johann Baptist Metz, *Faith in History and Society: Toward a Practical Fundamental Theology.* London: Burns & Oates, 1980, p. 45.

[24] Bruce A. Ackerman, *Social Justice in the Liberal State.* New Haven: Yale University Press, 1980, p. 11.

policies for a liberal society. Those who believe they have more than an opinion about what is true and good are entitled to their views, but must not pretend that they have validity in the public realm. If these views are theologically based, they will be met with bemused incredulity:

When somebody posits the existence of a disembodied Everyman . . . we are confronted with a different sort of problem – one of theology, not politics. For one thing, it is not clear what is meant when such spirits are said to exist; for another, it is not clear how they communicate their wants to us; for another it is not clear that they want bodies. This is not to say that a liberal . . . should take a hard materialist line on these issues. She need not deny the right of bodily citizens to define their life's meaning by positing the existence of spiritual beings and conducting dialogues with them. . . . [A]ny group of like-minded citizens have the right to worship God in any way they see fit. All such spiritual communions, however, must be founded on a *voluntary* decision by each communicant, affirming the value of his particular church's form of divine dialogue.[25]

The problem, of course, is that most groups of believers actually hold that they are encountering truth that is not merely true *for them*. And it is this view which cannot, in Ackerman's opinion, be admitted to the public realm. Public discourse for him can only be based on religious scepticism.[26] Neutrality and relativism are beyond question and the ultimacy of current forms of liberal democracy appears to be assumed. The barrier between the public and the private protects these assumptions from serious scrutiny and deprives the public realm of a resource which is capable of playing an important and constructive role.

The German social theorist, Jürgen Habermas, has produced a perceptive account of the genesis and predicament of the modern public sphere. For him the public sphere is essentially the place where 'public opinion' is formed by the conversation

---

[25] Ackerman, *Social Justice*, pp. 110–11.

[26] Brian Barry agrees with Ackerman on this. See his *Justice as Impartiality*. Oxford: Clarendon, 1995, pp. 177–88. Barry joins issue with Rawls's refusal to base his theory of justice on scepticism or indifference, and Nagel's suggestion of 'epistemological restraint' according to which one may be convinced of the truth of some doctrine but be unwilling to base policy upon it in a society in which some people reject the doctrine.

and debate of an engaged citizenry: it is 'a realm of social life where matters of general interest can be discussed, where differences of opinion can be settled by rational argument and not by recourse to established dogmas or customs'.[27] This provides a forum for what Habermas calls 'discourse ethics', and a place where practical political reasoning – something very similar to the practical wisdom of which Aristotle wrote – may take place.

The modern form of the public sphere emerged in England, Habermas argues, in the late seventeenth century, and was for long at the heart of healthy social and political life.[28] At least in principle the public sphere could provide a way of limiting and legitimating the activities of the state, and of rising above sectional and private interests to seek a collective good. The public sphere has, however, been impoverished and trivialised in recent times by certain aspects of modernity. For one thing there has been an increasing tendency to treat all issues in the public realm as technical rather than moral concerns, so that it is assumed that political problems are amenable to a quick fix on the part of a technician, an expert, rather than requiring a wrestling with the complexities and ramifications of the problem on the part of the wide range of people who are involved and bringing into the common discussion their varied insights and perspectives. This kind of discourse has been corroded by, among other things, the modern mass media which set up a spurious kind of communication which is more often a subtle manipulation of the public than the resourcing of a genuine debate.[29] The inherent democratic vitality of the public sphere has been seriously eroded. But Habermas continues to pin great hopes on the possibility of the restoration of its vitality and hospitality. In principle, he would welcome theology to the dialogue, and encourage participants to enquire whether theology might have a useful contribution to make.

[27] John B. Thompson and David Held (eds.), *Habermas: Critical Debates*. Cambridge, Mass.: MIT, 1982, p. 4.

[28] See J. Habermas, 'The Public Sphere' in Steven Seidman (ed.), *Jürgen Habermas on Society and Politics: A Reader*. Boston: Beacon, 1989, pp. 231–36.

[29] J. Habermas, *The Structural Transformation of the Public Sphere: An Inquiry into a Category of Bourgeois Society*. Cambridge, Mass.: MIT, 1988.

But he is not, to be honest, sanguine as to the possibility that theology might have something worthwhile to say.[30]

Increasingly in modern times, religion and theology are excluded more or less systematically from the public sphere and assumed to have little to say beyond personal and domestic matters.

THE RESURGENCE OF SOCIAL THEORY

In the 1950s there was much talk of what Daniel Bell called 'the end of ideology'.[31] The old gods of Nazism and Marxism had failed; now common sense and a pragmatic, hand-to-mouth approach was to be adopted – a piecemeal way of dealing with social problems rather than attempting to implement some blueprint of the new society. This was presented not simply as liberation from theories that had spawned actual tyrannies but as emancipation from a confused and moribund tradition of theoretical reflection on society. Karl Popper, in his immensely influential book *The Open Society and its Enemies* (1945), identified Plato, Hegel and Marx as the great apologists for inhumane tyranny. Philosophers, under the influence of linguistic analysis, for a time dismissed virtually the whole tradition of political philosophy as based on relatively simple linguistic or logical confusions. The public square was to be purged not only of theology but also of metaphysics and, indeed, the whole tradition of disciplined reflection on the nature and purpose of human society based on beliefs about human nature and the way things are. Now scholars and politicians could dismiss these grand speculations as so much hot air and get on with the rather prosaic, but vital, business of taking pragmatic political decisions independently of grand metaphysical or theological theories. These were now recognised to be not only misleading and pretentious, but also positively harmful.[32] Hitler had

---

[30] See Don S. Browning and Francis Schüssler Fiorenza (eds.), *Habermas, Modernity and Public Theology*. New York: Crossroad, 1992, especially David Tracy's and Habermas's contributions.

[31] Daniel Bell, *The End of Ideology*. Glencoe, Ill.: Free Press, 1960.

[32] A good example of this is T. D. Weldon, *The Vocabulary of Politics*. Harmondsworth: Penguin, 1953.

revealed the dangers lurking in the thought of Hegel and of Nietzsche; Stalin was the true heir of Marx. The grand theorists of the past could be shown to be confused and contradictory;[33] the legacy of such speculations was believed to be devastatingly destructive. The great totalitarian world-views of the twentieth century were adduced as evidence of the dangers of theory.

Marxism survived, compelling to some, particularly in Latin America and in the European academy, but deeply suspect to most. In eastern Europe and the Soviet Union it continued as a moribund official orthodoxy which commanded less and less heartfelt intellectual conviction. Outside continental Europe, only a few scholars like Leo Strauss, Eric Voegelin or Michael Oakeshott struggled to sustain an interest in the tradition of political philosophy as something of continuing relevance, because it taught that society must be based on truth and should reverence its roots. More or less in the wilderness, Friedrich A. Hayek warned of the dangers of the road to serfdom and simultaneously developed a system which sought to rehabilitate and update classical political economy as the theoretical base for a free society, while Popper denounced grand theory in favour of piecemeal social engineering. Around them conservative thinkers of some eminence gathered in the Mont Pelerin Society to look to the future when the pragmatic welfare consensus would collapse from its own inner contradictions.

Then, in the 1970s, to most observers' surprise, political theory revived. John Rawls's *Theory of Justice* (1971) was the harbinger; it sparked off an amazingly lively discussion and provoked a series of monographs. Along with Rawls, Nozick, Ackerman, Habermas, Walzer, Hayek and many others contributed to an immensely important and still on-going debate about justice. Some of these theories were quickly used consciously and systematically to undergird policy, two obvious examples being the use of Rawls by left-of-centre politicians in the States and Britain and the way Hayek came to the centre of the stage in Britain as the guru of Thatcherism, first through

---

[33] See, for example, John Plamenatz, *German Marxism and Russian Communism*. London: Longmans, 1951.

the Institute of Economic Affairs and then through Keith Joseph's endeavours to re-educate both politicians and civil servants.[34]

A partial reason for the revival of broad-gauge political theory was perhaps the apparent atrophy of the socialist tradition, which left an acute ideological vacuum. Few of the new theorists were far left-of-centre; the neo-conservatives gradually established a significant intellectual ascendancy. With the collapse of the Eastern Bloc, Francis Fukuyama captured the mood of the moment when he wrote of 'the end of history', which he saw in a profounder sense than Daniel Bell's as the end of ideology: liberal capitalist democracy has won, and no longer has any serious rivals, he argued.[35] Others see the present situation of the West as a far more problematic intellectual vacuum: not so much a victory of liberalism and decency as a house swept and garnished, ready for seven worse devils to enter in. Post-modernist thinkers rejected all universalising theory as inherently oppressive and believed that only a fragmentary approach could be truly emancipatory.

THE RESURGENCE OF CONVICTION POLITICS

There is a widespread and deep-seated conviction in the modern western academy that religion is either a trivial or a malign factor in political life. Both views – that religion is insignificant and that it is harmful – can be supported by evidence, which is not at all surprising when we are dealing with the multitudinous and varied phenomena which are labelled religious. The decline of religious observance and in the significance of the churches in the West has been dramatic except in the United States, where the situation is distinctly different. It is easy to argue that religion today in western countries is far less influential in the public realm than once it was. In addition, Freud and Marx and others have combined to suggest that the rhetoric and practice of religion are little more

[34] On this see Nick Bosanquet, 'Sir Keith's Reading List', *Political Quarterly*, 53 (1982), 324–41.

[35] Francis Fukuyama, *The End of History and the Last Man*. New York: Free Press, 1992.

than disguises for activities and processes which find their roots and their significance quite elsewhere. Religion is an infantile or pathological response to reality, or a subtle way of manipulating public opinion, or a reversed reality which perpetuates human alienation and bondage – assumptions such as these lurk around the atmosphere of many academic accounts of religion and its significance in the modern world. At most, religion could be no more than a cover for processes and interests which are in fact quite secular and different. Certainly the idea that religion might be more than reactionary and atavistic, that it might have a constructive and distinctive contribution of its own to offer, was unthinkable. Such attitudes are common but make it hard if not impossible to look clearly and dispassionately at the role of religion in public today.

In the actual realm of politics, the situation is markedly different from what it is in the academy. The days of the 1960s and 1970s when politicians like Harold Wilson in Britain dismissed as 'theology' any discussion of theory or principles seem very far away. For Wilson and his like, politics was a pragmatic matter, and they believed one could operate more or less independently of more general considerations. Politics was regarded as a process of horse-trading, in Horkheimer's words, 'mere business'.[36]

Then a great reversal took place. In Britain this was identified with the emergence of Thatcherism and its distinctive brand of 'conviction politics'. Margaret Thatcher and some of her closest colleagues felt the need to relate policies to principles rather than short-term expediency alone. A commitment to principles meant that one wanted to implement policies because they were right whether or not they would win the next election. And 'principles' involved reference to theory (in her case particularly the theories of Hayek) and also to religion. Margaret Thatcher took religion seriously, read her Bible and enjoyed discussion of theological themes. A determined effort

---

[36] Max Horkheimer: 'A politics which, even when highly unreflected, does not preserve a theological moment in itself is, no matter how skilful, in the last analysis, mere business.' Cited in Charles Davis, *Theology and Political Society*. Cambridge: Cambridge University Press, 1980, p. 133.

was made at one point to recruit 'court theologians', and the Institute of Economic Affairs began to concern itself with specifically theological issues.

A revealing episode was Margaret Thatcher's 'Sermon on the Mound', her address to the General Assembly of the Church of Scotland in May 1988.[37] This was quite unlike the bland congratulatory sentiments which had been contained in other ministerial speeches to the General Assembly. She presented a simple, clear and apparently biblical statement of what was obviously both her personal theology and what she believed were the Christian roots of her government's policies. Nothing quite like this had been heard in Britain from a Prime Minister since the time of Gladstone. What was she doing in that speech and what did she hope to achieve? She was certainly appealing over the heads of the church leaders, whom she found unsympathetic to her policies, to the rank and file of the churches – the General Assembly is a large gathering of some 1300 commissioners, half of whom are elders and the rest ministers. She was proclaiming her own Christian convictions and suggesting that her government was in the business of implementing a Christian view of things. She was appealing for understanding and support. Her speech was on the whole received unsympathetically: but that is not the point. The significant thing is that here we have a leading British politician who sees principles, and particularly Christian convictions, as central to a properly conducted public life, and who believes that the constituency of the churches is still politically immensely important.

Meanwhile there was a similar development on the Left. John Smith, who succeeded Neil Kinnock as Leader of the Labour Party, was a committed member and elder of the Church of Scotland who had always been known to take the implications of his faith for public life very seriously. He encouraged the remarkable resurrection of the Christian

---

[37] The text is available in various places, for instance in Hugh Montefiore's *Christianity and Politics*. London: Macmillan, 1990, pp. 86–90. Jonathan Raban has a detailed analysis of the speech in his *God, Man and Mrs Thatcher*. London: Chatto & Windus, 1989, pp. 8–20.

Socialist Movement, of which his successor Tony Blair is a leading member. Religious belief has returned in 'secular' Britain as a significant player in the public arena, to the bemusement of many intelligent observers.

The situation in the United States has different contours, but is no less paradoxical. On the one hand there has been an increasing tendency to suggest that the constitutional division between church and state requires American public life to be entirely secular, with prayers banished from the public schools and religious considerations disallowed in policy-making and in administration. On the other hand, the emergence of the New Christian Right has reminded us that religion not only continues to command the active allegiance of an amazingly high proportion of the American population but is also extremely influential in electoral politics. And what wins votes cannot but influence policy. Recent decades have seen the emergence of a whole range of pressure groups and think-tanks, and intellectuals of real eminence address the issues of religion in public life and the bearing of religion on public policy. [38]

While the concern to give political action a religious dimension has been growing, there has been a determined effort to redraw the constitutional boundary that divides church from state in such a way that religious considerations are systematically excluded from the public realm, religious arguments are declared improper in political debate, and religious activity is relegated to the private and domestic realm as, in Stephen Carter's words, 'a hobby'. Increasingly, Carter argues, it is assumed by people who should know better 'that religion is like building model airplanes, just another hobby: something quiet, something private, something trivial – and not really a fit activity for intelligent, public-spirited adults'.[39] It is seen as 'more a hobby than an object of hostility', and consistently trivialised. Religious arguments are not admissible to the public

[38] Among the more important studies of the American scene are Richard Neuhaus, *The Naked Public Square: Religion and Democracy in America*. Grand Rapids: Eerdmans, 1984, and Ian Markham, *Plurality and Christian Ethics*. Cambridge: Cambridge University Press, 1994.

[39] Stephen L. Carter, *The Culture of Unbelief: How American Law and Politics Trivialize Religious Devotion*. New York: Doubleday, 1993, p. 22.

square according to many influential theorists; in a liberal
society reference should only be made to axioms, standards and
principles that *all* can share – if such exist! Religious people
should voluntarily bracket off their private beliefs when they
enter public debate which must be conducted on strictly secular
principles.[40]

These developments raise in a sharp way issues which will be
our concern in this book. Can modern secular pluralism
provide the theories, insights and resources which are required
for the framing and implementation of public policy in a
modern democracy? Do secular theories on their own provide
an adequate basis for policy-making today? Is it in fact possible
to conduct debates on public policy in such a way that religious
and metaphysical insights are set aside, without a serious
impoverishment of the public sphere? It is not difficult to see
why intelligent, liberal people might wish to exclude religion
from public life. Religion has, indeed, often been divisive.
Religious views are frequently presented as if their proponents
have some privileged access to the truth which exempts them
from any need to show how the policies they propose might be
for the general benefit. Religion often goes with a kind of naive
idealism which pays scant respect to the facts of the case and
the constraints within which politics must operate; absolutism
in politics can be very destructive; simplistic utopias can be very
dangerous. All that may be admitted.

And yet, there is another line of argument that suggests that
a public sphere from which religion is excluded is deprived of a
great source of determination, hope and the vision 'without
which the people perish'. The strict application of this principle
would have excluded Martin Luther King's dream from American public life. Would a purely rational, liberal civil rights
movement have been anything like as effective in recruiting
enthusiastic and sacrificial support and pushing through change
in face of bitter resistance? Would the end of apartheid and the
building of a new South Africa have come more quickly and
more generously had Archbishop Tutu been confined to the

---

[40] Carter's whole discussion of these issues in contemporary America is particularly
illuminating.

pulpit and compelled to leave public affairs to the politicians? Can convictions, as against calculations of electoral advantage, be sustained in politics without the support of religious beliefs? Has secular liberalism shown itself as effective in naming and resisting great evils and appealing to conscience as religious movements, often small minorities, have shown themselves to be? Religion can generate passion in politics but, although passion can be destructive, a politics where 'the best lack all conviction' becomes a very evil thing.

A PUBLIC THEOLOGY FOR TODAY?

Is it possible for Christians to check their convictions at the entrance to the public forum without losing integrity? And if it is not, in a complex social and political situation in which it is clear that theology has been part of the problem and when it is by no means plain that it is widely recognised as being capable of offering a solution, is it possible that theology may have a modest but constructive and questioning contribution to make both to the theoretical discussions which undergird policy and to policy-making itself? Jeffrey Stout puts the issue into sharp focus:

Academic theology seems to have lost its voice, its ability to command attention as a distinctive contributor to public discourse in our culture. Can theology speak persuasively to an educated public without sacrificing its own integrity as a recognizable mode of utterance? . . . To gain a hearing in our culture, theology has often assumed a voice not its own and found itself merely repeating the bromides of secular intellectuals in transparently figurative speech . . . Can a theologian speak faithfully for a religious tradition, articulating its ethical and political implications, without withdrawing to the margins of public discourse, essentially unheard? Serious conversation with theology will be greatly limited if the voice of theology is not recognizably theological . . . Conversation partners must remain distinctive enough to be identified, to be needed.[41]

In response to such questioning a number of theologians, particularly in America, are attempting to produce a 'public

41 Stout, *Ethics after Babel*, 1988, pp. 163, 184.

theology', which is as it were specially designed to sail the seas of public debate. The term 'public theology' is itself a little striking. Most of its more articulate proponents are anxious not to be confused with the radical political theologians of Europe or with the liberation theologians, initially from Latin America and now from many countries and contexts around the world. These theologies address to their own contexts theologically grounded programmes which are consistently radical. In contrast, the public theologians are cautious about the very idea of a theological *programme* in the public sphere, and their inclinations are on the whole liberal or conservative rather than radical. They are more concerned with gaining an entrée to the existing public debates and being heard there, than with challenging the system or espousing any utopian cause.

Prominent among those who are attempting to define the nature and methods of 'public theology' is David Tracy. Tracy sees a necessity for theology to be sensitive to the three 'publics' it addresses: the church, the academy and the wider society. Each calls for a distinctive approach and specific emphases. The 'public theology' which particularly concerns us at present is that which is engaged in dialogue with the broader society and allows that society, at least to some extent, to set the agenda. The major concerns of that public theology which addresses what Tracy calls 'the public of society' are the organisation and allocation of goods and services, issues of social justice and of power and questions of culture.[42] For Tracy, public theology must present arguments and conclusions which may be examined by anyone independently of the specifics of a particular faith. This theology gains its right to enter the public arena, as it were, by accepting the standards of rationality and argument that are operative there.

At this point there arise two problems: it is now by no means clear that there *are* today generally accepted criteria of public rationality to which theology might conform; and a theology which eschews the offering of distinctive and perhaps challenging insights derived from its own heritage of faith on the

---

[42] David Tracy, *The Analogical Imagination: Christian Theology and the Culture of Pluralism.* New York: Crossroad, 1981, pp. 6–7.

grounds that they do not meet the standards independently set for public discourse may be both defrauding the public sphere of something that is true and important for it and simultaneously diluting its own message.[43]

Other public theologians, such as Ronald Thiemann, emphasise more strongly the necessity for a distinctively Christian public theology:

> Our challenge is to develop a public theology that remains based in the particularities of Christian faith while genuinely addressing issues of public significance. Too often, theologies that seek to address a broad secular culture lose touch with the distinctive beliefs and practices of the Christian tradition . . . In the process, the distinctive substance and prophetic 'bite' of the Christian witness are undermined.[44]

But there is also, Thiemann believes, the opposite danger – that a theology which is unable to move from the language of Zion to the language of the world will not communicate at all in public. And there is a third danger, which is this: there is a constant risk of theology being recruited to give support to dominant forms of discourse in the public sphere, so that the theologian sees things through the prism of his nation's interests or some influential ideology. The possibility that theology in the public realm might be part of what Foucault calls 'an insurrection of suppressed knowledges' is not easily accommodated.[45]

Thiemann and Robert Benne have recently developed public theologies on a Lutheran basis. Benne presents what he calls the 'paradoxical vision' of Lutheranism as full of relevant insights for the public realm, particularly as a corrective to an overly Calvinist stress in the past which has encouraged in recent times an optimistic social gospel and an exaggerated

---

43 See Tracy, *The Analogical Imagination*, and 'Theology, Critical Social Theory and the Public Realm' in Browning and Fiorenza, *Habermas*.

44 Ronald F. Thiemann, *Constructing a Public Theology: The Church in a Pluralistic Culture*. Louisville: Westminster/John Knox, 1991, p. 19. See also his forthcoming *Religion in American Public Life: A Dilemma for Democracy*. Thiemann's new book is an endeavour to implement the proposals in the earlier work.

45 Michel Foucault, *Power/Knowledge: Selected Interviews and Other Writings*. New York: Pantheon Books, 1980, pp. 81ff., cited in Lewis S. Mudge, *A Sense of a People: Toward a Church for the Human Future*. Philadelphia: Trinity Press, 1992, p. 120.

idea of what might be achieved through political action, which strangely came in the end to support approaches which were effectively Pelagian. The Lutheran paradoxical vision emphasises the limits of what can be achieved through politics in a fallen world. A sharp distinction between law and gospel provides an obstacle to any overidealistic endeavour to implement gospel norms or the ethic of the Sermon on the Mount in public life. A revised version of Luther's 'two kingdoms' doctrine provides a safeguard against theocratic projects and allows a proper degree of autonomy to secular realms while protecting the integrity of the church. Benne sums up:

The general presumption of the paradoxical vision is against direct action. The first has to do with the mission and integrity of the church. From the point of view of the paradoxical vision, the church's mission is not to wield power in the realm of the law, but to proclaim the gospel. True . . . the church is also charged with addressing the law to the society. This gives it warrant to engage in direct and intentional influence, albeit carefully and sparingly.[46]

Thiemann, as we have already seen, advocates a public theology which is rooted in Christian specifics, but although he is also a Lutheran, he is more cautious than Benne in calling on the Lutheran tradition of public theology. This, I think, is because he rereads the Lutheran tradition in the light of the struggle against Hitler in the 1930s and realises how easily leading proponents of that tradition were beguiled into passive acceptance or active support of Nazism by a conviction that qua theologians they could not address a word of challenge or rebuke to authorities who had an entirely independent mandate from God. Luther's doctrine of the two kingdoms can encourage a tendency to see the existing structure of things as a sphere of God's love and mercy, so that the crude facts of exploitation and suffering are sometimes overlooked. Thiemann, in an autobiographical passage, speaks of how shocked he was to discover that the theologians who had been presented to him in seminary as paragons of orthodoxy and

---

[46] Robert Benne, *The Paradoxical Vision: A Public Theology for the Twenty-first Century*. Minneapolis: Fortress, 1995, p. 217.

theological rectitude had compromised in the 1930s and colluded with Nazism. Robert Benne, in contrast, has moved steadily to the right in recent years and deploys a two-kingdoms theory for a fairly enthusiastic defence of capitalism.

This kind of 'public theology' has been criticised on a number of grounds. Liberationists regard it as little more than an ideological defence of capitalism, a kind of syncretism between Christianity and the mammon worship which they see as characteristic of modern industrial societies. Political theologians believe it is inadequately critical and see it as domesticated in the dominant culture. Others suggest that public theology has forgotten that the first task of the church is to *be* the church and thereby witness to an alternative, coherent set of beliefs and values in a world that has become disastrously fragmented. Only a theology which is rooted in the life of the community of faith and attempts as a 'church theology' to articulate a distinctive vision is worth hearkening to in the public realm; the public role of theology is essentially to confess the faith. Lewis Mudge describes this position:

[There are] those who say that the most important 'subjected knowledge' in modern Western culture is that of classical Christian faith itself. It is this faith, some say, which can both welcome the excluded and downtrodden, and, in a world of relativism, help human beings put their lives together around shared values. A valued tradition fully lived can then be free of the need to defend itself against reality definitions alleged to be held by all genuinely modern human beings. In this view, the Enlightenment vision of the world no longer has pride of place. The faith tradition can be the criterion of reality within which one lives, moves and has one's being.[47]

This last position, associated today particularly with names like Alasdair MacIntyre, Stanley Hauerwas, George Lindbeck and Hans Frei, is that with which I have most sympathy. If a choice were necessary, this is the position with which I would identify. But I do not think it is in fact necessary to make such a choice. Before recent decades, when theologians began rather nervously to attempt to delimit and define something called 'public theology' and give an account of its method,

---

[47] Mudge, *Sense of the People*, p. 80.

theologians simply by unselfconsciously doing as serious
theology as they could often exercised considerable impact in
the public realm. Reinhold Niebuhr who had such immense
influence both in US politics and in the study of international
relations is a case in point. His robust Christian realism
seemed to provide a more adequate account of the heights and
depths of human nature and a better way of discerning the
signs of the times than the main alternatives on offer. Karl
Barth likewise was a towering influence in the public realm in
Europe from the 1930s to the 1960s and an immensely
courageous leader in the struggle against Hitler – undoubtedly
a public theologian! He saw Nazism as *the* political problem of
the day for the churches as the result of a theological programme which he developed in the early 1930s. A theology
which faithfully followed its own agenda could not, Barth
believed, be other than political and prophetic. Barth's work is
an impressive account of the nature and priorities of a
Christian and church theology that takes both God's Reign
and the contemporary world with seriousness, but does not
allow the world to set the agenda.

This book is an attempt to explore the possibility that theology
might have, even in a pluralist, secular society, a modest but
constructive and questioning contribution to make both to the
theoretical discussions which undergird policy and to policy-
making itself. I concentrate on the central issue of justice,
outlining in the next chapter the present confusion about how
to understand and practise justice. In Part II I attempt to
ground the discussion in real situations and the issues which
arise for policy and practice by examining two particularly
complex, contentious and confusing areas of public policy –
poverty, and punishment with special reference to imprisonment – and enquiring whether there are theological insights
which may be constructively deployed in relation to them. In
Part III I examine some prominent secular accounts of justice,
asking whether any of them embody Christian insights in a
publicly accessible way and suggesting some of the issues which
arise in the transition from theory, through policy, to practice.

Finally, in Part IV, I suggest that there are distinctive Christian insights into justice which are commonly undervalued or neglected but can contribute constructively to policy-making and to practice.

'Nobody knows what justice is': the problem of justice in a morally fragmented society

POLICY-MAKING IN A MORAL VACUUM?

Barbara Wootton, the distinguished British social scientist, had for years been deeply involved in wage negotiations and in the development of official wages policies before she reflected on her experience in a magisterial study, *The Social Foundations of Wages Policy*.[1] In this book she carefully examines the procedures that have been followed in wage negotiations and the criteria that have been used. She correctly concludes that the central issue in the determination of wages is a moral rather than simply a technical matter and discerns the impossibility of reaching just determinations of wages in a context where 'nobody knows . . . what justice is'.[2] In this field, which is paradigmatic of so many areas of public policy today, she claims that 'moral actions must be performed without moral principles to guide them'.[3] This means that those who attempt to determine wage levels are 'engaged in the impossible task of attempting to do justice in an ethical vacuum',[4] for almost all the arguments deployed are in some way or other moral, but this is not commonly recognised, and there is no consensus about the nature of justice.

This situation, Wootton argues, is inherently conservative. In the absence of an agreed notion of justice against which

---

[1] Barbara Wootton, *The Social Foundations of Wages Policy: A Study of Contemporary British Wage and Salary Structures*. London: Allen & Unwin, 1962. Cf. her later *Incomes Policy: An Inquest and a Proposal*. London: Allen & Unwin, 1974.
[2] Wootton, *Social Foundations*, p. 162.
[3] *Ibid.*   [4] *Ibid.*, p. 120.

wages and differentials may be measured, the easiest thing is to appeal to history and precedent, striving on the whole to maintain real levels of remuneration and differentials between occupations more or less as they have been. Change needs to be justified, and proper and convincing justification is impossible in an ethical vacuum; the easiest course then is to maintain the status quo, and recognise precedent and public opinion as having some kind of moral authority. Even arguments that suggest that a worker is entitled to a wage that may keep the worker and dependents in a decent and acceptable style of life tend to assume the present social hierarchy and conventions: a dustman is 'entitled' to a great deal less than a high court judge because society continues implicitly to accept the legitimacy of such differences. And challenging huge salary rises awarded to themselves by the directors of privatized utilities while their workforce is being slimmed down or offered trivial increases is awkward in the absence of a generally accepted standard of just remuneration. The beneficiaries tend to reply to the critics that they are earning what they are worth, that the determination of wages is a matter for the market, and that they are earning what they deserve according to this amoral standard.

Barbara Wootton concludes that Parliament should in effect declare what justice is – in our kind of society there is no other way of settling the issue. The principles of justice are therefore to be decided politically, the legislature acting as a moral forum on behalf of the community.[5] This was indeed tried, and tried repeatedly, without marked success, whenever the legislature interested itself in wage negotiations and in industrial disputes about pay, which happened frequently.

The whole business of wage control and wages policy has almost collapsed since Wootton wrote. The proposal to leave the moral issue to the legislature was aptly derided by Hayek. That Parliament can determine what is just, he argued, is 'an illusion', and no one in their senses would wish to defend 'the atrocious principle . . . that all rewards should be determined

---

[5] This position has been developed theoretically by John Rawls in his argument that justice as fairness is a political not a metaphysical matter, as we shall see in ch. 5.

by political power'.[6] But Hayek's own solution is no more
satisfactory: the determination of wages, he believes, should be
left to the market, and is quite independent of considerations of
justice or fairness, provided some procedural rules of just
dealing are followed.[7] This is really another way of saying that
wage levels should be determined by power and scarcity, apart
from moral considerations.

Wages policy and its collapse, leading to present confusions
and uncertainties, is a good instance of how the lack of any
general agreement on justice leads to clearly identifiable problems for policy-making in a variety of fields and often leaves
conscientious policy-makers in a quandary. A vital component
is missing; there is no commonly acceptable account of justice.
But the most serious problem in this situation is not for the
policy-makers, who are normally powerful and prosperous
people with an assured position and a great deal of security, but
for the poor and the weak. In the absence of an agreed account
of justice a major moral constraint on the powerful and the rich
has been removed and the rewards tend to go predominantly to
those who are already prosperous. And in addition, as Barbara
Wootton pointed out, a major incentive for questioning the
present ordering of society has been neutralised. Similar problems are to be found in many other policy areas, a few of which
we will explore later in this book.

Barbara Wootton depicts:

a community determined, on the one hand, to fix standards of
remuneration that are fair and just as well as economically defensible;
and no less determined, on the other hand, to abdicate from all
responsibility either for the definition of general policy or for the
actual decisions made – a community, in fact, which is engaged in the
impossible task of attempting to do justice in an ethical vacuum.[8]

But she, and we, are not really dealing with a vacuum in which
'nobody knows what justice is'. The problem is that too many
people and groups have too many differing and often contra-

---

[6] F. A. Hayek, *Law, Legislation and Liberty*, vol. II: *The Mirage of Social Justice*. 2nd edn.,
   London: Routledge & Kegan Paul, 1982, p. 75.
[7] This will be investigated further in ch. 6.
[8] Wootton, *Social Foundations*, p. 120.

dictory accounts of justice. Too many people think that they know what justice is, and usually they understand justice in a way that suits their individual or collective interests. In such a context we have not so much a vacuum as an arena, or even a battlefield. Ideas of justice are wrought into weapons to be used in social conflict; each side claims that their case is just; and there is no arbitrator or judge to resolve the matter. Ideas of justice are used but rarely any longer have the capacity to limit or restrain. What has been lost is a sense of the objectivity of justice, that justice is grounded in reality, not simply something we devise and use for our purposes. But lurking in the wings is still an important, almost universally shared, conviction: self-interest, aggression, acquisitiveness, oppression, inequality need to be justified, and if they cannot be, then they are disguised. On this primal awareness something perhaps could be built, even if we are indeed in an age when, as Alasdair MacIntyre suggests, 'modern politics [and he would I think include modern economics] is civil war carried on by other means'.[9]

MacIntyre may help us to explore the implications of the situation exemplified for us by Barbara Wootton. There is today, MacIntyre suggests, no criterion to which appeal may be made. Politics is a game of sorts, but there are few recognised rules, no goal and no referee. The theorists and the philosophers may be good at explicating and exploring arguments and positions, but they have become incapable of resolving serious disputes:

Modern academic philosophy turns out by and large to provide means for a more accurate and informed definition of disagreement rather than for progress towards its resolution. Professors of philosophy who concern themselves with questions of justice and of practical rationality turn out to disagree with each other as sharply, as variously, and, so it seems, as irremediably upon how such questions are to be answered as anyone else. They do indeed succeed in articulating the rival standpoints with greater clarity, greater fluency, and a wider range of arguments than do most others, but apparently little more than this.[10]

[9] MacIntyre, *After Virtue*, p. 236.
[10] MacIntyre, *Whose Justice? Which Rationality?* London: Duckworth, 1988, p. 3.

This failure on the part of the philosophers to make progress towards resolving matters is not simply an academic problem (although it is that) but it raises very serious issues for society, and for policy in particular. The academics are no better than anyone else in making progress in this field. Their efforts mirror, and may even exacerbate, the confusions of society. MacIntyre famously sees the present situation as a more or less total breakdown, a new Dark Ages.

This book has more narrow concerns than MacIntyre's and is more hesitant to be apocalyptic. I will concentrate on the implications for policy-making and the knock-on effects on society and human flourishing of the present confusions about justice. These present serious problems, for theory as well as for practice, for ideology as much as for policy-making. Although I will take the existence of the church as a community of faith that is orientated towards the God of justice with profound serious-ness, and in that sense welcome MacIntyre's increasingly strong call to attend to the insights cherished in communities of shared faith, I am not wholly convinced by his suggestion that, 'What matters at this stage is the construction of local forms of com-munity within which civility and the intellectual life can be sustained through the new dark ages which are already upon us.'[11] Such communities may be of great importance for the sake of the whole, but must not be regarded as bolt-holes from the public debate about justice, community and human flourishing.

In her work on wages policy, Barbara Wootton was, largely unknowingly, operating within the parameters of traditional just wage thinking. Virtually all the considerations, arguments and criteria which figure in her books also appeared in the earlier discussion centuries before on how to determine a just wage. These factors are also to be found featuring in the debate whenever there is a really serious endeavour to seek justice in remuneration. Hayek is well aware of this history. He sees Wootton and others as striving to restore 'the futile medieval search for the just price and the just wage', which was necessarily abandoned when it was 'recognised that only that

---

[11] MacIntyre, *After Virtue*, pp. 244–5.

"natural" price could be regarded as just which would be arrived at in a competitive market where it would be determined not by any human laws or decrees but would depend on so many circumstances that it could be known beforehand only by God'.[12] Yet medieval and early modern just wage theory was a sophisticated form of analysis which took with equal seriousness the moral and the empirical or economic dimensions of the issue. Perhaps it did not so much collapse because it was the pursuit of a will-o'-the-wisp, as Hayek suggests, as find itself incapable of operating when its keystone was removed. This keystone was the belief that there is an objective, true standard of justice which constrains the exercise of power and protects the weak. When this is cast aside and rejected, it is not surprising that attempts to embody justice in specific spheres of life become increasingly doomed to frustration.

SOCRATES AND THE SEARCH FOR JUSTICE

This kind of situation is not without precedents apart from the Dark Ages, *pace* MacIntyre. What does seem to be new is the enthusiasm with which many thinkers embrace pluralism and a kind of moral relativism as if this were an achievement rather than a predicament. Wootton, in contrast, laments that today 'no Socrates walks the streets pestering us to find out' what justice is.[13] This may serve to remind us that Plato's *Republic* is set within an Athens which is full of new ideas, differing morals and various religions. The dialogue starts at the first festival of a new goddess, imported from the East. This setting is to remind us of the crucible of new ideas that was Athens at that time, the relativism and pluralism that was in the atmosphere. To Socrates and his closest disciples this is no tolerable resting place. For him, an easy tolerance of moral diversity can only be based upon ignorance and lack of commitment to rigorous enquiry. Throughout the dialogue, Plato is attempting to establish the existence of objective moral truths, and to reassess their nature.[14] Socrates enters into the dialogue with three

---

[12] Hayek, *Mirage*, p. 75.   [13] Wootton, *Social Foundations*, p. 162.
[14] Julia Annas, *An Introduction to Plato's 'Republic'*. Oxford: Clarendon, 1981, p. 10.

fundamental assumptions: that there is such a thing as justice; that it is not easy to know what justice is; and that knowing and doing justice involves a kind of ascesis, indeed a rigorous and lifelong engagement with the powerful psychic and social forces that obstruct our grasping and implementing or carrying out of justice. These are indeed assumptions that have been almost lost sight of in most modern accounts of justice – that justice has an objective existence and that there are powerful obstacles to even a partial realisation of justice.

In the early stages of the dialogue we encounter both efforts to reaffirm justice as a traditional value, wholly concerned with validating the existing order of things, and Thrasymachus' view that justice is the interest of the stronger. Plato in the persona of Socrates gradually works through to an architectonic account of justice: it is justice that holds a decent society together; it is the central, framing virtue of the good society and of the good soul alike. This understanding of justice cannot validate the existing order of things and can only be adequately expressed through the constitution of an ideal state and the kind of citizens who compose that state. This makes Plato 'a strange kind of conservative', for he teaches that 'the needs of justice require wholesale moral reform'.[15] According to Popper's rather hasty judgement, this makes Plato the father of totalitarian thought.[16] Judith Shklar, in contrast, affirms Plato's instinct that taking justice seriously involves adopting a critical distance from the present order:

According to Plato the normal model is an expression of deep ignorance. It is a bad joke, a circus. Far from altering unjust people, it only encourages and maintains their habits. Injustice, truly understood, is a condition of misdirected psychic energy, in which aggressive and acquisitive impulses expand, while rationality can barely assert itself . . . The normal model, far from establishing justice, merely allows personal disorder to become socially systemic; it simply perpetuates injustice.[17]

---

[15] *Ibid.*, pp. 12–13.
[16] See Karl Popper, *The Open Society and its Enemies*. London: Routledge, 1945.
[17] Judith Shklar, *The Faces of Injustice*. New Haven: Yale University Press, 1990, pp. 21–22.

Justice for Plato, then, has an objective existence; its function is to constrain and channel the use of power, and it shapes society in the light of an underlying account of human nature. Plato's analogy between the soul and the state reminds us that justice has to do with human flourishing: society and the individual exist for one another. Plato thus presents a broad, thick account of justice, what Julia Annas calls 'an expansive theory of justice', as the central virtue of the good society, which contrasts with the thinness of so many modern accounts. Despite Plato's lack of an historical sense and the pervasiveness of his hierarchical mind-set, so that justice for him cannot be the vindication of the victims, he still has much to teach us in our in some ways similar situation.

One last lesson to be drawn at present from Plato has to do with the search for consensus. The Socratic dialectical method might seem to involve such a quest. And in a sense it does. But Socrates' goal is truth, and he is not surprised when Cephalus, the representative of the uncritical acceptance of tradition and the customary ordering of things, withdraws with dignity from the debate, and when later on Thrasymachus, who is thirled to the radical falsehood that justice is the interest of the stronger, storms off in frustration. Socrates is seeking the truth about justice, not an easy blending of views; he hopes to carry his disciples with him on his journey, but he recognises that an intellectual *metanoia* is involved for all of them: minds and attitudes, personality and behaviour are to be changed. All views cannot be accommodated because of the constraint of truthfulness. Falsehood and evil have to be excluded, even if they are disguised as justice. No highest common factor consensus is possible for him.

Periodically in history societies have gone through basic uncertainties about justice and morality not *toto caelo* different from our problems today. But what is unusual about the modern situation is the apparent breakdown of the belief in an objective grounding of justice and in the need for an ascesis of justice, because human beings and human societies do not easily manifest justice. Everyone purports today to know what justice is, but hardly anyone believes that it is real, and something to be treated with reverence. This is hardly surprising, since most people and groups claim the right to define justice for themselves without challenge from others. Or they shrink justice to something thin and manageable which can exercise little moral constraint and is not hard to implement. In such a context the search, sometimes rather desperate, for a consensus which is a gathering together of what most people think and claims no further objectivity is understandable, but quite other than Plato's search for the truth about justice or indeed the main thrust of the pre-modern quest for justice.

THE PRIORITY OF INJUSTICE

Perhaps the question of justice is the wrong place to start. Those who concern themselves with careful discussion of the nature of justice are mostly the powerful and the influential. In courts of law it is the judges who determine what is just. This is not at all surprising, since justice is centrally about the deployment of power and position, and the kind of issues we have been discussing affect, or ought to affect, the powerful in their decision-making and in their implementation of policy. Yet there is a danger that reflection on justice which is through the prism of the interests of the powerful may be blind to the broader dimensions of justice. Thought about justice which is top-down tends to be elitist and partial, allowing the concerns and perspectives of the powerful to crowd out whole categories of people and disregard their insights and their interests. Plato, for instance, excluded slaves, workers and women from the whole discussion. Their destinies were to be decided for them by others, and women were to be allowed to be rulers in the ideal society only on condition that they set aside all particular attachments and anything that distinguished them from men. Greek thought was pre-eminently from the standpoint of the aristocracy, of the elite, even when it was most critical of the tradition. Socrates can even say (in the *Gorgias*) that 'injustice is the greatest of evils to the doer of injustice', and that doing injustice is a greater evil than suffering injustice.[18] Those who

---

[18] *The Dialogues of Plato*, tr. Jowett. New York: Random House, 1937, vol. 1, p. 570.

suffer from the injustices of the powerful have been pushed to the margins of concern; it is the effects of doing injustice on the unjust person's soul that really matter.

The exclusion of women from the discussion of justice until recent times has been cogently represented as a main cause of serious impoverishment and narrowing of the understanding of justice, in as far as justice becomes a matter of observing rules rather than a personalised care for community and human flourishing. Assumptions about the gender structure of society, it is argued, have fed into the understanding of justice, and women's experience has typically not been taken into account.[19] Other groups also have been excluded from the discussion and their experience disallowed, so that they can neither enrich nor challenge the dominant account of justice and their interests are often not fully reckoned with. Slaves, women and workers in the ancient Greek city state are the obvious examples. But in modern times we have to ask about the relation to theories of justice of women, aliens, people with learning or physical difficulties, and especially the poor. If the voice, the protest, the anger of the victims of injustice is not heard in a theory of justice, that theory shows itself to be radically deficient. Judith Shklar writes: 'No theory of either justice or injustice can be complete if it does not take account of the subjective sense of injustice and the sentiments that make us cry out for revenge.'[20] These are issues to which we shall return frequently in this book.

Although from ancient times it was recognised that injustice, acknowledged and experienced, sparked off a concern with justice, few theorists gave more than cursory attention to injustice.[21] This tended to give the impression that injustice is

---

[19] On this, see especially Benhabib, *Situating the Self*; Susan Moller Okin, 'Reason and Feeling in Thinking about Justice', *Ethics*, 99 (Jan. 1989), 229–49, and 'Justice and Gender', *Philosophy and Public Affairs*, 16 (1987), 42–72; Carol Gilligan, 'Do the Social Sciences have an Adequate Theory of Moral Development?' in R. Haan *et al.* (eds.), *Social Science as Moral Inquiry*. New York: Columbia University Press, 1982, pp. 33–51; and Judith N. Shklar, *Faces of Injustice*.

[20] Shklar, *Faces of Injustice*, p. 49.

[21] Hayek gives a useful bibliography to show that 'the primary character of injustice' has been a central concern from the beginning: Hayek, *Mirage*, pp. 162–4. But this reflects his view that injustice is the breaking of a rule, or the upsetting of a natural equilibrium, the latter a position that has been common since Anaximander, who

some kind of occasional aberration from a more or less normal state of justice, that injustice is not systemic and deeply rooted, but something like weeds in the garden which can, with persistence, be eliminated. 'The normal model of justice [writes Judith Shklar] does not ignore injustice but it does tend to reduce it to a prelude or a rejection and breakdown of justice, as if injustice were a surprising abnormality.'[22] Hidden in this assumption is the important conviction that justice, not injustice, is the characteristic of the proper ordering of things; confusion arises when people assume, as they often do, that this proper order is more or less the present structure of power. The liberation theologians and the feminists remind us that for multitudes of people today injustice, not justice, is the substance of their daily experience. Not surprisingly, this makes the victims of injustice excited and angry. People get angry about injustice, but 'it is difficult to get excited [about justice] except when it is refused or threatened'.[23] The voice of those who suffer from injustice is indispensable in the search for justice.

INJUSTICE AND MISFORTUNE

The scope of injustice is the subject of much dispute and misunderstanding. Some, like Hayek, develop a minimalist account of justice and argue that ill-fortune or distress which is not the direct consequence of a human act intended to harm one cannot be unjust. Thus the poor and the losers in market transactions can complain about bad luck or ill fortune, but cannot suggest that they are the victims of injustice or indeed victims at all. The immediate consequence is that they are not entitled to redress from those who have done them harm or from society on account of their misfortune. But the boundaries between misfortune and injustice are by no means as clear-cut

taught that injustice was the strife of opposites in which a proper balance was destroyed, and Heraclitus who saw conflict as the necessary path to justice as balance. See John Burnet, *Early Greek Philosophy*. London: Black, 1908, pp. 56, 71, 160, and *Greek Philosophy: Thales to Plato*. London: Macmillan, 1914, pp. 22, 48.

[22] Shklar, *Faces of Injustice*, p. 17.

[23] A. D. Woozley, 'Injustice', *American Philosophical Quarterly*, Monograph 7. Oxford: Blackwell, 1973, pp. 109–22 (109–10).

as most people suppose, as has now been superbly demonstrated by Judith Shklar. She argues that we tend to see misfortune rather than injustice when we are unwilling to act, to respond to a problem. We see the homeless beggar as the agent of her own misfortune when we are unwilling to help. If we see her as a victim of injustice she has a claim on us, especially if in any sense we are the agents of the injustice that has caused her plight or have at least colluded in the policies which have brought her to where she is. It is easier to see misfortune rather than injustice in the situation of others, yet we are quick to claim that ill-fortune that comes our way is in fact injustice, so that we are entitled to a remedy.

The definition of the boundary between injustice and misfortune is often a political matter. Judith Shklar instances the Irish Potato Famine of 1846–7 as an example. The official British line was that the fecklessness of the Irish had to a large extent brought their problems on themselves, so that they were unable to cope with the new potato blight. Since they were suffering from misfortune rather than injustice, they were not entitled to a remedy from government or, indeed, from their landlords. Assistance or any form of governmental intervention, whether delivered in terms of charity or of justice, would simply, it was argued, make the situation worse by exacerbating the idleness and dependency of the Irish peasantry which was substantially responsible for the crisis in the first place. It would be good for them to cope with their own misfortune by themselves. Certainly, nothing must be done or said to suggest that injustice rather than misfortune was involved. Similar arguments are repeated again and again about the poor and the unemployed: they are not victims; they are not entitled to help or to remedy; they do not deserve assistance; the problem has nothing to do with justice; and the broader community or the government is not responsible. The solution to misfortune is self-help. Thus the powerful frequently disguise their injustices.

Judith Shklar writes:

The very distinction between injustice and misfortune can sometimes be mischievous. It often encourages us to do either too much or too little. That something is the work of nature or of an invisible social hand does not absolve us from the responsiblity to repair the damage and to prevent its recurrence as much as possible . . . On the border between misfortune and injustice we must deal with the victim as best we can, without asking on which side her case falls.[24]

It is, in other words, unjust to refuse a remedy when such is within our power to those whose distress is not the result of an act of injustice. The victims of natural disasters have a claim in justice on our help. To say otherwise leads directly to quite immoral conclusions.

For the religious believer there is an added complication in drawing a neat boundary between misfortune and injustice. The question of theodicy, of justifying the ways of God to human beings, is unavoidable. For a person of faith, an 'act of God' is not simply removed from the sphere of justice; indeed, in as far as God is involved, the issue of justice must arise. Accordingly it is inevitable that theists should struggle with the question how a just and loving God can allow the Holocaust, or the death by cancer of a child, or some great natural catastrophe. How can faith in God survive the evils of existence? In fact an underlying cry of anguish and search for a just God and a structure of meaning in face of evil is an almost universal human quest. The alternative is a naturalistic fatalism or the kind of resignation which religion itself has sometimes encouraged. Behind it all is the need which Christian faith paradoxically both fulfils and denies for a justice which is wrought into the heart of things and gives some kind of ultimate meaning and hope even in face of disaster.

THE VICTIMS' VOICE

An affirmation of the priority of injustice does not necessarily lead to a special concern for the victims of injustice, for their situation, for their feelings and for their insights. Much ethical thinking has emerged in aristocratic circles, where the paucity of victims is not altogether surprising. Plato, as we have seen, suggested more than once that 'to do injustice is more to be

[24] Shklar, *Faces of Injustice*, p. 55.

avoided than to suffer injustice', for 'injustice is the greatest of evils to the doer of injustice'.[25] Such sayings can be interpreted in two ways. It is true that the victim in the sense of anyone outside the aristocratic and educated circle has disappeared from view, to be replaced as the *real* victim by the perpetrator of injustice. At first glance this seems outrageous and self-indulgent. But it is also surely a way of putting in a powerful form the moral gravity of acting unjustly. It is not in fact far from the teaching of Jesus' parable of the Rich Man and Lazarus. The earthly appearance is that it is Lazarus, the victim, who is in the problematic situation. But the denouement of the parable in Abraham's bosom reveals that it was the Rich Man who was all along in moral and spiritual jeopardy and who is finally condemned. Both Plato and the gospel seem at pains to underline the gravity of unjust behaviour and to suggest that, despite appearances, it is the victim who is ultimately privileged.

This is not to deny Shklar's argument that religion, like philosophy, has often conspired to conceal the victim from view by an inordinate concentration on the destiny of the oppressor's soul and by an encouragement to resignation on the part of victims of injustice, because non-resistant suffering is understood as the vale of soul-making. 'The pursuit of eternal salvation', Shklar writes, 'may function just like the aristocratic quest for self-perfection in shunting the victim of injustice aside.'[26] But it is not only in removing the victim from view that the Christian tradition sometimes has offended. It has also frequently taught the victims of injustice to glory in their victimhood, confident that ultimately the balance will be set aright.

Religion has colluded too in the pervasive tendency to blame the victims for the injustices from which they suffer. It is comfortable for the rich and powerful if they can believe that the victims are themselves responsible for their plight, that they are receiving their just deserts rather than acts of injustice at the hands of others. The Victorian distinction between the

---

[25] *Gorgias*, in *Dialogues of Plato*, vol. 1, pp. 587, 570.
[26] Shklar, *Faces of Injustice*, p. 32.

deserving and the undeserving poor constantly reappears. The undeserving are feckless, improvident, dishonest, unreliable; they deserve whatever happens to them. The deserving uncomplainingly strive to pull themselves up by their own bootstraps; they do not agitate or accuse, nor do they see themselves as victims. Those who blame the victims thereby disown responsibility for what has befallen them and do not recognise an imperative to help. Charity may be in order, but there is no question of restitution or reparation. The issue is no longer seen as one of justice or oppression; it is simply a matter of running adjustments to a social order and patterns of behaviour which are themselves regarded as basically just.

Victims, of course, often do not recognise themselves as such. Most people are reluctant to accept the label 'victim'. It has degrading connotations. It took the modern feminist movement to spread widely a conviction that women are victims of injustice. Victims often internalise the ideology of the oppressors. Slaves in the ancient world or in America in more recent times, Blacks under apartheid in South Africa, colonised peoples in almost any colony you care to name, frequently echoed the voice that told them their situation was right and proper, that it was good for them, that it was what they deserved, above all, that it was just.

In a classic empirical study, W. G. Runciman examined the feelings of acquiescence or resentment among the poorer sections of English society. One would suppose that in an unequal society those near the top of the social pyramid would be relatively content, and those near the foot would be dissatisfied and would believe that the system which involved deprivation for them was unjust. But all the evidence suggests that 'many people at the bottom of society are less resentful of the system, and many nearer to the top are more so, than their actual position appears to warrant'.[27] This kind of discrepancy between the situation of a group or an individual and how that situation is understood and assessed can be

[27] W. G. Runciman, *Relative Deprivation and Social Justice: A Study of Attitudes to Social Inequality in Twentieth-Century England.* Berkeley: University of California Press, 1966, p. 3.

interpreted in various ways. In a strongly hierarchical society like India, Brahminical Hinduism provided a variety of ways of justifying the social order: the main caste groups and their hierarchical ranking were part of the created order and therefore the system was itself divine and beyond question; each person fitted into a rung in the hierarchy which reflected achievements and failures in a previous life and was therefore just in the longer view despite the apparent injustices of the present life. Karma was a just system of rewards and punishments working within a social order which was itself morally neutral.

Social groups which felt unjustly treated have characteristically rejected such systems of thought, converting to another more egalitarian religion, presenting a myth that originally they were of high status of which they have fraudulently been deprived, presenting themselves as 'Dalits', the original owners and inhabitants of the land who have been cheated of their proper rights by incomers, or embracing a modern secular and egalitarian ideology.[28]

The situation Runciman discovered in England was in some ways similar, although rather less complex. Some people and groups who might be expected to express a vivid sense of resentment at their condition professed themselves quite content; others who in some cases appeared to enjoy more than they deserved were envious of a reference group above them and saw their own condition as unjust. The way forward in such a confusing situation was, Runciman argued, to have recourse to a theory of justice which provided criteria for judging more or less objectively whether groups or individuals were or were not being treated unjustly. Runciman opted for a Rawls-type theory of justice. In chapter 5 we will be considering Rawls's theory in more detail. Meanwhile we should simply note the importance of Runciman's conclusion that social policy depended upon having an account of justice which has some claim to objectivity; it could not simply be based on people's fluid sense of deprivation or opinions or feelings.

[28] See my *Caste and Christianity*. London: Curzon, 1980; and Louis Dumont, *Homo Hierarchicus*. London: Paladin, 1972.

The pioneering educational work of Paulo Freire in Latin America was devoted to helping poor peasants and slum-dwellers to name and possess their world, initially through basic education in literacy. Freire saw his task as enabling poor people to understand their true situation which was one of oppression, disfranchisement and injustice. Although Freire's influential work has been denounced as being driven by a quasi-Marxist ideology with which participants are subtly indoctrinated, it is none the less important as a reminder that it is not enough to base a theory of justice even on the untutored apprehensions of the victims.[29] We must seek some further objectivity, even while agreeing with Judith Shklar that 'No theory of either justice or injustice can be complete if it does not take account of the subjective sense of injustice and the sentiments that make us cry out for revenge.'[30]

A CHRISTIAN VOICE IN PUBLIC POLICY?

In a situation which may be a moral vacuum where 'nobody knows what justice is', or perhaps an arena full of conflicting voices, Christians claim to know what justice is. Their voices may be discordant, some more certain than others, some simply reflecting conventional secular opinions, some basically confused. But it is hard to take the source documents and the history of Christian faith seriously without affirming that this tradition has some things to say about justice. Christians, that is, believe that they know something about justice, and that this something must in a sense be true, objective and reliable if it is grounded in Christian truth. At least Christians should believe that they know where to look to find out what justice is and how to come to a deeper understanding of justice, for God is the God of justice as of love, and coming to know God and God's justice involves a distinctive form of ascesis through *metanoia*,

---

[29] See Paulo Freire, *Pedagogy of the Oppressed*. Harmondsworth: Penguin, 1972, and *Cultural Action for Freedom*. Harmondsworth: Penguin, 1972. A critical account of Freire is Dennis P. McCann, *Christian Realism and Liberation Theology: Practical Theologies in Creative Conflict*. Maryknoll: Orbis, 1981.

[30] Shklar, *Faces of Injustice*, p. 49.

repentance, change of mind, and through the effort to love God and neighbour and to do justice. Like Socrates, then, Christians can affirm that they know that there is such a thing as justice and that they know something of where to seek for it, and how to carry on the quest. They do not need to claim that they know a great deal about justice or that they can formulate a Christian theory of justice to set alongside other theories. They simply believe that if they are orientated in mind and action towards the God of justice they should have insights, questions and challenges to contribute to the on-going discussion about justice in our society today.

They are also aware of the dangers of self-indulgent talk. Karen Lebacqz is right to suggest that 'All the talk about justice today may not bring us any nearer to making justice a lived reality.'[31] The doing of justice is, for Christians, more important than getting our ideas straight. Indeed a main strand in the tradition suggests that only through loving and doing justice do we come to know God, and therefore to understand more deeply what justice is and the claim of justice upon us. This is why Christians are sometimes suspicious of *theory*. They know how easily it can become an excuse for inaction, a disguise for selfishness, a reason for failure to respond to the cry of the neighbour for justice. But they also know that unreflected activism can be a temptation, even for policy-makers.

I remember at an international ecumenical gathering listening to a long and carefully reasoned disquisition on justice delivered by a distinguished German theologian. After some time, a group of Latin-American women who had been becoming visibly impatient and angry burst out: 'We know what justice is – it is bread for our children. All this theorising is irrelevant.' The professor was nonplussed at first, and then it became clear that he was irritated by an intervention that he regarded as being beside the point, irrelevant to the serious academic exercise on which he was engaged. He tried, without success, to silence the angry women. They resented his bland assumption that he and his like should first sort out an

---

[31] Karen Lebacqz, *Justice in an Unjust World*. Minneapolis: Augsburg, 1987, p. 7.

acceptable theory of justice, and then, in the light of this achievement, people could consider what to do about hungry children in Latin America. They did not believe that detached academics really had the capacity to appreciate the reality of injustice and the urgency of doing justice. Accordingly, they thought his theorising went awry. The professor, for his part, while not without his share of intellectual arrogance, was justifiably suspicious of unreflected activism, of the danger of Christians neglecting the tradition of their faith and of the impossibility of basing policy entirely on spontaneous impulses to reach out to the victims of injustice. The mutual incomprehension of the two parties was sad. For a serious practical Christianity needs to relate to the tradition and to the world by way of careful and informed critical reflection, and Christian theologians should surely see their intellectual efforts as more a service of the poor and simple, of the victims and of the church, than a self-justifying academic game.

Konrad Raiser, the General Secretary of the World Council of Churches, has identified the problem we are addressing. Increasingly ecumenical pronouncements, he says, have concentrated on cries of protest against manifest injustice arising in various fields of social conflict. But these are hardly ever related to 'a consistent theory which integrates convincingly the biblical understanding of justice and is critically related to the contemporary debate among social philosophers, political scientists and lawyers'. Ecumenical statements characteristically are calls to protest and to action, or denunciations of specific injustices, and few attempts are made to define the sense of justice that is operative, either in relation to the Bible and Christian theology on the one hand, or to the way justice is understood in contemporary philosophy and jurisprudence on the other hand.[32]

There is no doubt that a serious Christian account of justice must attend very closely to the cry of the victims and see this as a major resource rather than a distraction from the task of

---

[32] Konrad Raiser, 'Reflections about Social Justice within the Ecumenical Movement' in H. G. Reventlow and Y. Hoffman (eds.), *Justice and Righteousness*. Sheffield: Sheffield Academic Press, 1992, pp. 154–5.

developing an account of justice. Karen Lebacqz is right when she says: '[J]ustice is experiential before it is theoretical. There is no "theory" of justice prior to the lived experience of the people. Theory is a "second act", following experience.'[33] It may not always be easy to recognise who the victims are, and victims often do not wish to be labelled as such. But the voice of the victims should be treated as a primary and privileged insight into the nature of injustice, which must not be pushed aside. Only those who take the side of the victims can really attend to their cry and hear the depths of their suffering and their anger. Those who are alongside are the ones who can hear; those who attend to the victims encourage them to speak. What is heard is often cries of protest, confused, passionate, sometimes misdirected. The Judaeo-Christian narrative, because it speaks of a God who attends to the cry of the oppressed, has often actually encouraged the oppressed to cry out. But Christian intellectuals, as typical modern academics, have sometimes regarded the cry from below as a distraction from their studies rather than a resource, as something that challenges the standards of detachment, impartiality and objectivity which should characterise serious study rather than something that enriches them with relevance and grounds them in a privileged field of experience.

Today we all, like Lesslie Newbigin, 'hear a long cry of anguish and distress. Who can be deaf to this cry?'[34] Although there may not be much that is specifically Christian in a longing for justice as such, although Christianity can whet the appetite for justice, it is good if we seek a response to the cry that is shaped by the Christian faith. Perhaps the task at the start is that of articulating the cry so that it is heard:

> Open your mouth for the dumb, for the rights of all who are left desolate.
> Open your mouth, judge righteously, maintain the rights of the poor and needy.[35]

---

[33] Lebacqz, *Justice in an Unjust World*, p. 65.
[34] Lesslie Newbigin, 'Whose Justice?', *Ecumenical Review*, 44 (1992), 308–11 (308).
[35] Prov. 31.8–9 (RSV).

Intellectuals are to take the side of the needy; there is no such thing as unbiased scholarship. But taking sides and providing a kind of megaphone for the cry of the needy does not exhaust the Christian responsibility. We need to find ways of seeking justice and responding actively to concrete situations of injustice which are shaped by the Christian tradition.[36] This involves disciplined reflection, starting with a hermeneutic of suspicion, questioning theories and interpretations with an eye to their actual functions, and trying to probe below the surface to the deeper realities of oppression and injustice. This is no modern project without historical precedent; religion has often been fundamentally at odds with received interpretations of justice and injustice, with the whole conventional wisdom.[37] The issues of justice must be related to the framework of Scripture and the whole biblical narrative, as well as to contemporary social analysis. This kind of approach not only provided an intellectual resource in the past for movements of social change and protest against injustice but also generated in the days of Christendom careful theories of the just price, the just wage, the just war and so forth, which were all intended to protect the poor and weak and constrain the selfish doing of injustice, holding up the stringent demands of justice in public policy.

Within the churches today there is a dangerous tendency to recycle tired and overidealistic slogans which in fact inhibit a proper sense of what can be done, and of the value of 'doing good in minute particulars'. One of the more notable of such slogans was coined at the Vancouver Assembly of the World Council of Churches in 1982: 'Without justice for all everywhere we shall never have peace anywhere'.[38] Sloganising and passing resolutions does not in fact change things, especially

---

[36] I am uneasy about Glenn Tinder's suggestion that we should 'give up the ideal of the just society' while responding to specific injustices, and indeed 'rebelling' against injustices. In the Christian tradition it is those who 'seek a city' and have a hope for the coming Kingdom who are likely to be most responsive to particular injustices. It all depends on the way one understands 'the ideal of the just society'. See G. Tinder, *The Political Meaning of Christianity: An Interpretation*. Baton Rouge: Louisiana State University Press, 1989, pp. 64–8.

[37] Shklar, *Faces of Injustice*, pp. 24–6.

[38] D. Gill (ed.), *Gathered for Life: Official Report of the 6th Assembly of the World Council of Churches*. Geneva: WCC, 1983, p. 132. This type of ecumenical thinking has been

when these statements are seen not as part of a deep and costly commitment to justice, but as the pronouncements of people who delude themselves that they are innocent by denouncing evils 'out there' in which they believe themselves not to be implicated and for which they have no responsibility. But for all that within the Christian church disturbing memories and hopes of a more just future are nurtured and in a world where there is much callousness about the sufferings of others and where most people do not care as much about justice as they pretend, there is the constant reminder that we were slaves in Egypt, delivered by the God who heard our cry and responded to it. The Christian church is, or ought to be, about empathy with those who suffer, sensitising people with the divine compassion to the needs of their neighbours. And despite the compromises of centuries, Gustavo Gutierrez was right when he said, 'Justice and right cannot be emptied of the content bestowed on them by the Bible.'[39]

Such an account of justice is to be embodied not only in words but also in the life of the church, which is called to be 'an agency of God's justice', as Lesslie Newbigin explains:

In its liturgy it continually relives the mystery of God's action in justifying the ungodly. In its corporate life and the mutual care and discipline of its members it embodies (even if very imperfectly) the justice of God which both unmasks the sin and restores relation with the sinner. In its action in the society of which it is part it will seek to be with Jesus among those who are pushed to the margins. But in all this it will point beyond itself and its own weakness and ambivalence, to the One in whom God's justice has been made manifest by the strange victory of the cross . . . It can continually nourish a combination of realism and hope which finds expression in concrete actions which can be taken by the local community and more widely, which reflect and embody the justice of God.[40]

Such, ultimately, is the Christian gift to public policy, and the basis of the Christian witness in the public realm.

---

roundly, and not entirely fairly, criticised by Ronald Preston in *Confusions in Christian Social Ethics*. London: SCM, 1994.

[39] G. Gutierrez, *The Power of the Poor in History*. London: SCM, 1983, p. 211.

[40] Newbigin, 'Whose Justice?', p. 311.

'As Christians,' writes Stanley Hauerwas, 'we will speak more truthfully to our society and be of greater service by refusing to continue the illusion that the larger social order knows what it is talking about when it calls for justice.'[41] But we also have to clarify the account of justice which lies at the heart of Christian faith and experience and see whether it may be constructively deployed in relation to tricky issues of public policy, which have such deep impact on human flourishing.

The second part of the book starts from the assumption that theory – and theology as a kind of theory – must be rooted in practice and experience. Only out of reflection on lived experience does clarification come. The discussion hinges on two particularly contentious policy areas – poverty and imprisonment as a form of punishment – and argues that in each of these areas there are some distinctively Christian insights and resources which are often neglected but may play an important role today if recognised as in some sense 'public truth'. These insights arise out of real experiences of confusion, uncertainty and oppression, and they come more as fragments, clues, questions, cries, than as a coherent system or a theory. Sometimes they may provide real illumination and suggest the way forward; often they give support and encouragement to those grappling with injustice and struggling to humanise structures that have become oppressive, divisive and degrading.

[41] Stanley Hauerwas, *After Christendom?* Nashville: Abingdon, 1991, p. 68.

PART II

Policies and practices

In chapter 2 we saw how Baroness Wootton argued that great difficulties arise for those involved in wage bargaining when nobody knows what justice is, when there is a fundamental uncertainty about whether an objective standard of justice exists, when there is a moral vacuum. In this Part I examine in some detail two important policy areas in which these problems may be exemplified. What happens to policy-makers, to those responsible for implementing policy, to people within a system attempting to work with integrity in the fulfilment of a vocation, to those whom the system or practice is intended to serve or help or change if there is fundamental uncertainty about justice, if society is morally fragmented, if serious-minded people feel that a moral vacuum exists? And what kind of resources are available to help in such confusing situations? Are there in these areas relevant insights and resources drawn from the tradition of Christian reflection on justice which might be helpful?

CHAPTER 3

Punishment and prisons

Prisons are major social institutions, key components in any modern system of criminal justice, and they are expected to be agencies of justice on behalf of society. Various understandings of criminal justice and of social justice are expressed in policies and practices of imprisonment. Yet at times when there is much uncertainty and confusion about what justice is, people become unclear what prisons are for, what they are intended to achieve and how they should operate. What happens in prisons shows remarkably clearly the problems that arise when there is pervasive uncertainty about what justice is, and issues of justice are raised in particularly sharp form for all those involved in imprisonment and the operations of the criminal justice system.

UNCERTAINTIES IN PENAL POLICY

In 1985 I was involved in a day conference on the theme 'Law and Order – Prospects for the Future'. Four powerful and perplexing themes emerged from that conference, which led some of us to feel that we must see if there were Christian resources which might illumine the confusing situation and suggest perhaps, if not solutions, at least ways forward towards a less brutal and ineffective, and a more just, penal system.[1]

(a) The first theme emerged from the elegant and intelligent presentation by the minister responsible for Scottish prisons. He gave the clear impression that there was in fact a coherent rationale or theory undergirding the Scottish prison system.

[1] The papers from that conference have been published as M. Rifkind *et al.*, *Law and Order – Prospects for the Future*. Occasional Paper, no. 10, Edinburgh: CTPI, 1986.

This had changed over time, he claimed, from a dominant emphasis on rehabilitation to something approximating to what is known as the 'justice model' – of which more shortly. This ideological development, he suggested, had been a cautious and thoughtful response on the part of policy-makers to the findings of empirical research, particularly on the 'effectiveness' of various forms of sentence and the balance between individual responsibility and social conditioning in criminality, to the development of social theory, and to public opinion.

(b) A second presentation gave a starkly different picture. The then Director of the Scottish Prison Service suggested that his organisation was bewildered and incapacitated by the fact that the public and their political masters loaded onto the prison system a series of widely divergent and often conflicting expectations. This made it very difficult to sustain coherent regimes or to provide prison staff with a sense that they were carrying out a consistent practice which made sense to them and to those who were being punished. This confusion was compounded, he said, by the fact that the prison service was not provided with the resources to carry out any of the tasks expected of it with full effectiveness.

(c) The third voice was that of the prisoner. Prisoners spoke of the awful conditions in many Scottish prisons, of over-crowding, of 'slopping out', of human ordure thrown out of windows at night, of the undertow of violence, of the intense pressure put on marriages and family relationships, of the sense that the system was both arbitrary and incoherent. In short, the prisoners' view was of a system that was often dehumanising and sometimes brutal, and in countless ways made people worse rather than better, less likely to become useful, law-abiding citizens, and more incapable of reintegrating effectively into society at the end of their sentence. Some prisoners were quite explicit in saying that the system was *unjust*.

(d) The final theme came from staff in the criminal justice system, and in particular prison staff, who had gone into the service (note that term!) with a sense of vocation, whether secular humanist or Christian. These were people who brought with them convictions, expectations, standards and values which they hoped to express in their work. They shared belief in the importance and value of human beings, the human need for loving relationships, the necessity of dignity, responsibility and respect. They believed in the worth of human beings, even the most apparently depraved, and the need for this worth to be recognised and respected. They saw their work as a vocation, as tending towards a goal, a *telos*.

As they talked, the staff made clear that they found a more or less acute sense of frustration and even oppression in their work within the criminal justice system, but felt it important to continue because they saw the system as confused and often harmful but not incurably corrupt, as the criminal justice system in Nazi Germany had been. When pressed, it became clear that the root of their discontent was the experience that the standards and understandings which shaped their vocations were sharply at variance with many of the operative standards of the system, just as these standards were often different from the standards and procedures which we had heard officially proclaimed as undergirding the system. In effect, their personal convictions about justice sometimes conflicted with the understandings of justice which were operative in the prisons.

These concerns were so serious that we were convinced that they deserved further detailed consideration, with particular openness to the possibility that Christianity might have some constructive contribution to make. It was also felt that our prison system might be a case in which the effects of the increasing moral fragmentation of our society could be seen in some detail, and in relation to which Christian responses to moral pluralism – or perhaps moral fragmentation – could be examined.

So in due course we established an interdisciplinary working group. It brought together people with a great deal of experience of working within the criminal justice system: prison governors, judges, a forensic psychiatrist, social workers, probation officers and chaplains. Then there were academics: moral theologians, a research student and two criminologists. And there was a member who had served a long sentence for murder and is now released 'on licence'. Most of the members were Christians, both Protestant and Roman Catholic, but a few were secular humanists with a sympathy for Christian values. The group met regularly over a period of two and a half years, held residential meetings, consulted with a wide variety of people, visited prisons, and held two consultations prior to the publication of its report in the form of Chris Wood's book, *The End of Punishment*.[2] As we met together and came to know one another, and attended to each other's experiences and views, we gradually worked through to an unusual degree of honesty and openness. At the end I think all the members of the group felt that their views had been substantially influenced by the shared experience of the group.

In the light of this experience I want to reflect on two areas – theory and theology – and draw some conclusions.

THEORY

Our group's discussions started, as such studies usually do, by considering the various theories of punishment – retribution, deterrence, rehabilitation and so forth. As we progressed we became increasingly uneasy about this approach through theory. While we tended to agree with Rowan Williams that from a Christian point of view, all the 'classical' theories of punishment have something to be said for them, and all have weaknesses, we felt such a position was rather academic in the sense of being distanced from actual practice.[3] Theory, the practitioners in particular felt, failed to illumine and clarify so much experience; theory was unable to explain a great deal that went on in the system, including many of the most important things. Our group divided into the two groups identified by David Garland: those who thought theory to be a distraction from the obvious practical issues which had to be faced in a penal system whose defects and purpose were fairly

---

[2] Chris Wood, *The End of Punishment: Christian Perspectives on the Crisis in Criminal Justice.* Edinburgh: CTPI/St Andrew Press, 1991. See also David Garland (ed.), *Justice, Guilt and Forgiveness in the Penal System.* Occasional Paper, no. 18, Edinburgh: CTPI, 1990, and *Penal Policy: The Way Forward.* Occasional Paper, no. 27, Edinburgh: CTPI, 1992.

[3] Rowan Williams, 'Penance in the Penitentiary', *Theology*, 95/764 (1992), 90.

obvious to everyone, and those who saw theory as not a flight from reality or necessarily a disguise for what is going on but as something which *when properly used* 'enables us to think about that real world of practice with a clarity and a breadth of perspective often unavailable to the hard-pressed practitioner'.[4] We also noted that some of the 'volatile and contradictory penal policy developments that we have recently witnessed in the UK' were based on arbitrary changes of theory or sudden shifts in popular mood.[5] Clearly this stage of our discussion raised a range of issues which demanded attention.

From rehabilitation to justice model

We recognised that in Britain, as in the US and elsewhere, there has been a major shift in the preferred theory from the so-called 'treatment' or 'rehabilitation' model of punishment to what is commonly called the 'justice model'.

This is not the place for a detailed account or analysis of this shift. But the main charges against rehabilitation should be mentioned. Central is the feeling – and it is no more than a feeling – that rehabilitation doesn't work. In general terms this means that systems that are, or that claim to be, based on rehabilitation or treatment do not seem to be any more successful in discouraging crime or recidivism than any other approach to punishment. Supporters of rehabilitation argue that it (like Christianity!) has never really been tried. It seems to be the case that it is almost impossible to find anything approaching a pure rehabilitation model in operation anywhere in Britain.

A more important charge, and one that in my experience is supported by many prisoners, is that the treatment model involves an unacceptable amount of discretion on the part of those who operate the system. In order to rehabilitate, they

---

[4] David Garland, *Punishment and Modern Society: A Study in Social Theory*. Oxford: Clarendon, 1990, p. 277.

[5] David Garland, 'The Punitive Society', Inaugural Lecture, University of Edinburgh, 24 May 1995, Typescript, p. 14. Garland instances the way carefully planned initiatives such as the Criminal Justice Act of 1991 and the prison reform programme suggested by the Woolf Report have been undercut.

must have some ability to control the length of sentence and modify the details of the regime. Furthermore, since rehabilitation is a form of therapy, a right is claimed to intrude into prisoners' 'private space'. Thus many people believe that rehabilitation is excessively arbitrary and discretionary, and involves imposing on offenders a particular view of human flourishing and the good without reference to the prisoners' own goals and values – a serious matter in a liberal pluralist society. Philosophically, rehabilitation involves using prisoners as means rather than ends – a Kantian objection recently powerfully reiterated by Agnes Heller.[6]

The commonly preferred alternative to the treatment model is some version of the 'justice model'. This stresses 'just deserts', a punishment that is proportionate to the offence. It is at heart a backward-looking approach, focusing on the offence rather than the offender, dealing with the past rather than attempting to constrain the offenders' future. Prisoners must be justly treated; although they have broken the law and are being justly punished, they still have rights. In particular, they have the right to choose their own values, goals and life-plans. Their inner space should be impregnable, unless they open it and freely ask for help. The punishment of prison is the deprivation of liberty and nothing else.

The first problem with this approach is a crucial one: without any purpose beyond 'humane confinement', prisons tend to become human warehouses. The prison becomes a group of people with no goal, no *telos*, no purpose apart from confinement. Even if the stress on prisoners' rights leads, as it should, to the maintenance of acceptable standards of accommodation and so forth, the prison cannot be a real community, let alone a recognised part and agency of the broader community;[7] it is not intended to do anything to or for the prisoners except keep them securely behind bars and, for a time, out of the broader community. As a group of witnesses pointed out to the May Committee of Inquiry into the United Kingdom Prison Ser-

---

[6] Agnes Heller, *Beyond Justice*. Oxford: Blackwell, 1987, pp. 160–80.
[7] On this see especially Andrew Coyle, 'Imprisonment: A Challenge to Community' in *Penal Policy: The Way Forward*, pp. 18–24.

could it, with archaic and overcrowded buildings, staff
s~~h~~rtages, a punitive public opinion, extraordinarily large
~~nu~~mbers of offenders given custodial sentences, and the justifi-
~~a~~feeling on the part of the staff that they were sitting on a
~~powd~~er keg which might explode into rioting and violence at
~~any m~~oment? It is not surprising that priority was often given to
~~contro~~l or containment, occasionally enforced with consider-
~~able ha~~rshness, even as the system was publicly proclaimed to
~~be direc~~ted towards either rehabilitation or justice or what-
~~ever~~. Theory, our group concluded, could, and sometimes
~~wa~~s a disguise for what was actually happening.

~~The gro~~up's theoretical discussions also suggested that diffi-
~~cult~~y arise from modern social theory's reluctance to
~~teleo~~logical questions, that is questions about goals and
~~ends, th~~e sort of questions that point to the future and
~~ask wha~~t a system or a practice is *for*. As Habermas has
~~shown~~ there is in the modern world a tendency to treat
~~the p~~ublic realm as technical rather than moral (or
~~politic~~s. Within a retributivist horizon, this encourages
~~a mec~~hanical and impersonal relating of penalty to
~~utili~~tarians the danger is that reducing the notion of
~~goo~~d to utility provides a very narrow base on
~~the j~~ustification of punishment.

~~An~~ impressive short book entitled *Why Punish?*
~~was~~ published by Nigel Walker, the highly
~~of~~ British criminology. This is a useful and
~~emi~~nently clear, critical and fair-minded, and
~~d~~etailed hands-on knowledge of the British
~~j~~ustice. But, as far as I can see, Professor
~~diffi~~culty in answering the question he poses
~~eviden~~t involves an engagement with the two
~~teleo~~gical theory – the Benthamite, leading
~~to ac~~tion, treatment and deterrence, and a
~~retribu~~tion, just desert, and the justice model.
~~precisio~~n and cogency, and always with fair-
~~ness, w~~ith which he disagrees, against retri-
~~butive u~~tilitarianism. But he is also aware of
~~the u~~tilitarian approach to questions of

---

vices, '"humane containment" suffers from the fatal defect that
it is a means without an end. Our opinion is that it can only
result in making prisons into human warehouses – for inmates
and staff. It is not therefore a fit rule for hopeful life or
responsible management.'[8] This is, of course, frustrating also
for many prison staff: their job is now simply to man the
perimeter fence and interfere as little as possible. It was not
surprising when a report on the English prison service by Ian
Dunbar in 1985 declared that with the collapse of the ethic of
rehabilitation 'a sense of futility has become pervasive and has
led to what some observers have called a moral vacuum'.[9] And
although many prisoners actually prefer the new type of regime
because it is predictable and non-intrusive, it does rather little
for them or to them and is certainly not intended (as certain
other regimes were) to enable them to come to terms with guilt,
feelings and behaviour patterns and plan for a different future.
It is in fact a system without an aim.

David Garland writes:

For nearly two decades now, those employed in prisons, probation
and penal administration have been engaged in an unsuccessful
search to find a 'new philosophy', or a new 'rationale' for punishment.
They have been forced to rethink what it is they do, and to reopen
foundational questions about the justifications and purposes of penal
sanctions, without so far having found a suitable set of terms upon
which to rebuild an institutional identity.[10]

The effects of this uncertainty are serious; but at such a time of
searching there is also an unusual openness to new ideas and
new possibilities.

One might well expect a system which is entitled a 'justice
model' of punishment to rest on and express a clearly articulated notion of justice but, apart from a general Kantian rather
than utilitarian stress on justice as retribution and the need to
adjust the punishment to fit the crime rather than the person,

---

[8] Committee of Inquiry into the United Kingdom Prison Service, *Report* [May Committee Report]. CMND 7673, London: HMSO, par. 4.24 cited by Anthony Bottoms in Garland, *Justice, Guilt and Forgiveness in the Penal System*, p. 8.

[9] Ian Dunbar, *A Sense of Direction*. London: Home Office, 1985, cited in Garland, *Justice, Guilt and Forgiveness in the Penal System*, p. 12.

[10] Garland, *Punishment and Modern Society*, p. 6.

must have some ability to control the length of sentence and modify the details of the regime. Furthermore, since rehabilitation is a form of therapy, a right is claimed to intrude into prisoners' 'private space'. Thus many people believe that rehabilitation is excessively arbitrary and discretionary, and involves imposing on offenders a particular view of human flourishing and the good without reference to the prisoners' own goals and values – a serious matter in a liberal pluralist society. Philosophically, rehabilitation involves using prisoners as means rather than ends – a Kantian objection recently powerfully reiterated by Agnes Heller.[6]

The commonly preferred alternative to the treatment model is some version of the 'justice model'. This stresses 'just deserts', a punishment that is proportionate to the offence. It is at heart a backward-looking approach, focusing on the offence rather than the offender, dealing with the past rather than attempting to constrain the offenders' future. Prisoners must be justly treated; although they have broken the law and are being justly punished, they still have rights. In particular, they have the right to choose their own values, goals and life-plans. Their inner space should be impregnable, unless they open it and freely ask for help. The punishment of prison is the deprivation of liberty and nothing else.

The first problem with this approach is a crucial one: without any purpose beyond 'humane confinement', prisons tend to become human warehouses. The prison becomes a group of people with no goal, no *telos*, no purpose apart from confinement. Even if the stress on prisoners' rights leads, as it should, to the maintenance of acceptable standards of accommodation and so forth, the prison cannot be a real community, let alone a recognised part and agency of the broader community;[7] it is not intended to do anything to or for the prisoners except keep them securely behind bars and, for a time, out of the broader community. As a group of witnesses pointed out to the May Committee of Inquiry into the United Kingdom Prison Ser-

---

[6] Agnes Heller, *Beyond Justice*. Oxford: Blackwell, 1987, pp. 160–80.

[7] On this see especially Andrew Coyle, 'Imprisonment: A Challenge to Community' in *Penal Policy: The Way Forward*, pp. 18–24.

obvious to everyone, and those who saw theory as not a flight from reality or necessarily a disguise for what is going on but as something which *when properly used* 'enables us to think about that real world of practice with a clarity and a breadth of perspective often unavailable to the hard-pressed practitioner'.[4] We also noted that some of the 'volatile and contradictory penal policy developments that we have recently witnessed in the UK' were based on arbitrary changes of theory or sudden shifts in popular mood.[5] Clearly this stage of our discussion raised a range of issues which demanded attention.

From rehabilitation to justice model

We recognised that in Britain, as in the US and elsewhere, there has been a major shift in the preferred theory from the so-called 'treatment' or 'rehabilitation' model of punishment to what is commonly called the 'justice model'.

This is not the place for a detailed account or analysis of this shift. But the main charges against rehabilitation should be mentioned. Central is the feeling – and it is no more than a feeling – that rehabilitation doesn't work. In general terms this means that systems that are, or that claim to be, based on rehabilitation or treatment do not seem to be any more successful in discouraging crime or recidivism than any other approach to punishment. Supporters of rehabilitation argue that it (like Christianity!) has never really been tried. It seems to be the case that it is almost impossible to find anything approaching a pure rehabilitation model in operation anywhere in Britain.

A more important charge, and one that in my experience is supported by many prisoners, is that the treatment model involves an unacceptable amount of discretion on the part of those who operate the system. In order to rehabilitate, they

---

[4] David Garland, *Punishment and Modern Society: A Study in Social Theory*. Oxford: Clarendon, 1990, p. 277.

[5] David Garland, 'The Punitive Society', Inaugural Lecture, University of Edinburgh, 24 May 1995, Typescript, p. 14. Garland instances the way carefully planned initiatives such as the Criminal Justice Act of 1991 and the prison reform programme suggested by the Woolf Report have been undercut.

vices, ' "humane containment" suffers from the fatal defect that it is a means without an end. Our opinion is that it can only result in making prisons into human warehouses – for inmates and staff. It is not therefore a fit rule for hopeful life or responsible management.'[8] This is, of course, frustrating also for many prison staff: their job is now simply to man the perimeter fence and interfere as little as possible. It was not surprising when a report on the English prison service by Ian Dunbar in 1985 declared that with the collapse of the ethic of rehabilitation 'a sense of futility has become pervasive and has led to what some observers have called a moral vacuum'.[9] And although many prisoners actually prefer the new type of regime because it is predictable and non-intrusive, it does rather little for them or to them and is certainly not intended (as certain other regimes were) to enable them to come to terms with guilt, feelings and behaviour patterns and plan for a different future. It is in fact a system without an aim.

David Garland writes:

For nearly two decades now, those employed in prisons, probation and penal administration have been engaged in an unsuccessful search to find a 'new philosophy', or a new 'rationale' for punishment. They have been forced to rethink what it is they do, and to reopen foundational questions about the justifications and purposes of penal sanctions, without so far having found a suitable set of terms upon which to rebuild an institutional identity.[10]

The effects of this uncertainty are serious; but at such a time of searching there is also an unusual openness to new ideas and new possibilities.

One might well expect a system which is entitled a 'justice model' of punishment to rest on and express a clearly articulated notion of justice but, apart from a general Kantian rather than utilitarian stress on justice as retribution and the need to adjust the punishment to fit the crime rather than the person,

---

[8] Committee of Inquiry into the United Kingdom Prison Service, *Report* [May Committee Report]. CMND 7673, London: HMSO, par. 4.24 cited by Anthony Bottoms in Garland, *Justice, Guilt and Forgiveness in the Penal System*, p. 8.

[9] Ian Dunbar, *A Sense of Direction*. London: Home Office, 1985, cited in Garland, *Justice, Guilt and Forgiveness in the Penal System*, p. 12.

[10] Garland, *Punishment and Modern Society*, p. 6.

we find that the justice model uses a rather vague and ill-defined notion of justice which is not easy to relate to the major protagonists in the contemporary debate about the theory of justice, some of whom we consider later in this book. The move from one model to another was made, it appears, largely for pragmatic reasons, rather than indicating a major theoretical shift in the basis of public policy. David Garland's summing up is fair:

[W]e are developing an official criminology that fits our deeply divided, and increasingly anxious society. Unlike the rehabilitative welfare ideal which, for all its faults, was linked into a broader politics of social change and a certain vision of social justice, the new policies have no broader agenda, no strategy for progressive social change, no means for overcoming inequalities and social divisions. They are, instead, policies for managing the danger and policing the divisions created by a certain kind of social organisation – and for preserving the political arrangements which lie at its centre.[11]

How can you have a 'justice model' when there is fundamental uncertainty about what justice is? Lord Justice Woolf in his report on the Strangeways riots recommended that prison regimes should represent a balance between security, control and *justice*. He does not spell out his understanding of justice, but it appears to include fairness, due process and an obligation to treat prisoners with 'humanity', that is to preserve their dignity and self-respect. A failure to deliver justice will alienate prisoners and is likely to lead to disturbances; an unjust and degrading prison system will erode the justice of the criminal justice system and indeed demonstrate the strength of injustice in the broader society.[12]

A main focus in the contemporary theoretical discussion is on social justice, as we shall see later in this book, and sometimes the concept of justice is fragmented, so that, for example, criminal justice and social justice are treated as if they have hardly any connection. Proponents of the justice model are particularly likely to separate criminal and social justice. A

---

[11] Garland, 'Punitive Society', p. 15.

[12] Rod Morgan, 'Just Prisons and Responsible Prisoners' in *Penal Policy: The Way Forward*, pp. 1–11, citing *Report of an Enquiry by the Rt Hon Lord Justice Woolf and His Honour Judge Stephen Tumim* [Woolf Report], Cm 1456, London: HMSO, 1991.

notable exception is Agnes Heller who, in her fine book *Beyond Justice*, defends a Kantian view of criminal justice in the context of a serious endeavour to recover the wholeness of the understanding of justice which was characteristic of the Christian and the classical traditions alike. What happens when a society separates social justice from criminal justice? Does it cease to ask questions about the social causes of crime and the social construction of criminality? Does it not operate with an excessively simple notion of responsibility? The sort of inconclusive fragmentation that is prevalent in the contemporary debate about justice can be a confusing impoverishment which in fact causes problems 'on the ground', as it were.

The limits of theory

As we progressed in our working group through the discussion of the major theories of punishment, an increasing mood of impatience on the part of many members became obvious. Practitioners, people actually involved in the criminal justice system (How far it is a *system* is an important and relevant issue into which I cannot enter here.) became increasingly convinced that none of the theories explained much of what in fact goes on and that some of the things that were left without explanation or theoretical justification were matters which have a profound effect on people, for good or ill. Theories, these members felt, cast a veneer of respectability over everything, or nearly everything, that happens, and can serve to disguise or conceal from public view that which is not in accordance with the theory.

Thus, when the official theory of British prisons was that their task was to rehabilitate prisoners, in some situations prisoners were locked in their cells for twenty-two hours of the day, the degrading business of 'slopping out' continued unabated, there were many instances of violent attacks on prisoners by officers or other prisoners, and there was a chronic and massive lack of facilities for therapy and of people trained in rehabilitation. Nor did a change in the dominant theory necessarily mean a significant change on the ground. How could it, with archaic and overcrowded buildings, staff shortages, a punitive public opinion, extraordinarily large numbers of offenders given custodial sentences, and the justifiable feeling on the part of the staff that they were sitting on a powder keg which might explode into rioting and violence at any moment? It is not surprising that priority was often given to control or containment, occasionally enforced with considerable harshness, even as the system was publicly proclaimed to be directed towards either rehabilitation or justice or what-have-you. Theory, our group concluded, could, and sometimes did, act as a disguise for what was actually happening.

Our group's theoretical discussions also suggested that difficulties may arise from modern social theory's reluctance to address teleological questions, that is questions about goals and purposes, the sort of questions that point to the future and enquire what a system or a practice is *for*. As Habermas has pointed out, there is in the modern world a tendency to treat issues in the public realm as technical rather than moral (or practical) issues. Within a retributivist horizon, this encourages an almost mechanical and impersonal relating of penalty to offence; for utilitarians the danger is that reducing the notion of the common good to utility provides a very narrow base on which to build a justification of punishment.

An elegant and impressive short book entitled *Why Punish?* has recently been published by Nigel Walker, the highly respected doyen of British criminology. This is a useful and important book, eminently clear, critical and fair-minded, and based of course on detailed hands-on knowledge of the British system of criminal justice. But, as far as I can see, Professor Walker has some difficulty in answering the question he poses in his title. His argument involves an engagement with the two main types of criminological theory – the Benthamite, leading to a stress on rehabilitation, treatment and deterrence, and a Kantian stress on retribution, just desert, and the justice model. Walker argues with passion and cogency, and always with fair-mindedness to positions with which he disagrees, against retribution and in favour of utilitarianism. But he is also aware of the need to set limits to a utilitarian approach to questions of punishment. Utilitarian arguments can be used, for instance, to justify disproportionate savagery in the punishment of an individual if this were to have dramatic and effective deterrent effects, reducing crime and thus benefiting society as a whole, using the offender as a means to a greater social good. So what Walker calls 'humanitarian limits' to utilitarianism must be established: 'It is a fact of history,' he writes, 'that it has been humanity, not notions of utility or desert, which has inspired opposition to death penalty, attainder, loss of civic rights, castration and other mutilations, flogging, transportation and solitary confinement.'[13]

But what is the source and justification of these 'humanitarian limits'? Walker is silent on this, although he suggests tacitly that they are axiomatic or self-evident. His argument shows a remarkable awareness that each of the two positions on offer – the retributivist and the utilitarian – is capable of producing and justifying behaviour that he would regard as 'inhumane'. But where does this attachment to humanitarianism, which is clearly prior to his attachment to utilitarianism, come from? Is it, perhaps, what Alasdair MacIntyre would call a 'fragment', surviving powerfully from an ancient world-view which was explicitly teleological, and depending on an ontology which neither retributivist nor utilitarian now share, but which is capable of addressing questions of purpose and the limits that purpose imposes?

Walker's book ends on a tentative note. He seems to acknowledge the limits of theories and the importance of fundamental attitudes, commitments and values, which have presumably been shaped by upbringing, beliefs and other such factors. Some, at least, of these may be the kind of fragments of which MacIntyre speaks. And the tentativeness of Walker's conclusion seems to support MacIntyre's suggestion that there are considerable difficulties in the way of a coherent and convincing treatment of fundamental issues of value in our kind of morally fragmented society.

---

[13] Nigel Walker, *Why Punish?* Oxford: Oxford University Press, 1991, p. 131.

THEOLOGY

From the start of our group's work there was a demand to present 'the Christian theory of punishment' which could then be put alongside the secular theories and might act as a corrective, complement, or reflection of some of them. The Christians in the group seemed to crave the reassurance that there was such a thing. The secular humanists asked the question, I think, partly out of curiosity, partly in the hope that perhaps within the tradition of discourse of which theology is the steward there might be helpful insights which might suggest a way forward in the handling of complex penal issues. When we said we could not put on the table alongside deterrence, retribution, rehabilitation and so forth *the* Christian theory of punishment, the comment was met initially with surprise. Were we acknowledging our incompetence as theologians, or did we regard ourselves as guardians of some arcane mystery which had no claim to being regarded as public truth? Or were theologians just loose cannons, firing wildly in all directions, rather than aiming consistently at a common target and a common enemy?

Initially most of the members of the group felt quite strongly that rehabilitation, the treatment model, had something inherently Christian about it, or at least was the approach most congenial to Christians and to a Christian view. Most also agreed with Hastings Rashdall's view that there was something inherently un-Christian about retributivism.[14] But as we looked more closely at the matter, and in particular as we attended to the common view of prisoners that rehabilitation was a disguise for the unattractive reality of what really went on in prison and authorised an unacceptable amount of arbitrary and discretionary action, we felt increasingly disenchanted with the possibility of baptising rehabilitation.

[14] Hastings Rashdall, cited in H. B. Acton (ed.), *The Philosophy of Punishment.* London: Macmillan, 1969, p. 13. It is important to note that one of the most influential early critiques of the treatment model was *Struggle for Justice: A Report on Crime and Punishment in America Prepared for the American Friends Service Committee.* New York: Hill & Wang, 1971. This Quaker report advocated something close to today's justice model, with arguments many of which were explicitly Christian.

So we determined as theologians to attend very closely to experience, to what was actually happening, seeing whether we could learn from the real situation and discern what was happening there. We thought liberation theology might teach us that insights arise particularly out of experiences of frustration, confusion, uncertainty and oppression, and that people in such situations who are committed to transformative action, to changing things, to seeking justice and loving people have a kind of privileged access to truth. Such experiences and insights, of course, must be brought into relationship to the tradition. So we quarried in the rich and diverse Christian tradition to see what we could find that interacted significantly with these experiences and provided illumination, challenge and motivation.

We also came up with an understanding of the theological task which was chastened by an awareness of the very ambiguous record of Christian involvement in penal affairs and rather suspicious of grand systems and theories. In a situation where the confusion in penal policy and penal practice is damaging to individuals and societies, might it be possible for theology to ask questions and give clues, insights, comments and suggestions which, even if fragmentary, might be helpful and illuminating in this corner of the public square? We thought it could. And we were encouraged to discover people like Antony Duff, the philosopher, who mined deep into the Christian tradition to discover resources for an account of punishment which is relevant to the needs of today, arguing that an acceptable understanding of punishment must be 'communicative, retributive and reformative'[15] and concerned with the restoration of relationships.

Some way into our group's discussions, a member with much experience of the prison system and a profound sense of Christian vocation said that there were two issues which were her primary concern. The first was that in the prison system hardly anyone was willing to face up to guilt, or respond to it in any way. The notion of guilt caused embarrassment in some

---

[15] R. A. Duff, *Trials and Punishments*. Cambridge: Cambridge University Press, 1986, p. 260.

quarters, or was considered a distraction from the serious business of treating personality disorders or psychiatric illness. Few people now had the time or interest to talk through feelings of guilt, or to discuss matters with prisoners who, rightly or wrongly, had no such feelings. Guilt in any sense other than the verdict of the court was something that many people either preferred to pretend did not exist or reduced to a survival from the past which should now be forgotten.

The second concern which this woman identified was forgiveness. Few people today, she said, regarded the penal system as having anything to do with forgiveness and society was singularly loth to forgive those who had paid the penalty for their offence. Nigel Walker clearly regards such issues as peripheral to the main thrust of the penal system. Forgiveness and mercy create 'minor awkwardnesses' for retributivists in particular, he says, while utilitarians may exercise mercy when they choose, for good reason, a penalty which causes least suffering to the offender. Hastings Rashdall, the theologian, goes further. For him, forgiveness is not a side issue, but 'forgiveness is opposed to punishment'.[16] This puts forgiveness in a different realm, separate from and opposed to punishment. Perhaps here, we thought, was a starting point for theological reflection. For these themes have been the subject of intense theological discussion down the ages.

Guilt

The law and, in particular, retributive theories of penal justice operate with a relatively simple notion of guilt. People are guilty if they have committed an offence, as defined by law and determined by the court. Guilt should be met with punishment which as far as possible should be proportionate to the offence. Offenders are guilty and deserve to be punished – that is their 'just deserts'. The rest – and that obviously means the vast majority of human beings – are innocent and do not deserve punishment.

---

[16] Cited in Acton, *Philosophy of Punishment*, p. 13.

Christian theology has some difficulties with this account. In the first place, Christianity teaches that guilt is universal. All have sinned, all are offenders, and therefore are guilty in the objective order of things. There therefore is, or ought to be, a solidarity in the state of being a guilty offender. Christians should find it impossible to divide people neatly into the guilty few and the innocent many. This conviction should make it possible for Christians to have fellow-feeling with offenders against the law; they should be able to echo John Bradford's remark on seeing criminals being taken to execution: 'There, but for the grace of God, goes John Bradford.'[17] Accordingly there should be no easy polarity between the guilty individual and the innocent society.

Nor is it possible for theology, despite the long history of casuistry and penitential tariffs, to produce a neat calculus of the gravity of an offence and the degree of guilt entailed. St Augustine, to the modern mind, was quite pathologically obsessed with the severity of his offence in the boyish prank of stealing, along with others, a few pears. But Augustine's retrospective conscience was shaped by his faith. Who can really say that his sense of guilt was misplaced, or excessive, or wrong?[18]

All this makes the situation more confusing and ambiguous than it was before. If we are all offenders, how dare we judge?[19] If only the one without sin may cast the first stone, how dare we punish our sisters and brothers? If it is hard truly to weigh the gravity of an offence, how may we provide commensurate penalties? Such questions might be taken to undermine the foundations of any system of criminal justice. That may well be the case. But it is also possible that, if kept constantly in mind, such questions may humanise the system and make it more constructive by stripping it of arrogance and pretentiousness, and showing that despite being necessary it is human and fallible and inadequate.

---

[17] Attributed to a Puritan, John Bradford, 1510–55.
[18] Augustine, *Confessions*, II. 9.
[19] See, for example, Matt. 7.1–5.

Forgiveness

There was a time when most people in western societies had some awareness that they were offenders, people who stood under the judgement and the forgiving grace of God, people who had sins to confess. Our guilt, they believed, is taken away, expunged, by God. The whole community was understood as standing together, in solidarity, as forgiven offenders. Forgiveness is offered freely and is to be received with joy and responded to in life. But forgiveness is not cheap and does not lead to a turning of the blind eye to the gravity of offence – indeed, precisely the opposite:

Forgiveness cannot, if it is a virtue, be a matter simply of *ignoring* the serious wrong which the criminal has done, or pretending that it never happened: if forgiveness is to be consistent with a proper regard for the values which the criminal has flouted, as well as with a proper concern for the wrong that has been done, it must also be consistent with an attempt, perhaps through punishment, to bring him to recognise and repent that wrong.[20]

This shared experiential base has been widely eroded in modern societies and replaced with more individualistic notions which make it easier for the society to become punitive because it believes it is not implicated in offence.

Consider this order for the reception back into the congregation of a forgiven offender, coming from the Scots Calvinist tradition, and dating from 1564:

If we consider his fall and sin in him only, without having consideration of ourselves and of our own corruption, we shall profit nothing, for so shall we but despise our brother and flatter ourselves; but if we shall earnestly consider what nature we bear, what corruption lurketh in it, how prone and ready every one of us is to such and greater impiety, then shall we in the sin of this our brother accuse and condemn our own sins, in his fall we shall consider and lament our sinful nature, also we shall join our repentance, tears and prayers with him and his, knowing that no flesh can be justified before God's presence, if judgement proceed without mercy . . .
[The minister turns to the penitent and says:]

[20] Antony Duff, 'Punishment, Repentance and Forgiveness' in Garland, *Justice, Guilt and Forgiveness in the Penal System*, p. 45.

You have heard also the affection and care of the Church towards you, their penitent brother, notwithstanding your grievous fall, to wit, that we all here present join our sins with your sin; we all repute and esteem your fall to be our own; we accuse ourselves no less than we accuse you; now, finally, we join our prayers with yours, that we and you may obtain mercy, and that by the means of our Lord Jesus Christ.

[The minister addresses the congregation:]
Now it only resteth that ye remit and forget all offences which ye have conceived heretofore by the sin and fall of this our brother; accept and embrace him as a member of Christ's body; let no one take upon him to reproach or accuse him for any offences that before this hour he hath committed.[21]

In this 'theological fragment' we find a number of convictions of great importance, which are rare in the modern world. Individual offenders demonstrated not only their own sins but the fallen human condition. The community therefore should respond both with punishment and redemption, indeed with punishment which is oriented towards redemption. Offenders were not to be shown to be different, but to exemplify the human condition. The offender retained always an 'intimate link' with the community. Even if the offender was for a while to be excluded from the community, the goal was reconciliation and reception back after repentance and forgiveness. David Garland comments on such Calvinist practices, shaped by Protestant theology:

[T]he sinner-offender was not conceived as 'Other' but rather as a kind of Protestant Everyman, a living example of the potential evil which lies in every heart and against which every soul must be vigilant. In keeping with this conception, the dénouement of each public ceremony was aimed not at the vanquishing of the enemy, but instead at the reinclusion of the atoned and repentant sinner.[22]

Forgiveness is seen as a costly, objective reality which comes from God and should be recognised by the community, by the victim and by the offender alike – indeed all of them constantly

---

[21] Order of Excommunication and of Public Repentance in John Cumming (ed.), *The Liturgy of the Church of Scotland, or John Knox's Book of Common Order*. London: J. Leslie, 1840, pp. 140–1, 145, 148.
[22] Garland, *Punishment and Modern Society*, p. 207.

stand in need of this forgiveness and need to learn how to participate in the giving as well as in the receiving of forgiveness. And forgiveness, reconciliation, reception back into fellowship is the goal of punishment, the *telos* which alone can justify the punishment of the offender.

Such an understanding of forgiveness and its place, derived directly from the Christian tradition, we recognised as in some sense 'public truth', with relevance to public policy as well as to personal relations and the life of the church.

Discipline

Another way of explaining and justifying a system of punishment which was suggested in our group was to regard it as *discipline*. We attempted to explore the theological and biblical understanding of discipline rather than following Foucault's exploration of punishment and discipline as 'methods of correct training' to achieve 'docile bodies' and compliant behaviour.[23] We did not wish to be locked into an assumption that discipline was simply a term for rigorous social control. The roots of the word mean learning, that is the person disciplined should learn and grow through the process and the broader group may also learn through the declaratory aspect of discipline and the fact that the group as a whole is involved in the process. Discipline, Christianity teaches, is necessary for disciples, those who are responding to a person rather than being under a rule and are following a way rather than obeying a law. Discipline is therefore a personal rather than a mechanical matter. An offender does not so much trigger a machine which administers a penalty as breach a relationship which requires healing; and in the process the offender should grow and learn. Through discipline, people are brought back into fellowship and held in fellowship. Through discipline in a context which is just and loving both the worth of the victim and the offender's worth and responsibility and potentiality are recognised and affirmed.

[23] Michel Foucault, *Discipline and Punish – The Birth of the Prison*. New York: Vintage Books, 1979. The word 'discipline' in the title is a rather odd translation of 'surveiller'.

This is not to say that discipline is pleasant or easy. Even an academic discipline is often hard, painful and difficult. One undertakes it for the sake of the goal, of the *telos*. Discipline is not cheap. Human relations are not maintained or enhanced or repaired without cost. A loving family without discipline is inconceivable; but a family in which there is much punishment is sick. Discipline is not properly to be understood primarily as regimentation or the infliction of pain. It is rather the maintenance and restoration of the structure of relationships, allowing people to grow and develop together.

The common Greek word for discipline is *paideia*. This means education, discipline, the upbringing of children, culture.[24] It is a concept which looks towards the fulfilment of maturity, adulthood, freedom, responsibility. The classic New Testament exploration of this notion is in Hebrews 12. Here the Christian life, the life of discipleship, is compared to a race, for which we must undergo the discipline of training – hard and not always pleasant, but necessary for the end of running the race. The runners look to Jesus, who himself underwent the *paideia* of the cross, of hostility and of disgrace for the sake of the joy that was set before him. Disciples are encouraged to see hardships as God's discipline of them, as training for the race of faith, as sure signs that God is treating us as his children, that God takes responsibility for us.

A proper understanding of discipline on our part leads to self-discipline, taking responsibility for ourselves and our behaviour. God disciplines us because he cares for us; if God left us to stew in our own juice, it would betray a lack of concern for us and our welfare. Unlike earthly parents for much of the time, God disciplines us for our good, not in an arbitrary but in a loving way. Earthly parents discipline us 'at their pleasure'; God disciplines us 'that we may share his holiness' and have fellowship with him. And, finally, God's *paideia* is for our encouragement: 'Therefore lift your drooping hands and

24 See Werner Jaeger, *Paideia: The Ideals of Greek Culture*, tr. G. Highet. 2nd edn., New York: Oxford University Press, 1945. There is a careful treatment of *paideia* in the New Testament in G. Kittel and G. Friedrich (eds.), *Theological Dictionary of the New Testament*. tr. G. W. Bromily. Grand Rapids: Eerdmans, 1967, vol. V, p. 596.

strengthen your weak knees and make straight paths for your feet'.[25] Those who receive God's discipline can run the race, attain the goal and receive the prize. And the race is a relay; we run and we win in solidarity, not in isolation.

Justice

Justice is, of course, the key issue in any system of criminal justice. Questions of justice have been woven into our whole discussion. Today there are many conflicting notions as to its nature. Retributivist notions of justice, as we have seen, look back to the offence, calculate the desert of the offender, and try to adjust the penalty accordingly. Some other notions of justice concentrate on the person and look to the future. But since our society is in such a muddle about justice, there is much confusion. In such a situation there is a particularly acute danger that concepts of justice may be used and manipulated so that they serve sectional interests or disguise what is really going on.

   Christians will wish to affirm and explore some basic convictions, to offer and commend some 'theological fragments', which I will mention here and explore later. God is just and loving. We experience true justice in God's dealings with us, finding that at the heart of justice is mercy and love, that God's justice is for our good, although it is often disturbing to our ideas and our behaviour. God's justice is challenging to conventional and classical accounts of justice as fairness and giving to each what is due. The labourers in the marketplace (or some of them!) complain because they are treated equally, because they are accepted totally, without regard to their work, achievement and desert.[26] The elder brother in the parable of the Prodigal Son is angry because his younger brother does not get what's coming to him, his just deserts, but is simply accepted without reserve back into the bosom of the family. The elder brother complains that it is not fair.[27] Was he right? On an understanding of justice as fairness the answer can only be 'yes'. But

---

[25] Heb. 12.12–13 (RSV).   [26] Matt. 20.1–16.   [27] Luke 15.11–32.

God's justice is more than fair, not less than fair. It is a creative rather than an arithmetic fairness. It points to the true nature of justice, to which human justice and human fairness are mere approximations at the best.

But is this practicable? The answer must be 'yes' and 'no': one cannot by legislation oblige people to be generous, merciful and forgiving. But generosity and mercy may be elicited as a response to God and to the neighbour. And without the 'seasoning' of mercy, generosity and forgiveness, justice – and criminal justice in particular – becomes rigid and mechanical, destructive of the very qualities that are necessary for the maintenance of a decent social order.

Another classical Christian tradition sees criminal justice as not so much *paideia* as a dyke against sin. In a fallen world, it is essential that sin be restrained lest chaos and violence intervene. This way of thinking is particularly at home in the two-kingdoms or two-cities thought of Augustine or Luther: the justice and holiness of the heavenly city cannot be replicated in the earthly city, where the best that can be expected is a pale reflection of the justice of the heavenly city. But it is vital that it is a reflection, an anticipation, a partial manifestation of the same thing. Those who take God's justice seriously must strive to make the justice of the earthly city a closer approximation to the divine justice. The justice of the Rule of God alone can give the authentic flavour of justice to human systems of justice. Without this, they are in danger of becoming hard, mechanical and unforgiving.

But in practice most systems of criminal justice are, as Foucault suggests, forms of social control, heavily punitive, concerned with blaming, scapegoating and exclusion. Unlike discipline, vengeance and retribution are essentially backward looking; they are in danger of locking people into their past rather than opening the future for them. Much punishment is about boundary maintenance and assumes that we can preserve an innocent community by exorcising the guilty. The wrath of the community and the wrath of God are visited upon the offender. We should recognise that all these themes appear in the Bible. But the vital thing to note is that a dominant theme in the New Testament is that Jesus has taken the blame upon himself and absorbed it, as it were. Those who follow in the way of Jesus should acknowledge this and recognise that it now becomes necessary to rethink what we mean by punishment in the light of what we know about the justice of God.

I shall return in Part IV to a rather more detailed discussion of these 'theological fragments', attempting to place them in context and give them more body.

Four general conclusions seem to emerge from this chapter. First, the contemporary penal crisis reflects confusions and uncertainties which suggest some validity to Alasdair MacIntyre's account of the predicament of modern pluralist societies. In the absence of a firm and enduring moral consensus, it is difficult to know what to do, policy tends to swing erratically, and people get hurt and frustrated. The issues of prisons and criminal justice in such a time are particularly intractable. If the absence of one generally agreed theory of punishment meant a human flexibility in policy and practice, it would not be a problem. But what we have is a muddle, encouraging erratic policy shifts, an increasingly punitive public opinion, and demoralisation in the system.[28]

Secondly, theology's role in such a context should be modest, disturbing and constructive, offering, but not imposing, insights, values and convictions – 'theological fragments' – and hoping that some of them may be tested and accepted as 'public truth'. I have suggested here a number of theological fragments which seem to be relevant to the crisis in criminal justice.

Thirdly, while theology does not (thank God!) any longer have the role of legitimating the penal system, it should provide support and encouragement as well as stimulus and perhaps guidance to the people who are endeavouring to fulfil their vocations within the system, on behalf of us, often in frustrating conditions.

Fourthly, the church and theology have a rather special access through the congregation to public opinion and have a

[28] Williams, 'Penance in the Penitentiary', 91.

responsibility to confront unthinking, destructive and punitive attitudes. Michael Ignatieff makes the point with admirable clarity:

The abuse of justice in prisons continues to repose on the lazy, unreflecting belief on the part of the general public that prisoners deserve nothing better. The very idea that the degradation of prisoners degrades all of us because it is in the name of all of us that they suffer their penalties – this idea is one which must be fought for and proclaimed unceasingly because it is unpopular, because it stands opposed to the great moral weakness of our age. This weakness is not, as some people think, a general lack of moral principles, but on the contrary, indignant moral posturings by people too lazy to think through the consequences of strong emotions.[29]

Finally, our group affirmed that a church that takes it upon itself to speak on such matters must take the principles it commends to society seriously in its own life. The church, as a preliminary and partial manifestation of God's Rule, should exemplify in its behaviour, procedures and structures the justice of God. Only in the light of its experience of the justice, mercy and love of God may the church assess systems of criminal justice. Not only should the church speak out about criminal justice but also by its being it should witness to and celebrate God's justice, love and mercy.

[29] Michael Ignatieff, 'Imprisonment and the Need for Justice', *Theology*, 95/764 (1992), 98.

CHAPTER 4

Poverty

We have seen how when 'nobody knows what justice is', when there is deep uncertainty and frequent changes of mind leading to reversals of policy, the difficult business of organising and running 'just prisons' becomes even more complex, confusing and difficult. And we have also seen how insights into justice sometimes emerged from those in the situation, struggling with it and seeking to transform and humanise it.

In such a moral climate it is also very difficult to understand and respond rightly to poverty. While no one denies that imprisonment should be an agency of justice, and many of the disagreements arise from conflicting views on what justice is, some people see poverty as a central issue of social justice while others deny that it has anything to do with justice. The whole notion of social justice is vigorously debated, with some thinkers like Hayek treating it as no more than a dangerous and misleading will-o'-the-wisp, while others, like Rawls, see it as the central component of the concept of justice. In this chapter we examine poverty, and we shall discover that the way we understand poverty, how we respond to it, and our fundamental values and beliefs are inextricably intertwined. There is thus a great deal of confusion today about how we should understand poverty, what it is, how best to respond to it and how to deal justly in relation to poverty as an issue. Construing poverty and its causes, and fashioning policies to deal with poverty which have a claim to be just, are matters of intense, inconclusive and often acrimonious debate. 'Poverty', Pete Alcock writes, 'is essentially a contested concept', but nevertheless, '*it is still a problem*.[1] It is important to remember in this discussion that we are not just talking about ideas, but about people, about community and human flourishing or human degradation. And we are also considering how ideas, beliefs and behaviour on the one hand and policy on the other influence and shape one another. In this confusing situation is it possible that from among the poor and those struggling with poverty fresh insights into justice may emerge? The whole enterprise of liberation theology and experience from around the world today suggests that this might be so.

POOR PEOPLE

In discussing poverty, we are talking about people – poor people, certainly, but ourselves as well. Our interpretations of, and responses to, poverty are in fact indications of how we respond to people who are our neighbours and whether we feel committed to loving them and doing justice to them or not. Let us therefore start with an experience familiar to most of my readers, like me middle-class, non-poor people.[2]

In a litter-strewn street in a run-down inner-city area we see an old, ragged man, in a threadbare raincoat, shuffling down the street towards us. There is something heavy in the pocket of his coat. He has some days' stubble on his chin, his hair is uncombed, and he looks as if he needs a bath. He carries a bulging plastic bag. He pauses to sift through a litter bin, and then wanders slowly towards us, peering around him all the time as if looking for something he has lost.

How do we interpret this situation? How should we respond to it?

The old man might be an eccentric professor of Greek, a text of the *Iliad* in his pocket, who suspects that he has absent-mindedly 'posted' an important letter in the litter bin. But we are not likely to see the situation in that way unless we actually know the professor.

---

[1] Pete Alcock, *Understanding Poverty*. London: Macmillan, 1993, p. 4.
[2] This is adapted from David Donnison, *A Radical Agenda: After the New Right and the Old Left*. London: Rivers Oram Press, 1991, pp. 9–10.

More likely, we will think the bulge in the man's coat is a
bottle; that he is rifling the rubbish bins in the hope of finding
some fag ends to smoke; and that the bag contains all his
belongings.

We are a little afraid of him and embarrassed if he holds out
his hand to us and asks for money. Rationally, we feel that if we
give him money it is unlikely to help him, and it certainly will
not ease our conscience. We don't know how to react; we
inwardly wish he were off the scene, invisible.

What do we call him? We don't know his name, so we attach
a label to him to describe what we think we are seeing: he is a
bum, a wino, a junkie, a vagrant, a tramp. The labels we use
indicate that he is not 'one of us', but an alien who does not
belong in our community. He is likely to move on before long.
Meanwhile, unlike us, he is 'a problem', who will be looked
after by other agencies from those we use. We will not meet
him in our doctor's surgery, or the golf club, or the super-
market. He and his cronies (and social rejection and hardship
drive him into company that we find strange and alarming)
hover on the fringes of society. But we are aware that their
number has increased significantly in recent times, and we
suspect that this is at least in part because of changes in policy
and economies in public expenditure.

Does this man have a claim on us and, if so, of what sort? Is
he in any real sense our neighbour? We know that individual,
person-to-person responses are rarely helpful and are often
demeaning to both sides. Small change is a kind of bribe to
persuade the man to go away and terminate a relationship
which is embarrassing. There seems no possibility in this
encounter of meeting the man's deeper needs – for care,
respect, self-esteem and a recognition of his worth, expressed in
part in the provision of the material things he needs. Our brief
relationship with him is a parody of care. What then of the
system which creates or tolerates his poverty? Do we not have
to say that it is unjust?

Is it enough that society should provide special services for
him – night shelters, hostels, detoxification units and so forth? Is
this any more effective a response than a few pence in the

hand? Often these services are provided in ways which reinforce
the patterns of life which are part of the problem, which
continue to stigmatise and label the people who use the services,
and in fact strengthen public fear, hostility and suspicion
towards the poor.

There are dangers involved in labelling people too easily,
and in responses which in fact broaden the gulf between the
poor and the non-poor and make empathy harder. Our words,
the labels we use, show whom we believe to be our neighbour,
part of our community, with claims on us. The very language
that we use indicates whether we regard the issue as a question
of justice, or of charity, or something that is in no way our
responsibility. Poor people are people like us, our neighbours;
we share with them a nature and a destiny; we are bound
together in community. And so we have to struggle with the
questions of what justice demands and of what justice is in this
situation and its like.

Academic uncertainties

That is the human reality which we attempt to address in more
academic discussions of poverty. But here too there is much
confusion and uncertainty. This was demonstrated for me some
years ago at a conference. The lead speaker was a distinguished
social scientist who had devoted a great deal of his attention
and research to the question of poverty. Poverty, he said, was at
its nub a matter of the maldistribution of material resources,
and the heart of poor people's problem was that they didn't
have enough money. Lack of material resources led to many
other serious problems – stigma, exclusion from community,
social conflict and so on – and poor people had fewer life
chances, worse health, shorter life expectancy and less education than people who were better off. The problem was thus
essentially a simple one – bad, meaning radically unequal,
distribution of material resources, mostly caused by identifiable
policies. But the evil consequences were pervasive and affected
the whole of society for the worse. Since the problem at its
heart was relatively simple, so was the solution: a few major

redistributive measures on an egalitarian basis effected through
the fiscal and benefits systems could in a relatively short space
of time more or less solve the problem of poverty and establish
social justice, provided there was the political will to wage such
a war on poverty for the sake of the health of society as a whole.
What had been caused by policies could be cured by policies
which expressed an egalitarian notion of social justice. The
resources for the abolition of poverty were already available; it
was simply an issue of whether they would be justly deployed.

The speaker's analysis was essentially simple – although
backed up by a formidable amount of empirical research – and
the remedy he proposed was also simple. He suggested that the
removal of poverty in a country like Britain was a goal which
could be achieved in a relatively short space of time.

The second speaker was from one of the countries of Eastern
Europe, where the communists were at that time still in control.
She endorsed the first speaker's account of poverty as mainly a
matter of maldistribution of material resources, but then went
on to question the adequacy of the policies which were
proposed to 'cure' poverty. These were precisely the measures,
she said, which they had adopted in her country in the 1940s.
Land reform had made land available for the first time for poor
peasants. Nationalisation had removed the grossly inflated
salaries common in top jobs in monopolies. Differentials in
earnings had been substantially reduced. Full employment had
made labour scarcity rather than unemployment a major
economic concern. Such measures produced many good fruits,
she went on, and for that they were grateful. But they still had
poverty, albeit some of it carefully hidden, and it was growing.
They had found that they could develop no strategy on the old
basis for eliminating or even containing the spread of poverty.
It was as if the first speaker's remedy had been tested and found
ineffective. Accordingly, he was hardly pleased.

The third speaker was a specialist in world development
questions. His primary focus was on global issues of poverty
rather than on poverty in Europe. He had had much experience
of living with poverty-stricken communities and groups around
the world and of listening to their stories and experiences. He

knew at first hand what absolute poverty and starvation meant, and spoke of the appalling rate of increase in global poverty. He had listened to the voice of the poor, sometimes surprisingly joyful despite unspeakably dreadful conditions of life, as they struggled together for justice.

As he spoke it became clear that he was engaging with real people and communities rather than an abstract, impersonal problem. Poverty, he suggested, was a kind of global sickness, not a problem 'out there', in which rich people and nations were not implicated, but which they had the capacity to solve. Indeed, he suggested, poor people and poor communities frequently preserved values and virtues which rich people and rich communities had lost. In this sense, the rich were the problem, not the poor. And the rich and prosperous were called to attend to the experience and the insights of the poor. The poor had resources of a non-material sort which might help to remedy the characteristic impoverishment of the rich. Poverty, in his account, was seen as much more than a lack of material resources, although the way material things were deployed was always charged with profound spiritual and ethical significance. Indeed he asserted that the Kingdom of God and its justice could more often and more readily be identified among the poor than among the rich; it was there that the seeds of God's future were to be found. When evil appeared to hold sway without restraint, that was the time that the Kingdom became visible.

As a consequence he suggested that the response to poverty must be far more varied, profound, participative and reciprocal than either of the first two speakers had suggested. Any approach to poverty which did not listen to the voice of the poor expectantly, and assumed that poverty was a problem involving a proportion of the population only, which might be solved by policy measures on the initiative of the rest, was fatally flawed, for it inherently confirmed the materialism which was in fact at the heart of the distinctively modern contours of poverty, its causes and its cure. It was not enough to grab power, nationally and internationally, and use it on behalf of the poor. The poor could help everyone to recover a sense of

community and conviviality in which ultimately materialist
values were transcended. The issue was one of spirituality as
well as of policy and power.

The voice of the poor people at the conference was angry
and a bit disjointed. They were irritated at so many people who
did not in fact know in their own experience the realities of
poverty talking about it with so much apparent authority. They
clearly did not like being treated as 'a problem', the solution to
which lay in the hands of others. They had a fierce pride in
their communities and what they had achieved through community action, in festival societies, self-help groups and organisations like Women's Aid. They resented being patronised.
They asked for justice, not charity.

Despite the fact that no one at the conference represented
the increasingly influential view that poverty has nothing to do
with justice, the speakers were in pretty fundamental disagreement with one another. But the audience was left with a proper
sense that while the problem is gigantic in the so-called 'developed world', it is even more immense in the 'developing
countries', and in fact the issue is a global one because it relates
so directly to the new global economy. Everyone agreed that
the scale of poverty today was an outrage to the conscience,
that it was a profound injustice, and that something must be
done. But there agreement stopped. We were left with a deep
uncertainty about how to construe poverty and a sense of
strange incapacity as to how to respond, how to harness the
sense of moral outrage to a constructive way forward. 'I was
left', one participant said, 'with a sense of helplessness.'

CONSTRUING POVERTY

Everyone thinks they know more or less accurately what
poverty is. And in the sense that they can point to it, that they
can recognise it, and that they regard it as an evil to be avoided
or remedied, they are right. Every account of poverty contains
implications for the proper response. But few people will
happily regard *themselves* as poor, for poverty is a disgrace, a
stigma, so that many people who by objective material stan-

dards are poor do not regard themselves as poor, manage successfully to conceal their hardship, and preserve their dignity and independence. Is it fair, then, to call them poor and to treat them as poor? Besides, a few people, usually for religious reasons, will voluntarily embrace poverty and discover in it deep spiritual values. But enforced poverty is of course a very different thing from poverty freely chosen as a way of life with a distinctive spirituality, an optional lifestyle emphasising self-denial and identification with the poor.

Absolute poverty means living on the edge of starvation, lacking the resources – food, clothing, shelter – necessary to sustain life and health. 'A family is poor', wrote Keith Joseph and Jonathan Sumption, 'if it cannot afford to eat.' Accordingly, they argued, we need an absolute standard which is 'defined by reference to the actual needs of the poor and not by reference to the expenditure of those who are not poor'. A decent society should be sympathetic to those in absolute poverty, and this sympathy should be reflected in policies and in institutions. The issue here is compassion, not justice.[3]

Strenuous, but ultimately unsatisfactory, efforts were made over many years by early students of poverty to develop objective criteria of absolute poverty which would be valid with only minimal adjustments for climate, etc., in various countries and contexts. The World Health Organisation, for instance, declared that 3,000 calories a day were required by a moderately active man and 2,200 by a moderately active woman. To define absolute poverty you require to know what people need in order to survive; and if they are provided with that, they are no longer poor. But needs are notoriously difficult to define precisely. These criteria were never satisfactory, and partly because they dealt with human beings as if they were simply biological machines rather than social beings who have a complex sense of identity and self-worth, and corresponding needs, rooted in the fact that they are relational beings, partly because it became increasingly obvious that poverty is a social

---

[3] Keith Joseph and Jonathan Sumption, *Equality*. London: John Murray, 1979, pp. 27–8.

construct which cannot be separated from the values, attitudes and beliefs of people in a particular culture, society and age.

The anthropologist Peter Worsley writes:

Notions of what constitutes an adequate diet, let alone adequate pay or an adequate standard of living in general are culture-specific norms, defined by people in specific societies, according to *their* criteria of what constitutes want or plenty, not standards deemed appropriate for them – often arbitrarily – by social workers, statisticians or nutritionists, and measured against some universal biological yardstick. Social wants, not asocial biological needs, define health and wealth.[4]

It really is not helpful to suggest that an eighteenth-century French peasant would regard the poorest unemployed factory worker of today as living in great luxury, or that a slum-dweller in the chawls of Bombay would regard the typical modern inhabitant of the slums of Liverpool or Harlem as rich. For in other respects, the eighteenth-century French peasant and the inhabitant of the Bombay chawl are in a better, and certainly a very different, position from the poor of the modern western world.

Poverty, it became clear, means different things in different contexts; and it is a graduated and relative rather than an absolute phenomenon, more or less the same in every age and situation. Even Adam Smith proposed a standard of poverty relative to his age:

By necessaries, I understand not only the commodities which are indispensably necessary for the support of life but whatever the custom of the country renders it indecent for creditable people, even of the lowest order, to be without. A linen shirt, for example, is strictly speaking not a necessity of life . . . But in the present time . . . a creditable day labourer would be ashamed to appear in public without a linen shirt.[5]

Peter Worsley pointed out in 1984 that at that time the official measure of poverty used in Britain was in real terms twice that adopted by Rowntree in 1899, and in real terms the poor in Britain were still seven times better off than the poor in India.

---

[4] Peter Worsley, *The Three Worlds*. London: Weidenfeld & Nicolson, 1984, p. 206.
[5] Adam Smith, *The Wealth of Nations* (1776), in Alcock, *Understanding Poverty*, p. 59.

'The relevant reference group . . . for immigrants to Third World cities,' he continues, 'is not any class in the First World, not even the rich or the privileged workers in their own country, but more often those in the villages and towns they have come from. What looks like the "backside of hell" to the outsider, is often experienced by the shanty-town dweller as improvement.'[6]

Social scientists and historians have demonstrated the important differences between poverty in the newly urbanised societies of Asia and in the more traditional countryside, and between poverty in Victorian cities and poverty in the same cities in the late twentieth century. In some situations the poor in the urban slums are in fact the more adventurous and upwardly mobile sections of the population; in others, slum-dwellers are mainly the failures and misfits of the broader society. A typical British poor area in the 1930s suffering from unemployment and deprivation was sustained by a sense of solidarity which has now been substantially eroded. Jeremy Seabrook argues that life in the Bombay chawls is in fact better than poverty in inner-city Britain today, for although the degree of physical deprivation is far higher in India there is a sense of shared destiny and of hope in the future.[7] Many visitors have been surprised how often in physically outrageous conditions in 'Third World' countries there is an ebullient sense of joy and an eager welcome to strangers.

The people who say that a family is only poor if it cannot afford to eat are in fact making a political point, for in developed countries this extreme kind of poverty is rare and it cannot count as a major disease of society. They are suggesting that poverty is a small and manageable problem. Nevertheless, in situations where there is little absolute poverty, poverty exists as a major, and growing, social problem. Poverty cannot properly be understood as only the extreme end of the scale, any more than sickness can be defined as occurring only when a person is under intensive care or on the operating table. Absolute poverty is a very dreadful thing; but it is the extreme

6 Worsley, *Three Worlds*, p. 205.
7 Jeremy Seabrook, *Landscapes of Poverty*. Oxford: Basil Blackwell, 1985.

instance of a social ailment which needs to be addressed as a whole.

Efforts to develop understandings of relative poverty and ways of measuring relative poverty must start from the question, relative to what? The simplest, and indeed the most obvious, approach is to relate poverty to the general level of income in a society: a family is poor if it has an unacceptably low level of income in comparison with the rest of society. On this general basis successive governments in Britain fixed the levels for National Assistance, then Supplementary Benefit, and then Income Support, as floors below which people were not to be allowed to fall. The leading social scientist specialising in poverty in Britain, Peter Townsend, in his major study, *Poverty in the United Kingdom*, developed what he claimed was an objective relative standard of poverty and suggested that there was a 'poverty threshold' at about 150 per cent of the Supplementary Benefit level. People with incomes less than 150 per cent of the Supplementary Benefit level were on the margins of poverty and peculiarly liable to sink into increased deprivation.

The criteria of poverty proposed by Peter Townsend and others produced truly alarming figures for the incidence and growth of poverty in Britain. His study, published in 1979, concluded:

By the state's standard, there were 6.1 per cent of the sample in households, and 8.1 per cent in income units who, when their net disposable incomes were averaged over the previous twelve months, were found to be living in poverty. They represented 3,300,000 and 4,950,000 people respectively. A further 21.8 per cent in households and 23.2 per cent in income units were on the margins of poverty, representing 11,900,000 and 12,600,000 respectively . . . By the state's own definition, therefore, there were between 15 and $17\frac{1}{2}$ million in a population of some $55\frac{1}{2}$ million who were in or near poverty.[8]

Other studies on a similar basis produced no less startling results: nearly a third of the population was poor or on the threshold of poverty. High unemployment and the rapid increase in the number of the elderly were main contributors to these alarming statistics.

[8] Peter Townsend, *Poverty in the United Kingdom*. Harmondsworth: Penguin, 1979, p. 895.

The basis of Peter Townsend's work was challenged by those who suggested that his method was shaped by egalitarian value assumptions so that broadening differentials in income or increasing economic prosperity almost inevitably increased the statistics of poverty. Furthermore, the size of the problem had been so exaggerated, the critics suggested, that resources were actually being diverted from the poorest in an effort to improve the lot of one-third of the population.

Another way of construing poverty is to relate it to people's attitudes. Poverty, on this account, is what most people think it is; the definition of poverty is based on consensus rather than any kind of objective criteria. And in this case consensus is closely related to empathy: poverty is a standard of living that you would find distressing and unacceptable for yourself or your near relatives. In public opinion surveys, people were asked to specify what might be a minimum level of acceptable living in Britain today. In a way this was a Rawlsian attempt to discover, on the basis of thinking oneself into the other person's shoes, whether there was a consensus about what poverty is. Mack and Lansley's study, *Poor Britain,* in the early 1980s was based on a large-scale survey to discover whether there was in fact any agreement about a minimum acceptable level of living in Britain today. They asked their respondents to choose from a list the items they regarded as indispensable. The responses suggested that there was a widely held consensus that families and individuals with less than about 150 per cent of the old Supplementary Benefit level were poor and measures should be taken to help them. They repeated their research in 1990, and showed that there was now a slightly higher expectation of what was necessary to keep out of poverty, and that there had been a significant increase in the number of poor people.

Although this on the whole confirmed Peter Townsend's approach and conclusions, it provided a fragile and volatile basis for policy. Electoral results tended to show that people voted according to their purses rather than their consciences. The same people as occupied the moral high ground when responding to public opinion pollsters voted in elections to defend their own economic interests. In addition, public opinion changes and varies from one country to another. It seems at present, for example, that public opinion in the United States is markedly more hostile towards the poor than it is in western European countries. Even in a country like Britain, research shows that there is much suspicion of the poor. Peter Golding and Sue Middleton's study shows that a considerable majority of the sample of those questioned considered that benefits for the poor were too high and too easy to get, and that too much was being spent on welfare. Low wage earners tended to be particularly suspicious of the poor and those on benefits; little poverty was believed to exist; the poor were generally blamed for their poverty and were felt to have become 'the spoilt darlings and cheats of the welfare state'.[9]

Although poverty in developing countries often goes with a lively sense of solidarity, it is increasingly the case that the poor in developed countries are marginalised and excluded and their worth denied. Poverty is deeply destructive to self-esteem, to families and to communities. So David Donnison, at that time Chairman, wrote in the Report of the Supplementary Benefit Commission for 1978:

To keep out of poverty, people must have an income which enables them to participate in the life of the community. They must be able, for example, to keep themselves reasonably fed, and well enough dressed to maintain their self-respect and to attend interviews for jobs with confidence. Their homes must be reasonably warm; their children should not feel shamed by the quality of their clothing; the family must be able to visit relatives, and give them something on their birthdays and at Christmas time; they must be able to read newspapers, and retain their television sets and their membership of trade unions and churches. And they must be able to live in a way which ensures, so far as possible, that public officials, doctors, teachers, landlords and others treat them with the courtesy due to every member of the community.[10]

In western societies at least, poverty is experienced as shame, lack of capacity and exclusion.[11]

---

[9] Peter Golding and Sue Middleton, *Images of Welfare*. Oxford: Martin Robertson, 1982.

[10] David Donnison, *The Politics of Poverty*. Oxford: Martin Robertson, 1982, p. 8.

[11] A. Sen, *Poor, Relatively Speaking*. Dublin: Economic and Social Research Institute, 1982.

But if poverty is experienced as exclusion, it is also argued that there are cultures of poverty which establish ringfences around the poor and give them a psychology of resignation and dependence. The various forms of 'poverty trap' make escape difficult. Some who speak of the culture of poverty regard poverty as a pathological way of life which is passed from generation to generation in poor communities. For them, the disease infects poor communities, not society as a whole. Shrewd observers have discerned the emergence of large and increasing 'underclasses' in western societies – groups of people effectively and permanently excluded from the choices and opportunities available to others, and living on the margins of the society, with their own mores, and alienated from the mainstream.

There is much confusion today about how to understand poverty. No value-free understanding is possible, and the values expressed in a particular account of poverty also shape the possibilities of response, to which I now turn.

RESPONDING TO POVERTY

There are three general ways of responding to poverty, which relate to three ways of understanding the issue and often overlap. For some people poverty is seen as a kind of cultural or psychological pathology. Accordingly, the culture of poverty must be destroyed and poor people helped or provoked to climb out of poverty. Other people view poverty as a self-contained social problem which can be isolated from the other items of social policy and treated as a separate entity. Policies to deal with poverty should be sharply focused, and are direct responses to specified needs. Yet a third group regard poverty as structural, a kind of disease of society as a whole which can only be cured by treatment which affects the whole system.

The first approach often goes with the once fashionable distinction between the 'deserving' and the 'undeserving' poor, which is still influential in some quarters. It played a great role in nineteenth-century philanthropy and social policy, with its suggestion that for the most part the poor were responsible for their own condition. Their poverty had been caused primarily by their own fecklessness, idleness and ignorance. And the solution lay largely in their own hands. The 'deserving poor' were those who were the innocent victims of misfortune, such as old people with no families to care for them, or the children of paupers. Such people deserved a judicious charity, carefully arranged so that they did not settle comfortably into dependence on the largesse of others. Victorian philanthropists were sometimes at pains to remove the children of poor people from their families so that they should not learn sloth and intemperance at home from their parents, but should be taught industry and thrift in an institution, and thus be enabled to become useful members of society. The undeserving poor were regarded as an ever-present threat to social order and as actually or potentially criminal. The poor laws provided ways of controlling the undeserving poor and inciting them to change their ways and escape from the culture of the underworld. They were not properly seen as worthy of charity, but the poor laws provided a kind of safety net for them against utter destitution while being sufficiently uncomfortable to discourage any tendency to dependency on others. Churchmen like Thomas Chalmers saw 'pauperism' as essentially a spiritual matter and thus properly the province of the church. Others emphasised the role of individual philanthropy.

While it is not fashionable today to talk about the deserving and the undeserving poor, the logic of the poor laws still lurks in the atmosphere. This is clear in repeated efforts to blame the victims for their lot, and make sweeping generalisations about the laziness of the unemployed, the wickedness of 'welfare scroungers', and the dependency of the poor on the largesse of others. Conservative thinkers like George Gilder proclaimed that 'real poverty is less a state of income than a state of mind and . . . the government dole blights most of the people who have come to depend on it'.[12] He goes on to argue that 'since the war on poverty was launched, the moral blight of dependency has been compounded and extended to future genera-

---

[12] George Gilder, *Wealth and Poverty*. New York: Basic Books, 1981, p. 12.

tions by a virtual plague of family dissolution'. But poverty, in this view, can also be a powerful spur to economic achievement. Thus a degree of poverty so regarded can be an engine for economic development and growth. Only, people must be left to climb their own way out of poverty. Poverty is not seen as a responsibility of the whole community. An extreme advocate of this position is the American Charles Murray who suggests that it would be better if all state support for the poor were withdrawn.[13]

The second approach sees poverty as a social problem which should be handled in isolation. The tendency here is to assume that the poor will be with us always, but to attempt to alleviate the lot of the poor. To do this it is necessary that measures should be carefully targeted so that those in real need are the ones who benefit. But targeting involves identifying poor people as a problem which others have the capacity to solve. And in order to target successfully one has to distinguish the people to be helped, usually by some form of means test, which is commonly experienced as invasive and degrading, so that many poor people through a proper sense of pride refuse to apply for benefits or go through the humiliating interrogation about their resources that targeting usually involves. To be labelled poor is a stigma (A theologian might be excused the reflection that stigma and stigmata originally referred to the wounds of crucifixion, simultaneously marks of disgrace at the hands of humans and of glory in God's eyes!) that most people find degrading. As a consequence, many sorts of targeting are not fully effective – help does not get to where the real need is. People are encouraged to define themselves as poor so as to qualify for benefits; 'thus it may well happen that poverty is simultaneously alleviated and perpetuated'.[14] It is difficult to have a form of targeting which does not involve some kind of

---

[13] Charles Murray, *Losing Ground: American Social Policy, 1950–1980*. New York: Basic Books, 1984, and *The Emerging British Underclass*. London: Institute of Economic Affairs, 1990.

[14] Zsusa Ferge, 'Comments on the Poverty Debate' in *Poverty Today*. Occasional Paper, no. 7, Edinburgh: CTPI, 1986, p. 13.

poverty trap, making it hard for people to move out of poverty without losing resources in the process.

The third approach tends to see poor people as victims of unjust social processes, as symptoms of a disease of society. The only solution to poverty is the establishment of social justice for the existence of poverty reveals the sickness of society. As in smallpox it makes no sense to treat the blisters without engaging with the disease, so advocates of a structural approach tend sometimes to be impatient with those who adopt a targeted approach because they are believed to be treating the symptoms rather than the disease. Occasionally those who adopt this position may be cavalier and dismissive about efforts to help directly those who suffer from poverty. In a truly just society, the advocates of a structural approach believe, there will be no poverty; the gulf between rich and poor which is inherently unjust and threatens social solidarity will be overcome. The object of social policy should be the elimination rather than the mere alleviation of poverty.

We are left, then, with considerable uncertainty about how to respond appropriately to poverty. For some people it is a problem 'out there', which we, the non-poor, have the capacity to solve if we so will – or perhaps political action can solve it on our behalf. Yet political action seems to engender a false and disabling dependency in some, and there is now much evidence that many measures intended to benefit the poor have in fact benefited the more prosperous to a far greater extent.[15] Sad experience has taught that throwing money at problems does not often resolve them, and may make them worse. For others, poverty is a problem of social justice in which everyone is implicated and all must strive to resolve. Some, from left as well as right, believe that only the poor themselves are capable of dealing appropriately with poverty. In their very different ways, both Jürgen Habermas and George Gilder believe that justice demands that we must attend to the poor and help them to take control of their own destiny.

But there are those who teach that no action is in fact

[15] See, for instance, Julian Le Grand, *The Strategy of Equality*. London: Allen & Unwin, 1982.

necessary, and any intervention is harmful in the long run, for the beneficent trickle-down effects of market operations over time improve the lot of the poor immeasurably more efficiently than any 'wars on poverty' or fundamental structural changes – in John Kenneth Galbraith's words, 'if one feeds the horse enough oats, some will pass through to the road for the sparrows'![16] But little empirical evidence supports the efficacy of trickle-down. Indeed, in Britain during the decade 1979–89, when average incomes rose by 30 per cent, the incomes of the poorest ten per cent of the population *fell* by 6 per cent.[17] The Joseph Rowntree Foundation's *Inquiry into Income and Wealth* demonstrated that in Britain income became rapidly less equal in the 1980s, that the lowest income groups did not benefit from economic growth, that since 1977 the proportion of the population on a perilously low income more than trebled, and that the United Kingdom was exceptional in the pace and extent of the increase in inequality in the 1980s. This, the report pointed out, had serious effects on the family, especially on children, and on the fabric of society.[18] We have in most western countries an increasing incidence of poverty, however defined, a wide recognition that this is a major issue – perhaps *the* major issue – of social justice today and great uncertainty as to how to respond effectively.

THEOLOGICAL CLUES

Is it possible that Christian faith may have something to offer in clarifying the issues, exposing the motivations and suggesting ways forward in such a confusing and depressing discussion? Or is the text, 'The poor you will have with you always', quoted by Jesus from Deuteronomy in the context of the criticism of the lavish generosity of the woman with the alabaster box of ointment,[19] a mandate for resignation in face of poverty, or a

[16] J. K. Galbraith, *The Culture of Contentment*. London: Sinclair-Stevenson, 1992, p. 29.
[17] Alcock, *Understanding Poverty*, pp. 262–3.
[18] Joseph Rowntree Foundation, *Inquiry into Income and Wealth*. 2 vols., York: Joseph Rowntree Foundation, 1995.
[19] Deut. 15.11 cited in Matt. 26.11, Mark 14.7 and John 12.8. It is interesting that Luke's account changes the focus of the narrative from the issue of poverty to the question

suggestion that the only Christian reaction to the perennial problem of poverty is voluntary charity with no relation to issues of justice? I think not.

I once heard an Indian theologian declare that the Christian gospel was a programme for the eradication of poverty in fifteen years. Such a trivialisation of the theological contribution to the discussion of poverty is stunning in its naiveté and its reductionism. But it at least emphasises that the Christian faith nourishes a passionate concern for the poor, and insists that poverty should be put high on the moral agenda as an issue of justice. Nor can theology provide an alternative analysis of the nature of poverty to that produced by social scientists. Yet even if theology can neither draw up the strategy and tactics for a war on poverty or produce a rigorous analysis to displace or operate alongside other ways of construing poverty, it can offer to the discussion important emphases and insights.

The first and most important of these is the affirmation that poverty is an issue of justice. It is this because poor people bear a disproportionate burden of pain. Their life expectancy is markedly less than that of more prosperous people, their health is worse, they have fewer life chances and their family and other relationships are under constant pressure. Christians believe that justice is to do with relationships. Good relationships are expressed and strengthened by a just distribution of material things; poverty and deprivation put pressure on family and other relationships; and poor people tend to be marginalised by the broader community.

Another central concern affirms the blessedness of the poor. They have a special, privileged place in the heart of God, and God gives them his blessing. The place of the poor in the Bible has been explored in detail by many scholars, who uniformly agree that God is depicted as the One who has a special care for the poor and will vindicate them.

With typical concreteness, the Bible does not engage with an abstract problem like poverty or pauperism, but with poor *people*, and their lot and standing in God's eyes. The poor are

of Jesus' relation to a woman of doubtful reputation. Luke as a whole is particularly committed to the cause of the poor.

people, made in the image of God, with claims and contributions to make. Instead of being labelled as a problem, the poor are treated as people who have gifts and claims to bring into the interactions of society. Indeed, it is more common in Scripture for the wealthy to be seen as in a problematic situation. In the parable of the Rich Man and Lazarus, for instance, by the end of the story it is not the poor man, Lazarus, who is in trouble, but the Rich Man, who is separated by a great gulf from the blessedness of Abraham's bosom, precisely because he had failed to see or respond to the need of the poor man at his gate.[20] The issue is here stood on its head: the problem in the eyes of the poor (as R. H. Tawney pointed out)[21] and in the eyes of God is not so much poverty as wealth. Poverty is an affliction of the whole society, as Jeremy Seabrook points out vividly:

The poor live in a distortion of the society we all inhabit; a more naked version, a cruder exemplification of its values. The reason why the voice of the poor is stifled is that they tell us too much about ourselves; our bartered freedoms and diminished autonomy and dying control over our lives.[22]

Thus in poverty we have an issue of how society is structured and how people relate to one another. Seabrook is right to say, 'The poor cannot be freed from the cruel visitations of their poverty unless the rich are at the same time emancipated from the diseases – physical, moral and spiritual – of their wealth.'[23] Poverty is a systemic problem; it can only be uprooted if there is change in values, in attitudes and in the social order.

José P. Miranda has argued convincingly that the Bible has a central concern with justice for the poor. The poor have a right to justice for justice is God's will for them. And charity or other forms of voluntary or palliative action fall seriously short of the teaching of the Bible.[24] This puts the question of poverty at the

[20] Luke 16.19–31.
[21] 'What thoughtful rich people call the problem of poverty, thoughtful poor people call with equal justice a problem of riches.' R. H. Tawney, Inaugural Lecture, 1913, in Pete Alcock, *Understanding Poverty*, p. xi.
[22] Seabrook, *Landscapes of Poverty*, p. 95.   [23] Seabrook, *Landscapes of Poverty*, p. 5.
[24] José P. Miranda, *Marx and the Bible: A Critique of the Philosophy of Oppression*. London: SCM, 1977.

centre of the public agenda, not as a marginal problem to which charity is an adequate response but as an issue which concerns the justice of God. Justice for the poor is restitution to them of what is properly theirs. The poor have a claim on the rich. Thus we have to speak, with R. H. Tawney, of the need for a demanding 'intellectual conversion' to a new concern for justice and the poor.[25]

The poor are a challenge to the church. 'The poor', wrote Gustavo Gutierrez, 'raise the question of what "being the church" really means.'[26] Is a church in which the poor do not belong truly the church of Jesus Christ? If one accepts in full seriousness the patristic adage, *ubi Christus ibi ecclesia* (where Christ is, there is the church), surely we must discover among the poor both the Christ who chooses to identify with them and the true nature of the church. The concept of the church as a perfect society, powerful and wealthy, parallel to the state and able to pontificate to the state, has few attractions for the poor even if it claims to speak on their behalf. For it is not their church; they do not belong to it, except as dependants. In such a church, as in the broader society, they are powerless and marginalised. In important senses, this church and class society are mirror images of one another; the place of the poor is the same in each, although the church may be more benevolent in its attitudes and dealings. What it does not often do is set aside its institutional arrogance and attend to the poor, listen to what they have to say and welcome the gifts and insights that they bring. Nor does it often risk taking a stand on their side, challenging oppression head-on, or sacrificing its own wealth, security or standing.

The poor therefore challenge the power structures of the church and the centralisation of authority in the hierarchy, together with the church's implication in class society despite its claim to transcend the social and political order. The challenge is intended to renew and reform rather than destroy the church. Sobrino suggests that the poor may be the resurrection of the true church; through the poor whom he loves Jesus

---

[25] R. H. Tawney, *The Acquisitive Society*. London: Bell, 1921, p. 230.
[26] G. Gutierrez, 'The Poor in the Church', *Concilium*, 104 (1977), 11.

Christ is recreating the entire church.[27] Yet the poor are a
constant irritant to a complacent and triumphalistic understanding of the church; their presence makes reality unavoidable. Their claim and their condition keep alive the questions
of God, and of the Kingdom, and of justice and ensure that the
church cannot be finally domesticated within the power structures of society. The poor bring to the church an understanding
of fellowship, sharing and, solidarity, which is a reminder that
an important dimension of catholicity is the sharing of one
another's burdens.[28]

The poor also stand as a test of the justice of any society, and
a challenge to materialism, for in God's eyes the poor are
blessed, and in God's Kingdom of justice they are vindicated.

But are not such 'theological fragments' on poverty of such
generality that they can make no impact in the complex and
difficult business of policy-making? Are they not so idealistic
that they do not fit into the hard-headed debates of modern
politics? Is the church really capable of responding to the
challenge of the poor? These are hard questions with no easy
answers. There are, however, instances in recent times which
suggest that Christian insights, if properly and responsibly
deployed, can in fact have a considerable influence in public
debate. The churches do continue to have some influence over
what people believe and how they behave, and, if the economist
Julian Le Grand is right, this can be of crucial importance:

To understand what people believe is crucial to understand the way
they behave; and to change the way they behave, it is crucial to
change what they believe. Indeed ideology can often override self-
interest . . . A change in beliefs can even induce people to reduce
their power and privilege.[29]

There are welcome signs that many churches are today having
the courage to speak out.

Notable among these is the pastoral letter on the United
States economy issued by the Catholic bishops and published in

[27] Jon Sobrino, *The True Church and the Poor*. London: SCM, 1985, p. 93.
[28] These two paragraphs are taken from my *Theology and Politics*. Oxford: Blackwell,
1988, p. 138.
[29] Le Grand, *Strategy of Equality*, p. 155.

1986 after extensive public discussion of three drafts.[30] Although this was explicitly a *pastoral* letter addressed to the Catholic community in the first place, it was also intended to be a contribution to public debate, and it turned out to be one of the most creative and stimulating contributions for many years. Both the drafts and the final version were highly controversial, but the bishops' theological, moral and economic judgements were so carefully measured that it was impossible to dismiss the document as utopian, moralistic or based on inadequate analysis, although it explicitly endeavoured to present and commend a 'moral vision'. Furthermore, although the document was controversial, its aim was to open, not to conclude, a responsible and morally informed debate about the implications of economic policy. The bishops did not attempt to constrain the consciences of believers or others by laying down a definitive Christian economic policy; they simply suggested priorities and considerations which were essential if economic activity was to be morally acceptable. Among these the position of the poor has a central place:

Decisions must be judged in light of what they do *for* the poor, what they do *to* the poor, and what they enable the poor to do *for themselves*. The fundamental moral criterion for all economic decisions, policies and institutions is this: They must be at the service of *all people, especially the poor*.[31]

Furthermore, 'the poor have the single most urgent economic claim on the conscience of the nation'.[32] Individuals and the nation, not only the church and Catholics, were called upon to make a fundamental 'option for the poor', assessing public policy 'from the viewpoint of the poor and powerless', because 'those who are marginalised and whose rights are denied have privileged claims if society is to provide justice for all'.[33] It was essential to overcome exclusion and enable the poor to be active, contributing participants in society: 'The deprivation and powerlessness of the poor wounds the whole community. The extent of their suffering is a measure of how far we are

---

[30] US Catholic Bishops, *Economic Justice for All: Catholic Social Teaching and the US Economy*. Washington: National Conference of Catholic Bishops, 1986.
[31] *Ibid.*, par. 24.   [32] *Ibid.*, par. 86.   [33] *Ibid.*, par. 87.

from being a true community of persons. These wounds will be healed only by greater solidarity with the poor and among the poor themselves.'[34]

The pastoral letter included a major discussion of poverty which expressed profound concern at its recent dramatic increase and made clear that the church, unlike most other major social institutions, had day-to-day contact with the human reality of poverty through its parishes and its pastoral and charitable work. In their letter the bishops wanted to strengthen the commitment and involvement of individuals, Catholic and non-Catholic, in responding to poverty, and the commitment of the church to the poor. But action in the area of public policy was also essential. 'Private charity and voluntary action are not sufficient' and 'Alleviating poverty will require fundamental changes in social and economic structures that perpetuate glaring inequalities and cut off millions of citizens from full participation in the economic and social life of the nation.'[35] For the issue of poverty is at its heart a question of justice.

In other contexts, too, the churches have made similar contributions to public debate, stressing the centrality of the issue of the poor. The 1985 Church of England report *Faith in the City* addressed the problem of urban deprivation and the degeneration of the inner cities. Like the US bishops' letter, it was addressed primarily to the church – and its problems in maintaining a serving presence with the poor – and to Christians, but it also of necessity addressed issues of public policy, calling for a major programme of regeneration for the inner cities and a special concern for the poor. 'Poverty', the report suggested, 'is not only about shortage of money. It is about rights and relationships, about how people are treated and how they regard themselves; about powerlessness, exclusion, and loss of dignity. Yet the lack of an adequate income is at its heart.'[36] *Faith in the City* aroused prolonged controversy, being roundly denounced by a government minister as 'Marxist' just

---

[34] *Ibid.*, par. 88.   [35] *Ibid.*, par. 187.
[36] Archbishop of Canterbury's Commission on Urban Priority Areas, *Faith in the City: A Call for Action by Church and Nation*. London: Church Information Office, 1985, p. 195.

before publication. Debate and action flowing from the report continues, and it can be argued that it directly provoked a new concern with urban regeneration on the part of the government.

The Church of Scotland published a report on the distribution of wealth, income and benefits called *Just Sharing*, in 1988. This report, produced by an interdisciplinary working party, attempted to face the facts of maldistribution in Scotland, and see in human and community terms what these facts meant for individuals, for families and for the nation. It tried to convey something of the experience of poverty to a readership which was largely non-poor. Then a section on interpretation and reflection looked at facts and experiences in the light of the Christian tradition. And finally the report suggested ways of response in three areas: personal life style, the life of the church and how it deploys its resources, and public policy. Once again, a church report provoked controversy, and once again a church affirmed the public relevance of the preferential option for the poor.[37]

All these statements are at one in seeing poverty as a crucial issue of justice. They operate with very similar understandings of social justice, derived from Scripture and the tradition of Christian social teaching, but also rooted in the day-to-day experience of struggling to be the church and proclaim good news to the poor in areas of great deprivation and poverty at home and around the world. They all see justice as demanding a far more equitable distribution of material things as an expression of neighbour-love and a reinforcement of community solidarity. They all see justice as demanding also empowerment and participation: people must be enabled to take responsible charge of their lives and of their communities.

[37] Duncan B. Forrester and Danus Skene (eds.), *Just Sharing: A Christian Approach to the Distribution of Wealth, Income and Benefits.* London: Epworth, 1988.

PART III

Theories and theologies

In Part II we have discussed some of the confusing difficulties 'on the ground', as it were, that arise when there is fundamental uncertainty about what justice is. These difficulties can be both destructive and threatening to practices and to policy-making and implementation.

In this Part we turn to consider what resources may be found in recent theories of justice. In chapter 3 we saw how many people are today rather suspicious of theory, believing it to serve sometimes to conceal what is really happening, or to justify the intolerable; and often theory is felt to be so remote from the actual issues that arise in practice that it is no longer believed to be relevant to action and to understanding.

But nonetheless theory is indispensable to illumine situations and reveal what is going on, and to guide towards coherent and consistent practice and policy.

In this book I am not concerned with an 'in-house' academic debate about theories of justice, but rather with the movement between theory, policy and practice. The kind of questions I will address in this Part are these: Do theories of justice illuminate what is going on? Do they articulate the demands of justice? Do they give effective guidance to practice? What kind of policy outcomes may they generate, and what kind of policies do they justify? What are the effects of these policies? Are these theories, or any of them, capable of motivating people to seek justice even if the establishment of a greater degree of justice goes against the self-interest of individuals and groups? How adequate are secular theories of justice to an age when nobody knows what justice is? In a secular, pluralist society can these theories, or any of them, serve as the Christian voice in the public sphere?

I will give special attention to the notion that justice is fairness, associated with the thought of the American philosopher John Rawls, to issues concerning the relation of the market and justice, exemplified in the theory of Frederick A. Hayek, to Habermas's thought on the kind of justice that is necessary if we are to have a decent, participative social order, and to the challenging and constructive contribution of some leading feminist thinkers to the contemporary debate about justice.

The dialogue between theology and social and political theory today is complicated, for various reasons. On the other hand all these theories have emerged in a Christian or post-Christian context, and some Christian assumptions are embedded in them. There is also a pervasive assumption today that Christian theological language is no longer permissible in the public sphere. On the other hand theologians for the most part have lost the art of public discourse, or engage with secular theories with undue deference to positions which are at variance with fundamental insights of Christian faith.

I intend, in dialogue with some major players in the contemporary debate about justice, to see what relevant insights they have to offer, and to examine from a theological angle their validity and cogency.

CHAPTER 5

Fairness is not enough

Fairness is clearly a good thing, and a quality that is closely involved with both love and justice. A family in which the children are systematically treated in an unfair way is hardly likely to be a loving family, unless apparent or real unfairness can be justified by the demands of love. Preferential treatment for a child with special difficulties can appear to the other children to be unfair favouritism, but it should be possible to explain that the unfairness is only apparent, and is required by love. Real unfairness is incompatible with love. Similarly in a community people expect fair treatment and are aggrieved if they do not, in their opinion, receive it. Preferential treatment for women, for ethnic minorities and so on is sometimes regarded by others as unfair, and wage disputes are character-istically arguments about what is regarded as a fair wage. Although few would suggest that love *is* fairness, and no more, most people assume that justice is fairness, or at least regard fairness as a kind of rule of thumb for just treatment.

'Justice as fairness' was the slogan the American social theorist John Rawls chose to explain in simple terms the nub of his theory. The sophisticated argument in his *A Theory of Justice* (1972), that justice is fairness, has shown itself to be immensely influential and important. It has sparked off a major academic debate which still shows little sign of abating. When the book first appeared it immediately demonstrated that Anglo-Saxon social philosophy was not dead, as many had believed. Rawls has vigorously defended and developed his theory in dialogue with a wide range of interlocutors. Recently he has presented a refine-ment and elaboration of his position in *Political Liberalism* (1993).

It is not only in an academic forum that Rawls's ideas are influential. In America they speak about 'the Rawls generation' – politicians, policy-makers and opinion formers who have found in Rawls's theory a convincing secular understanding of justice which commands wide, but by no means universal, assent and has an obvious bearing on public policy. And in Britain too it is not hard to see the profound influence of Rawlsian notions, for example, on the report of the Commission on Social Justice established by the late John Smith to set priorities and give a sense of direction to the Labour Party, and it is hoped eventually to the nation – a report I will discuss further.

Rawls's theory, despite the elegant simplicity of its central notion, is complex and intellectually demanding. It can be interpreted in a variety of ways. It has been called Christian by Stuart Hampshire, Hobbist by Anthony Flew, individualist by Robert Nozick, illiberal and socialist by Daniel Bell.[1] Perhaps one of the reasons for its popularity was the increasing implausibility to many of the Marxist ideology, especially after 1968. In Rawls there seemed to be an alternative egalitarian theory which was radical and reformist but seemed not to demand the adoption of a whole world-view. And not a few Christians have seen in Rawls something of the secular meaning of the gospel, and believed that Rawls offered the opportunity to embrace with others from very varied backgrounds a theory which articulated in a non-theological way central insights of the Judaeo-Christian tradition. There has, then, been a Christian appropriation of Rawls. But there have also been many, Christians and others, who have felt that Rawls's position is unsatisfactory, for a variety of reasons.

In this chapter I will examine Rawls's theory of justice as fairness, which has played so significant a role in recent social thought and has had a considerable impact on the public realm. I will discuss whether this theory, or some modification of it, is rich enough and strong enough to provide the basis for a public policy that strives to be just, and I will make some

[1] J .W. Chapman, 'Rawls's *Theory of Justice*', *American Political Science Review*, LXIX (1975), 588.

comments on the effects of the emphasis on fairness in some aspects of public policy. Rawls's theory is attractive to many for a variety of reasons. He is a powerful thinker who presents his views with vigour and rigour, and asserts the central importance of justice; as in the Bible and like Plato, Rawls gives it priority in the social order. 'Justice', he writes, 'is the first virtue of social institutions, as truth is of systems of thought. A theory however elegant and economical must be rejected or revised if it is untrue; likewise laws and institutions no matter how efficient and well-arranged must be reformed or abolished if they are unjust.'[2] He affirms the primacy of justice and acknowledges that 'a public sense of justice is what makes secure association together possible'. Justice is fundamental and priority should be given to it in ordering society, for without it things fall apart.

His distinctive view of justice is attractive because it corresponds to a fundamental instinct – we all believe that fairness is a good thing. In a way the theory legitimates and gives intellectual dignity to our untutored hunch that fairness is important, and it offers the possibility of a theory which could provide a tolerant pluralist society with an adequate level of ideological agreement by commanding far wider support than any of the alternatives on offer.

TWO READINGS

At the beginning it was possible to read Rawls in two different ways.[3] In the first, Rawls's project was seen as an attempt to produce a universal, rational and ahistorical theory of justice,

---

[2] John Rawls, *A Theory of Justice*. Oxford: Oxford University Press, 1971, p. 3.

[3] Rather unhelpfully, Rawls refers to these as two 'stages in the exposition of justice as fairness . . . in the first stage justice as fairness should be presented as a free-standing political conception that articulates the very great values applicable to the special domain of the political, as marked out by the basic structure of society'. The second stage 'consists of an account of the stability of justice as fairness, that is, its capacity to generate its own support'. ('The Domain of the Political and Overlapping Consensus', *New York University Law Review*, 64:2 (May 1989), 233–55 (234).) Even if Rawls meant them to be two stages when he wrote, it is clear that the theory has been read, and defended (by Rawls himself and others) in terms of two very different *readings*.

applicable everywhere and at all times. On this reading, in the 'Original Position' human nature is stripped down to its time-less essentials; those behind the Veil of Ignorance set aside, along with their interests and knowledge of their condition, their specific culture, their historical and geographical location, and their relation to a particular community and tradition. The suggestion is that they would then operate more or less as any rational human being in any setting would be likely to behave. These people would then be given the task of choosing the principles of justice in the society in which they are to live. Although Rawls admits that the people in his Original Position have 'a certain psychology' arising from 'various assumptions about their beliefs and interests',[4] on this reading it appears that justice has the kind of objectivity which arises from resting on an ontology, on an understanding of the nature of things, and thus it has the ability to maintain a critical distance from specific situations and from tendencies to twist notions of justice to accommodate them to selfish interests.

The second reading is the one which Rawls increasingly firmly insists reflects his intentions in writing. Here he claims to be producing a theory which 'matches the fixed points of our considered convictions'.[5] It reflects what most people believe. But it is not simply a distillation of unconsidered prejudices; justice as fairness rests on 'our' considered judgements; and 'we' are typical citizens of a modern liberal democracy. Thus his theory of justice is a kind of 'dogmatics' of liberalism – the exploration and elaboration from the inside of a system of belief. On this reading he does not appeal to some antecedently established moral order. The principles of justice should 'match our considered convictions of justice or expand them in an acceptable way'.[6] There should be a 'reflective equilibrium' between the theory and our convictions. The theory, in short, is not simply a reflection of public opinion. It interacts with considered convictions, which undergo a kind of internal critique. But on this reading Rawls's theory cannot appeal to any deeper or universal moral order. Principles emerge 'which

---

[4] John Rawls, *Theory of Justice*, p. 121.   [5] *Ibid.*, pp. 279–80.   [6] *Ibid.*, p. 19.

match our considered judgements duly pruned and adjusted'.[7] But on what basis does this pruning and adjustment take place? What makes the theory after pruning more fruitful than before? And what if the branches that are removed are essential to the continuing health of the main stem? This is, in Paul Ricoeur's words, 'a complex process of mutual adjustment between convictions and theory'.[8] But what if it degenerates into a reshuffling of prejudices and nothing more?

A central problem with this second reading is that it is not easy to see how such a theory of justice can indeed be more than a refinement of the conventional wisdom of the age. But the attractiveness of the reading is that it suggests a model of a kind of open, tolerant conversation about justice which might prove a useful force for social cohesion in a pluralistic society with a diversity of world-views, religions and fundamental commitments.

This may be a reason why Rawls has increasingly strongly stressed the second reading of his theory. In a 1985 article, Rawls emphatically rejects the view that *A Theory of Justice* claims any kind of universal truth.[9] He wishes to avoid making philosophical or metaphysical claims because 'in a constitutional democracy the public conception of justice should be, as far as possible, independent of controversial philosophical and religious doctrines'.[10] Justice as fairness, he suggests, is founded not even upon liberalism as a comprehensive moral doctrine, but on 'the basic intuitive ideas found in the public culture of a constitutional democracy'.[11] His theory is not a metaphysical doctrine, but a political matter. That is, it is a fundamental principle of political ordering which is endorsed by the vast majority of people in a modern constitutional democracy no matter what their varying overarching moral, religious and philosophical beliefs might be. Justice, then, mirrors the opinions of most people; it cannot act as the critic of these

---

[7] *Ibid.*, p. 20.
[8] Paul Ricoeur, *Oneself as Another*. Chicago: University of Chicago Press, 1992, p. 237.
[9] John Rawls, 'Justice as Fairness: Political not Metaphysical', *Philosophy and Public Affairs*, 14:3 (Summer 1985), 223–51.
[10] *Ibid.*, 223.
[11] *Ibid.*, 246.

opinions, and the possibility that 'considered convictions' might themselves be unjust seems to be excluded.[12]

The Original Position and the Garden of Eden

The first reading of Rawls's theory hinges upon the hypothetical scenario of the 'Original Position', in which human beings are stripped down to the essentials, and then, behind a 'Veil of Ignorance' as to their own abilities and status and resources, have to choose the principles of justice that should govern their society.[13] This is a sophisticated variant of a familiar device, used in most forms of social contract theory, to illumine the basic purposes and principles for which society and government were established. It tends, in all its various forms, to emphasise the priority of the individual to society; society and its governance are understood as devices established to advance and protect the basic interests of individuals. It also is a way of outlining an understanding of human nature: if human beings are like that, they would choose, or need, to live in such a society with a particular kind of government and structure.

The human beings under consideration have emerged from nowhere, 'sprung out of the earth . . . like mushrooms', to use Hobbes's vivid image.[14] They have no past, no affective links, no special interests to defend. They are human beings simpliciter. But the particular writer's presuppositions become obvious as the hypothetical situation is developed, and the reader is invited to test the narrative against experience: 'Are human beings fundamentally like that, and if so what kind of society must we have?' they are asked. Thus Hobbes, understanding human beings as basically competitive and antagonistic to one another, teaches that the state of nature would be

---

[12] This is a point made by Ronald Dworkin: see Daniel Bell, *Communitarianism and its Critics*. Oxford: Clarendon, 1993, pp. 214–15.

[13] T. M. Scanlon's more Kantian variant has commended itself to many people. Here there is no Veil of Ignorance. The participants need to justify their principles and proposals so convincingly to the rest that they have to agree to the universalisation of these principles. ('Contractualism and Utilitarianism' in A. Sen and B. Williams, *Utilitarianism and Beyond*. Cambridge: Cambridge University Press, 1982, pp. 103–28.)

[14] Cited in Susan Moller Okin, *Justice, Gender and the Family*. New York: Basic Books, 1989, p. 21.

a state of war in which human existence would be 'nasty, poor, brutish and short'. In his scenario, people are driven by fear of others to give up their freedom and accept an authoritarian sovereign. Locke, with a less threatening account of human nature, sees people as entering into a covenant to ensure greater security of life and property by setting up a government to act, with limited powers, as their trustee. Rousseau, again, sees the social contract as a way of marshalling and articulating the General Will over against the diverse wills of individuals; the General Will must shape society since the individual will is selfish and divisive.

Rawls's people in the Original Position are rational, self-interested human beings, capable of choosing what is good for them and of developing and sustaining a coherent life-plan over their whole lives. They are assumed not to be inclined to take risks, to gamble on achieving some great good, almost enjoying the danger that failure will leave one less well off. They have no religious beliefs, or family attachments – although Rawls suggests that they are 'heads of families' and thus probably male. This may betray 'the abstract and disembedded, distorting and nostalgic ideal of the autonomous male ego', which Seyla Benhabib believes 'the universalist tradition privileges'.[15] But the justification for the introduction of 'heads of families' seems to be as no more than a device to ensure that a concern for justice between generations is built into the hypothetical scenario; parents are assumed to see the interests of their children as at least implicated in their own.[16] Apart from this, the realm of feeling is bracketed off, as in Plato, as a disturbance to sober, rational judgement; judgements must be impartial, so particular affections are a distraction from the task in hand.[17]

Self-interestedness is assumed, but the device of the Original Position is calculated to develop a limited kind of empathy, for

---

[15] Benhabib, *Situating the Self*, p. 3.

[16] On this see especially the work of Susan Moller Okin. She sees Rawls as inheriting from Kant a moral world that excludes women, and populating his Original Position with heads of families. Okin, 'Reason and Feeling in Thinking about Justice', *Ethics*, 99 (June 1989), 229–49; 'Justice and Gender', *Philosophy and Public Affairs*, 16 (1987), 42–72; and now *Justice, Gender and the Family*.

[17] On impartiality in Rawls see Brian Barry, *Justice as Impartiality*, ch. 3.

each participant has to imagine what it would be like to be in another person's shoes, supposing that person became disadvantaged by the processes of society, or had some initial handicap or defect. The Original Position can thus generate something like the Golden Rule, of doing to others as you would they would do to you. But essentially people in the Original Position lay down principles of justice based on fear that they might turn out to be at the foot of the pile and needing protection and help. As with Hobbes, fear is a powerful spur to seeking a society which will as far as possible eliminate the causes of fear.

The Original Position for Rawls is a device for securing some kind of objectivity in reasoning about justice, rising above narrow and short-term self-interest. Rawls even follows Hobbes in seeking a moral theory which is developed *more geometrico*: 'We should strive for a kind of moral geometry with all the rigor which this name connotes.' But he acknowledges that his own work is highly intuitive and falls short of this ideal.[18] His own ideal of detached, logical reasoning which takes no account of particulars or empirical realities is instructive – but open to question. And yet it is interesting that so much of his argument hinges on an Original Position, which is in fact displayed as a narrative, a work of fiction, in which people who have a series of typically modern liberal needs and expectations, and in this regard are rather depressingly similar to one another, work out together the requirements for a society composed of those who in this way 'agree to share one another's fate'.[19]

But the Other in question, who participates with one in the Original Position, is not any longer a particular person, with all the quirks and particularities that go to make another individual. The Other is 'disembedded and disembodied', in Seyla Benhabib's words. 'Moral impartiality is learning to recognise the claims of the other who is just like oneself,' she writes, and continues that in this strange world all significant differences have to be erased; there are no longer mothers or boys, or

---

[18] Rawls, *Theory of Justice*, p. 121.   [19] *Ibid.*, p. 102.

sisters, or wives. Women's experience in particular is excluded, and along with this, women's distinctive insights into the good and the right. In fact, when human nature is claimed to be pared down to its essentials, we are left with a privileged male.[20]

By way of contrast it might be instructive to consider the highly specific and concrete way in which Jesus answers the question about justice. The lawyer who believes he has kept the rules of justice wants Jesus to declare him 'just'. He asks, 'But who is my neighbour?', expecting, presumably, the kind of answer that would come from behind the Veil of Ignorance: your neighbour is someone just like you, in whose place you might find yourself one day. But Jesus responds with a story, a parable, in which all the characters have quite specific roles and expectations. For him, the Veil of Ignorance must be swept aside before the demand of justice, which is always concrete, can be clarified. The neighbour who meets the demands of justice is the despised alien, the heretic, the one who was marginalised. It is he who acts justly in meeting the needs of the poor Jew, lying battered and terrified by the roadside. The priest and the Levite who, professionally as it were, should have known what justice is and what it demands of us, show themselves incapable or unwilling, because of fear, to act justly. Fear and self-interest together conspire *against* just action. And Jesus tells the lawyer who wishes to be declared just to go and do as the Samaritan did. For in the parable he now has a concrete example of acting justly, of the demand of justice.[21]

Rawls's procedure is to develop the principle in the hypothetical Original Position, and then seek its embodiment in practice and in policy. But what if the concrete has a real priority? Is Rawls perhaps in danger of falling subject to R. H. Tawney's stricture: 'to state a principle without its application is irresponsible and unintelligible'?[22] It is easier to explicate both the content and the demand of justice more clearly through concrete instances or narratives and parables.

[20] Benhabib, *Situating the Self*, p. 157.
[21] Luke 10.25–37.
[22] R. H. Tawney, *'The Attack' and Other Papers*. London: Allen & Unwin, 1953, p. 178.

The Judaeo-Christian tradition presents an alternative, more concrete, account of the Original Position in the story of the Garden of Eden and of the Fall. Here the original and proper condition for human beings is one of justice, expressed in confident and caring relationships with God, with one another and with the natural environment. Behind their very different Veil of Ignorance, Eve and Adam make a false choice, fear and shame enter in, and the two are banished from the Garden with the knowledge of good and evil – of justice – but without having eaten of the fruit of the tree of life, and with a damaged capacity to meet the demands of justice. The original harmony is broken; the earth is under a curse; and in a broken world the justice of the Original Position is present primarily as a memory and as a hope. While the demands of justice are constantly present, the nature of justice is never fully known.

We perhaps cannot get very far in developing an understanding of justice without a story of an Original Position, provided that story helps us to focus on the specific demands of justice, and helps us to see what a just society might, or will, be like. Working with a Christian, rather than a Rawlsian, account William Blake stressed the priority of the particular with characteristic pungency when he wrote:

He who would do good to another must do it in Minute Particulars:
General Good is the plea of the scoundrel, hypocrite & flatterer,
For Art & Science cannot exist but in minutely organized Particulars
And not in the generalizing Demonstration of the Rational Power.[23]

Only in particular acts and in a society whose moral order is 'minutely organized Particulars' can justice be known and its demands responded to.

Overlapping consensus: Babel or Pentecost?

As we have seen earlier, Rawls has increasingly stressed that his account of justice makes no claim to universality or to truth; it is 'political not metaphysical' and rooted in a consensus, that is,

---

[23] William Blake, *Jerusalem*, ch. 5, in *Complete Writings*. Oxford: Oxford University Press, 1966, p. 687.

in the convictions that most people in a modern liberal democracy share.[24] A society needs a consensus about justice if it is to hold together, and the social theorist's task is to explore this consensus critically, seeking to expose its inner coherence and commending it to the society. Boundaries are thus placed around the arena of public political discourse: it has to do with the area of the consensus and does not have the equipment to evaluate what lies outside, or to assess other societies which operate on radically different assumptions. The theorist cannot, for instance, denounce the understanding of justice in a caste society where there is a broad consensus that human beings are *not* equal, because all that is available as the basis for such judgements are the principles that are widely held in liberal societies which do not necessarily have any finality.

Rawls develops his understanding of consensus in his recent book *Political Liberalism* (1993). He freely recognises the existence in a liberal society of a range of differing 'reasonable comprehensive world-views'.[25] For a well-ordered society, however, it is necessary that there should be a generally accepted political notion of justice: 'It is a society in which everyone accepts, and knows that everyone else accepts, the very same principles of justice', and in which the society's basic institutions are generally acknowledged to be just.[26]

Within a liberal society there are, and ought to be, a range of world-views accepted and tolerated, perhaps even encouraged because they contribute to the rich diversity of the society. 'Justice as fairness,' he writes, 'does indeed abandon the ideal of political community if by that ideal is meant a political society united on one (partially or fully) comprehensive religious, philosophical, or moral doctrine.'[27]

There are, of course, problems in giving this degree of weight to a consensus. Ronald Dworkin has cogently argued that the principles of justice we support 'must be principles we accept

---

[24] Rawls, 'Justice as Fairness: Political not Metaphysical', esp. 230.
[25] John Rawls, *Political Liberalism*. New York: Columbia University Press, 1993, p. 59.
[26] Rawls, *Liberalism*, p. 35.
[27] Rawls, 'The Priority of Right and Ideas of the Good', *Philosophy and Public Affairs*, 17:4 (1988), 251–76 (269).

because they seem right rather than because they have been captured in some conventional practice. Otherwise political theory will be only a mirror, uselessly reflecting a community's consensus and division back upon itself.'[28] Werpehowski's suggestion that the critical appropriation of shared understandings and seeking a proper coherence among them provide opportunities of justifying and deepening conventional notions of justice is helpful, but he does not, in my view, totally overcome the force of Dworkin's objection.[29] If one rejects on principle the possibility of an objective moral order it is not easy to achieve critical distance from the conventional wisdom. A consensus about justice may be false. Most people would agree that the consensus about justice that the Nazis established in Germany was false, but on Rawlsian grounds it would have been hard to say so. All one would have been permitted to affirm would be that it is *different* from that dominant in liberal democracies.

Rawls develops the idea that there is an 'overlapping consensus' between the various reasonable comprehensive doctrines in which the political and public concept of justice as fairness finds its home.[30] Public political reasoning, he suggests, can be based *only* on this overlap.

This overlapping consensus has a number of important characteristics. The idea of the right which is enshrined in it is 'a conception of politics, not of the whole of life'.[31] This means that the idea of justice as fairness is not a comprehensive doctrinal scheme, but can and must co-exist with a wide diversity of ideas of what is good and what is true. But justice as right has priority, which means that it sets limits to the permissible ways of life in the society, and 'admissible ideas of the good must respect the limits of, and serve a role within, the political conception of justice'.[32] Ideas of the good which are incompatible with justice as fairness must be excluded. A Nazi

---

[28] Cited from *The New York Review of Books*, 30 (21 July, 1983), 43–6, by William Werpehowski, 'Political Liberalism and Christian Ethics: A Review Discussion', *Thomist*, 48 (1984), 93

[29] *Ibid.*

[30] Rawls, 'Justice as Fairness: Political not Metaphysical', 246; *Theory of Justice*, p. 388.

[31] Rawls, 'Priority of Right', 253.   [32] *Ibid.*

understanding of justice or the good, for instance, would not be acceptable in a liberal democracy like the United States.

Thus a society can be united around a common under-standing of justice expressed in just institutions while still providing for many differing comprehensive views of reality. The boundary between comprehensive views and the over-lapping consensus may not always be clear; Seyla Benhabib, for example, doubts whether one can defend liberalism on the basis of overlapping consensus alone without recourse to a shared understanding of the human being.[33] And there are, of course, radically different accounts of human nature and human destiny widely accepted in democratic societies, which may make them rather more communities of people 'locked together in argument' than Rawls seems to think desirable.[34] In such a society the state must be neutral or evenhanded in the way it deals with reasonable comprehensive systems of doctrine and varying understandings of the good; its own principles are 'independent of any particular comprehensive doctrine'.[35] Yet justice as fairness does incorporate certain understandings of the good, so that it is committed to the encouragement of virtues such as co-operation, civility, tolerance, reasonableness and a sense of fairness.[36]

There is, of course, a problem here. Operating in the public realm and striving to be as tolerant as possible in relating to the diverse world views and concepts of the good that are lively within its society, a government has from time to time to decide issues where no clear guidance comes from justice as fairness. An obvious case is perhaps abortion, where public opinion is radically polarised, where there is no consensus, and where decisions cannot be taken which are independent of contentious beliefs about the status of the foetus. And there are a range of other cases, some of which I will discuss later, where necessary decisions can only be responsibly taken with reference to convictions which lie outside or beyond justice as fairness.

[33] Benhabib, *Situating the Self*, p. 77.
[34] The phrase is from John Courtney Murray, cited in Browning and Fiorenza, *Habermas*, p. 161.
[35] Rawls, 'Priority of Right', 256.   [36] *Ibid.*, 263.

There are a number of important difficulties facing Rawls's notion of the overlapping consensus. The most obvious is that there are those who advocate with great vigour some form of liberal democracy, but vehemently reject the Rawlsian notion of justice as fairness – Hayek, Nozick and Alasdair MacIntyre, to mention but three prominent examples. Yet Rawls nonetheless assumes that all reasonable comprehensive doctrines in a well-ordered liberal democratic society will endorse in their varying fashions fairness as explicated by Rawls as that understanding of justice which is applicable in the public realm. No one comprehensive doctrine on its own can today provide 'the content of public reason on fundamental political questions', Rawls argues.[37] Only the overlap is capable of doing this. And Rawls believes that the part of the various reasonable comprehensive doctrines which lies outside the overlapping consensus provides a variety of alternative ideological foundations for justice as fairness;[38] he is benignly confident that all these doctrines, despite their differences, in their varying fashions endorse justice as fairness as the only account of justice which can be operative in the public realm.

But what of that part of the reasonable comprehensive doctrine with which we are concerned which lies outside the overlapping consensus on justice as fairness? What if this contains, as I believe it does, qualifications of the adequacy of justice as fairness, supplementation and enrichment? As I read Rawls, these views are excluded from public political discourse, making many of the most interesting and significant things that the Christian tradition has to say about justice no more than domestic concerns of the churches – and, more seriously still, impoverishing and narrowing public political discourse. In effect distinctive views which do not directly endorse justice as fairness are excluded from public political discourse. Religion as such is relegated to the private realm, and its voice is not welcome in the public square unless it comes to endorse consensual views. In the public sphere one should refrain from religious language or references to the distinctive resources of a

---

[37] Rawls, *Liberalism*, p. 134.   [38] *Ibid.*, pp. 12, 126.

particular tradition. Religion is regarded, in Stephen Carter's term, as a 'hobby' without public relevance, no longer even arousing hostility.[39] This trivialises the nature of a religion such as Christianity and disables it from making its authentic contribution in the public sphere. It is not only in the past that religion has helped to define, sustain and reform the political values of a liberal state. But it is only capable of doing this if the possible political relevance of that part of the religious system that lies outside the consensus, that is, which is not generally accepted by most people in the society, is recognised. If we eliminate metaphysics and theology from the public realm we have nothing to put in their place, and end up with a truncated and unsatisfactory notion of justice and of the nature of society.

It has been claimed that Rawls has recently to a significant extent moved his ground on the place of religion. In his early writings he regards religion as inherently divisive and therefore disruptive in the public realm. He now regards religious arguments as admissible provided that in the last analysis they are compatible with the generally acknowledged criteria of public reason and can be translated into secular terms. Religion may strengthen believers' commitment to the ideals of civility and liberal democracy. But this rather grudging admission of religion into public discourse does not, I think, represent a fundamental change in Rawls's position.[40]

Basing a notion of justice on an overlapping consensus rather than any kind of ontology or belief about reality results in a view of justice which is thin and unlikely to be able to constrain selfishness or elicit passionate commitment. For the Rawlsian consensus is entered into on the assumption that it serves everyone's interests, that the demands of justice do not call for serious limitations on the self-interest of anyone. If the principles of justice are satisfied, 'everyone is benefited'.[41] Rawls assumes that humans are inherently selfish people: 'in choosing

---

[39] See Stephen Carter, *The Culture of Disbelief*. New York: Doubleday, 1994, pp. 21–2, 51.
[40] See the important symposium on 'Political Liberalism: Religion and Public Life', in which Rawls discusses these issues with Martha Minow, Michael Sandel, Ronald Thiemann and Cornel West, in Harvard Divinity School, *Religion and Values in Public Life*, 3:4. Cambridge, Mass.: Harvard Divinity School, 1995.
[41] Rawls, *Theory of Justice*, p. 80.

between principles each tries as best he can to advance his interests'.[42] A questionable assumption appears to be built into his understanding of consensus: justice is in everyone's interests; it calls for no sacrifices; it does not conflict with the reasonable aspirations of anyone. In the original condition, people are not motivated by benevolence, or a concern for the interests of others, yet the circumstances force inherently selfish people to take the interests and the good of others into account.[43] Selfishness generates a sense of justice and a degree of altruism. Even the Difference Principle, to which I shall return later, benefits everyone.

Two comments might be made on this kind of measured consensualism: it has little in common with the visionary accounts of justice which have motivated most great movements for social transformation and reform; and it appears not to have taken the measure of human selfishness and sin, and the human capacity to twist justice into a weapon for the powerful in the defence of vested interests. Any account of justice which is, as Rawls wishes his to be, 'the first virtue of social institutions, as truth is of systems of thought',[44] must be robust enough to face real conflicts of interest and of understanding, and visionary enough to evoke a passionate commitment capable of calling forth self-sacrifice and challenging self-interest.

The idea of an overlapping consensus is intended to lay down the parameters of public debate in a pluralistic society that is in danger of becoming a Babel of discordant voices. Rawls's objective is a kind of political Pentecost in which authentic communication and dialogue about policy and the social order become possible. The goal is admirable, but I doubt whether the overlapping consensus can overcome Babel or usher in a new Pentecost.

The Difference Principle and poor Lazarus
Out of the Original Position Rawls argues that a package of three co-ordinated principles of justice as fairness emerge. These are the principles of equal liberty for all, of equal

---

[42] *Ibid.*, pp. 142, 144.   [43] *Ibid.*, pp. 147–8.   [44] *Ibid.*, p. 3.

opportunity, and of what Rawls calls the Difference Principle. This last is outlined as follows:

Assuming the framework of institutions required by equal liberty and fair equality of opportunity, the higher expectations of those better situated are just if and only if they work as part of a scheme which improves the expectations of the least advantaged members of society. The intuitive idea is that the social order is not to establish and secure the more attractive prospects of those better off unless doing so is to the advantage of those less fortunate.[45]

This concern for the least advantaged which Rawls builds into his theory is admirable. Inequalities are only to be justified when they are to the greatest benefit of the least-advantaged members of the society.

Where does the Difference Principle come from? It is not entirely easy to see it as emerging necessarily from the Original Position where the participants might well choose equal basic liberty together with equality of opportunity and see no special reason for building in a special protection for the weakest, especially if this in some way, however slight, limits the freedom and the equality of opportunity of the rest. On the second reading of Rawls it is not hard to see the Difference Principle as originally derived from the Judaeo-Christian tradition and now so deeply embedded in western culture that it is regarded as more or less self-evident. 'Considered convictions', as Rawls himself acknowledges, are shaped by a variety of factors, not least religious belief. Thus, while disclaiming *direct* recourse to metaphysical and religious belief, he can call upon such principles if he finds them commonly accepted in today's society. 'What justifies a conception of justice is not its being true to an order antecedent to or given to us, but its congruence with our deeper understanding of ourselves and our aspirations, and our realisation that given our history and the traditions embedded in our public life it is the most reasonable doctrine for us.'[46]

For some commentators Rawls's Difference Principle demon-

---

45 *Ibid.*, p. 75.
46 John Rawls, 'Kantian Constructivism in Moral Theory', *Journal of Philosophy*, 77:9 (Sept. 1980), 515–72 (519).

strates the deep conservatism of his theory. They see it as relevant only in inegalitarian class-structured societies, and as implying a gently reformist approach within a general acceptance of the existing ordering of things, which is believed to be in general fair.[47] This may well be an accurate account of Rawls's position; no one I know of has suggested that Rawls is a revolutionary. But it does not remove the importance of the emphasis put on protecting and promoting the interests of the weakest in any society that claims to be fair, and it provides a justification for 'affirmative action' on behalf of the disadvantaged.

Is the Difference Principle a secular transcription of what is now called the 'preferential option for the poor'? Would it provide redress and vindication for poor Lazarus in Jesus' parable, lying at the Rich Man's door? The Difference Principle, if taken in full seriousness, would certainly ensure that Lazarus' interests would be taken into account in any policies which affected the Rich Man's resources. But it would not, I think, call upon the Rich Man to do anything to respond to his needy neighbour's condition, unless the Rich Man saw this as in some way serving his own reasonable self-interest.

God's solidarity with the poor and excluded is inseparable from the command to respond with sacrificial and spontaneous generosity to the needy neighbour. Timothy Jackson may be right in suggesting that 'Rawls's contractarianism systematically subverts ethical *motivation*.'[48]

THE CHRISTIAN RECEPTION OF RAWLS

Some Christian theologians, such as David Tracy, welcomed Rawls's work as defining a genuinely public debate about justice, to which theologians would be as welcome as anyone.[49] There are others who endorse Rawls's theory of justice as

[47] Wieslaw Lang, 'Marxism, Liberalism and Justice' in Eugene Kamenka and Alice Erh-Soon Tay (eds.), *Justice*. London: Edward Arnold, 1979, p. 142.

[48] Timothy P. Jackson, 'To Bedlam and Part Way Back: John Rawls and Christian Justice', *Faith and Philosophy*, 8:4 (1991), 423–47 (433).

[49] David Tracy, *The Analogical Imagination*. New York: Crossroad, 1981, pp. 9–10.

fairness as the only form that a Christian notion of justice can take in the public arena of a modern democratic pluralist state. Harlan Beckley, for instance, believes that Rawls's theory holds out the possibility of maintaining a distinctive Christian world-view and ethic alongside a shared secular conception of justice. Specifically, he argues that the Christian notion of love affirms Rawls's view, so that on this Rawlsian basis Christians can establish common cause with others in the search for justice. Beckley adopts Outka's rather desiccated account of Christian love as 'equal regard' to argue that Christians should affirm justice as fairness.[50]

But there are problems, and serious ones, in adopting this position. Christian love surely demands a willingness to sacrifice our interests for the sake of others. Even Reinhold Niebuhr spoke constantly of 'the relevance of an impossible ideal' and believed that an account of justice which was not constantly challenged and refreshed by love quickly degenerated into less than justice.[51] Rawls himself taught that 'the sense of justice is continuous with the love of mankind' and suggested that the principles of justice are required to guide love when there are a number of competing claims to love.[52] But in his account of the relation of love and justice, Rawls clearly gives priority to justice and regards love as supererogatory, or optional. If Jackson is right in suggesting that Rawls's account of justice cannot be construed as 'anything other than immoral self-interest (prudence in the narrow sense)',[53] then a gulf is obvious between any adequate account of love and the Rawlsian theory of justice.

Rawls's theory involves assumptions about human beings and human society which are not obviously compatible with a Christian view. His society has no history and is held together by a shared account of justice and right, rather than any

---

[50] Harlan R. Beckley, 'A Christian Affirmation of Rawls's Idea of Justice as Fairness', Part I, *Journal of Religious Ethics*, 13:2 (1986), 210–42, Part II, *Journal of Religious Ethics*, 14:2 (1987), 229–46.

[51] See Henry B. Clark, 'Justice as Fairness and Christian Ethics', *Soundings*, 56:3 (1973), 359–69 (365).

[52] Rawls, *Theory of Justice*, p. 476.

[53] Jackson, 'To Bedlam and Part Way Back', 431.

commitment to a common good. It is only the rational moral
beings that Rawls posits who can participate in the decision-
making of the Original Position, and become responsible
citizens of the resultant society.[54] In *Political Liberalism* Rawls
reaffirms this position:

> I have assumed throughout, and shall continue to assume, that while
> citizens do not have equal capacities, they do have, at least to the
> essential minimum degree, the moral, intellectual, and physical
> capacities that enable them to be fully co-operating members of
> society over a complete life.[55]

What then of the senile, the mentally handicapped and others
such? Are they in fact citizens or members of the community?
Children and the elderly are perhaps provided for by the fact
that he states that those in the Original Position are 'heads of
families', who have an emotional involvement with their children, and presumably with their parents as well, so that they
have a sense of shared interests. But what about aliens and
people with severe learning difficulties or physical disabilities?
Are they indeed citizens or members of the society, with their
own contribution to make and entitled to be treated as human
beings and valued members of society? Is there not here a sharp
tension with the view which sees the marginalised and despised
as having a privileged place in the Kingdom, and as having
special gifts to bring for the enrichment of community, as Jean
Vanier has reminded us so effectively? Rawls does not seem to
have any way of adjudicating the claims to equal or preferential
treatment of the senile, children, aliens and people with
learning difficulties because in the absence of a metaphysic,
even with the Difference Principle, he cannot take them fully
into account. Gregory Jones's judgement is not, I think, too
harsh:

> Rawls's theory represents a progressive subordination to a different
> vision of human personhood and political community than Christians,

---

[54] Rawls, *Theory of Justice*, pp. 142–50; 'Kantian Constructivism', 546; and 'Justice as
Fairness: Political not Metaphysical', 233–4. See also L. Gregory Jones, 'Should
Christians Affirm Rawls' Justice as Fairness? A Response to Professor Beckley',
Journal of Religious Ethics, 16:2 (1988), 251–71 (258–9).

[55] Rawls, *Liberalism*, p. 183. Cf. pp. 33, 272.

at least, should want to affirm . . . The basic vision is corrosive of our understanding of what it means to be a person and to be part of a community.[56]

But, although some Christian thinkers are rather quick to baptise Rawls or jump on the Rawlsian bandwagon, there is I think much in Rawls that the Christian theologian should wish to affirm.

In the first place, it is of the greatest importance that Rawls, like the Judaeo-Christian tradition and Greek philosophy, gives priority to justice. Issues of justice for him cannot simply be swept aside in the pursuit of efficiency and economic prosperity. Justice is what holds together a decent society.

Secondly, Rawls affirms and assumes human equality. Here, even if he is mirroring a common conviction in liberal societies, it is a conviction which has its roots deep in the Judaeo-Christian tradition. Equality is not universally assumed – the Brahminic interpretation of Hinduism, for instance, proclaims the fundamental inequality of human beings, divided into castes. And equality is under heavy attack in the post-Christian West today. Perhaps Christians could help Rawlsians by suggesting a possible grounding for the belief in equality. It was the Christian moralist and historian, R. H. Tawney, who said: 'In order to believe in human equality it is necessary to believe in God'![57]

Thirdly, a Christian theologian would surely wish to affirm Rawls's Difference Principle as at least a partial expression of a Preferential Option for the Poor. The concern for the least-advantaged which Rawls builds into his theory is admirable. Inequalities are only to be justified when they are to the greatest benefit of the least advantaged members of the society.[58] Once more we appear to have here an assumption which was originally derived from the Judaeo-Christian tradition and now is so deeply embedded in western culture that it is regarded as

[56] Jones, 'Should Christians Affirm Rawls' Justice as Fairness?' pp. 258–9. See also Richard L. Fern, 'Religious Belief in a Rawlsian Society', *Journal of Religious Ethics*, 15:1 (1987), 33–58; and Arthur F. Holmes, 'Biblical Justice and Modern Moral Philosophy', *Faith and Philosophy*, 3:4 (1986).

[57] J. M. Winter and D. M. Joslin (eds.), *R .H. Tawney's Commonplace Book.* Cambridge: Cambridge University Press, 1972, p. 53.

[58] Rawls, *Liberalism*, pp. 6–7.

more or less self-evident. But perhaps Christians would wish to put the Difference Principle closer to the heart of what they mean by economic justice than Rawls's system would allow.[59]

Fourthly, I would like to affirm the importance of fairness as a central component of any adequate account of justice but to suggest that it involves a dangerous distortion and narrowing of the understanding of justice to say that justice *is* fairness, or that fairness is the only account of justice adequate in the public realm. If justice is, as Rawls claims, 'the first virtue of social institutions' it is the fundamental principle of social cohesion and of the good society. But is 'fairness' capable of sustaining such a role? Is it not in fact one aspect of a full account of justice, albeit a very important one?[60]

The right to fairness

There is surely a major moral distinction between claiming fairness for myself and for my group as a right and a concern that others should be treated fairly, even if this sometimes means that I have to give up something to which I have a claim. Only too often we have seen the notion of justice transformed from being something that motivated concern for the poor and the weak, and the search for a better society, into a weapon for the protection of vested interests, a slogan used in social conflicts which actually exacerbates those conflicts. A concern for the rights of the poor and the excluded degenerates into a willingness to do battle for the rights of one's own group.[61]

There is a world of difference between a society in which

---

[59] See Ronald F. Thiemann, *Religion in American Public Life*, p. 120.

[60] Cf. Lloyd L. Weinreb: 'The theories of Rawls and Nozick are as convincing as they are because each of them elaborates one aspect of the complete idea of justice and excludes the other.' (*Natural Law and Justice*. Cambridge, Mass.: Harvard University Press, 1987, p. 240.)

[61] I am aware that there is an important and growing literature about Rawls's understanding of rights and how Rawls's theory might be applied, particularly in welfare policy. I am here concerned not so much with this discussion as with the implications of the vulgar understanding of fairness. But it does seem to me that Rawls does not sufficiently take into account the implications of his acceptance of an adversarial social order in which the philosopher is not king. See, for example, Frank I. Michelman, 'Constitutional Welfare Rights and A Theory of Justice' in Norman Daniels (ed.), *Reading Rawls: Critical Studies on Rawls' 'A Theory of Justice'*. New York:

each individual or group demands fairness for itself as its right, and defines fairness on its own terms, and a society which is committed to seeking fairness for the other and believes that justice has some objective grounding. Hayek is at his most telling when he argues that the search for fairness becomes a disruptive force in modern societies. He suggests that different groups with strong opinions as to the wages and benefits to which they are entitled come into conflict with one another and disturb the integration of society. The search for fairness, he writes, 'must become a divisive force because it produces not a reconciliation of, but a conflict between, the interests of the different groups. As the active participants in the struggle for social justice well know, it becomes in practice a struggle for power of organised interests in which arguments of justice serve merely as pretexts.'[62]

From a very different position we find a similar argument emerging. In a remarkable book, *What Went Wrong?*, Jeremy Seabrook argues that the understanding of justice in Britain has deteriorated, narrowed and become divisive and destructive.[63] He interviewed a number of elderly people who had been active in the labour movement in the 1920s and the 1930s. In these hard decades they had been idealists, visionaries, making great personal sacrifices for a just society that would be fair, caring and humane. Today, Seabrook found most of his respondents disappointed, even bitter. What has eventuated, they told him, is a parody of what we strove for. A sense of community in which people care for one another has been eroded; people assume that everything can be cured only by more money. The hope of a just society has given way to the 'money militancy' of interest groups. The rhetoric of justice is still used, but it is now cynically deployed in the defence of privilege and of differentials. Justice is understood as getting the best possible deal for one's group; each group claims what it

Basic Books, 1978, and Rex Martin, *Rawls and Rights*. Lawrence: University Press of Kansas, 1985.
[62] F. A. Hayek, *Mirage*, p. 137.
[63] Jeremy Seabrook, *What Went Wrong? Working People and the Ideals of the Labour Movement*. London: Gollancz, 1978.

believes to be its rights, even if often at the expense of others. In Britain, all this climaxed in the 'Winter of Discontent', when unions and groups, still using the language of justice, fought and struggled with an apparent callousness about the common good and the marginalised. An attenuated understanding of justice seemed incapable of constraining collective selfishness, or sustaining a preference for the weak and poor whenever such a preference impinged upon immediate material interests. What one might call a 'vulgar Rawlsian' account of justice showed itself to be socially divisive.

Here we surely have an apt demonstration of the dangers of thought and behaviour which assumes the 'adversarial view of human relationships' so illuminatingly discussed by Grace Jantzen:

> John Rawls' *A Theory of Justice* is based squarely on the assumption that people are in competition with one another for goods and resources, and that the function of ethical theory is not to try to reduce this competitive adversarial stance and replace it with mutual care and community, but simply to provide a framework which would ensure that, given human greed, the distribution of the goods takes place as fairly as possible.[64]

Jantzen thus reminds us that justice must be more than fair treatment within unchanged and basically unjust structures.

'Fairness' in popular political usage is an overused term without an objective referent. As a result there is no way of adjudicating conflicting claims to fairness. Barbara Wootton reports that in the 1974 election campaign in Britain, Prime Minister Edward Heath's most hard-worked adjective was 'fair'. But, she continues, ' "fairness" and impartiality have no meaning in the absence of any relevant standard of reference. Without such a standard the word "fair", even in Edward Heath's speeches, is as meaningless as other less reputable four-letter words in current usage.'[65] As a result of such fundamental uncertainty as to what fairness means, she argues that in pay

---

[64] Grace Jantzen, 'Connection or Competition – Identity and Personhood in Feminist Ethics', *Studies in Christian Ethics*, 5:1 (1992), 1–20 (4–5).

[65] Barbara Wootton, *Fair Pay, Relativities and a Policy for Incomes*. Fawley Foundation Lecture. Southampton: University of Southampton, 1974, p. 5.

settlements we have 'a system in which the weak go to the wall and have also to pay the price of the successes of the strong'.[66]

Rawls cannot, of course, be blamed for such uncontrolled political rhetoric, or for its consequences. After all, he has provided a set of criteria for justice as fairness. But some sustained efforts to develop a Rawlsian basis for public policy display the issues. The report of the Commission on Social Justice established by the late leader of the Labour Party in Britain, John Smith, for example, was largely Rawlsian in its inspiration. In Rawlsian fashion the Commission claimed to base their work on the 'considered convictions' of most people in Britain: 'We are confident', the Commission affirmed, 'that at least in our belief that there is such a thing as "social justice", we reflect the common sense of the vast majority of people', and 'we have attempted to articulate some widely-held feelings about the character of our society'.[67] In other words, they claimed to be expressing an existing consensus rather than gathering support around a fresh vision.

The Commission's 'four principles of social justice' were distinctly Rawlsian in tone: first, in a free society all citizens are of equal worth; secondly, citizens are entitled to have their basic needs met; thirdly, there should be the widest possible access to opportunities and life chances; and, finally, although inequalities are not necessarily unjust, unjust inequalities should be reduced and where possible eliminated. Rawls's Difference Principle is there in the Commission's thinking, but it can easily be missed by a quick reader. And besides, Rawls urges that policies should maximise the well-being of the worst-off, but does not specify what degree of inequality of resources would be fair. At the key point in Rawls there lurks an uncertainty about what justice is which is disconcerting for the policy-maker.

Nevertheless, the Commission is quite clear that justice at its heart is fairness, but does not see this as demanding major structural or systemic changes; justice calls for adjustments in

---

[66] *Ibid.*, p. 18.
[67] Commission on Social Justice, *The Justice Gap*. London: Institute for Public Policy Research, 1993, pp. 4, 19.

the direction of fairness within a social and economic order which is accepted in its broad outlines. The Commission is emphatic that a fair society will be economically successful, or, to quote the title of a Fabian Pamphlet by Gordon Brown, *Fair is Efficient*.[68] Social justice and economic prosperity, in other words, belong naturally together; there is no need for a trade-off or compromise between fairness and efficiency. Economic success and social justice belong together, 'social justice is not simply a moral ideal but an economic necessity'. This is a comforting, but not wholly convincing doctrine. Similarly, the specific proposals of the report, most of which are admirable, are presented as if they would not damage the interests of any significant group in society. No one need make sacrifices for justice; fairness improves the condition of everyone: such seems to be the message of the Report, effectively concealing the fact that justice is usually costly and fairness is not necessarily in the interests of everyone.[69]

Beyond fairness

If justice is to be the first virtue of social institutions, the principle that informs and holds together a healthy society, it must surely be more than fairness claimed as a right. People expect of their political leaders more than fairness – and often receive less! Let me explain what I mean by justice as more than fairness in terms of an illustration, which happens to be true.

A young social worker is a houseparent in a residential community for young adults with learning difficulties, some of whom also have physical difficulties and emotional problems. She has a habit of taking on extra and of being available for people out of hours, she does not isolate herself in her room when she is off-duty, but is at pains to develop friendships, and

---

[68] Gordon Brown, *Fair is Efficient*. Fabian Pamphlet 563, London: Fabian Society, 1994.
[69] Commission on Social Justice, *Social Justice: Strategies for National Renewal*. London: Vintage, 1994. For commentary see Andrew R. Morton (ed.), *Justice and Prosperity: A Realistic Vision?* Occasional Paper, no. 34, Edinburgh: CTPI 1995, and *What Justice Demands: A Response to the Social Justice Commission Report*. London: Christian Socialist Movement, 1995.

generously pours herself into building and sustaining community and relationships, and affirming the worth of the residents
by the way she treats them and the way she relates to them
individually and as a group. The residents know that she cares
for them, but she can be a firm disciplinarian when disruptive
behaviour threatens the peace of the community. She is
recognised to be a fair person – but not like the schoolmaster
who was known as 'a brute, but a fair brute', is more than fair
and even-handed in her treatment of others, and is seldom
insistent on her rights, on fairness for herself. Sometimes she
will work extra shifts to help out a friend. Occasionally residents
or other staff members take advantage of her generosity. Sometimes she gets very tired.

Her boyfriend says that much of this is not fair – and in a
sense he is correct. He urges her to play it by the book and set
precise limits to her contribution. But she refuses to allow the
language of fairness to impose strict bounds on the extent of her
contribution. It is not that she rejects the importance of fairness
in the way the community is run. But a community in which
everyone is demanding fairness for themselves is very different
from a community in which there is a stress upon fairness to
others, and a willingness to go beyond fairness.

But there is a problem here. It really is not possible to
conceive of a polity run on the principles of love alone. In
collectivities larger than the family – and, even there, much of
the time – we have to deal with justice as a form of love. Even
in the family and in face-to-face relationships, fairness is the
best soil in which love may grow. But a society or a polity in
which the fundamental principle of justice has been narrowed
down to fairness, in which justice is not in some obvious sense
an expression of love, is impoverished and inhumane.

There is a major moral distinction between claiming fairness
for myself and my group as a right and a concern that others
should be treated fairly. A justice which is more than fairness
demands just societies and just social institutions. The justice
that the Lord requires is more than fairness. We narrow and
impoverish our understanding of justice at our peril.

CHAPTER 6

Justice and the market

In the previous chapter we considered the account of justice propounded by John Rawls. This saw justice as the central value in a decent society, shaping both behaviour and social institutions. Rawls is concerned with processes and institutions as well as outcomes. He believes that a just society reflects a belief in human equality and that society should have a special concern for the poor and the weak. Justice gives guidance on the distribution of advantages, responsibilities and liabilities within a society. As far as possible, a just society should set right the unjust outcomes of social institutions and strike an acceptable balance between liberty and equality. We also saw that Rawls's account of justice does not claim to be rooted in the nature of things or in any specific metaphysical or religious beliefs. Rather, it is an articulation and refinement of what most people in a modern liberal democracy believe; it rests on what he calls an 'overlapping consensus'.

Despite the problems that we discussed in the previous chapter, it is not hard to see why Rawls's theory of justice has become something of a prevailing orthodoxy among left-of-centre politicians and policy-makers in America, Britain and some other western democratic societies. In the aftermath of the apparent collapse of the varied socialist ideologies, Rawls seems to provide an alternative theoretical framework which is less grandiose, but capable of providing a defence of the extension of the social experiments of the New Deal, the welfare state and so forth. It seems to sustain some central socialist values while setting aside the utopian expectations and the suspect accounts of history and of human perfectibility which gave an unreal skew to much socialist reflection. Rawls may point to a simpler, more pragmatic way to many of the same ends, and the idea that his theory of justice rests on an overlapping consensus is reassuring to people who respect the values of others in a pluralist society, who believe that shared values are important, and who see the need for a public forum for the discussion of values and policies.

The existence of a consensus on justice was more credible in 1971, however, when Rawls published his *A Theory of Justice* than it is today. Since then the so-called New Right has launched a frontal attack on the priority and utility of consensus as such, and radically rejects the content of the Rawlsian understanding of justice and the kind of policies to which it gives support. In the Great Society which New Right thinkers celebrate, human flourishing has little to do with justice. Individuals and families seek their own varied goods through participating in a range of social institutions, particularly the market, which are neither just nor unjust in themselves but which have an almost miraculous capacity to fulfil human needs.[1] Justice is not concerned directly with outcomes or with control, but is rather the basic and relatively simple procedures which are necessary for the smooth running of these institutions. Here we have a narrow-gauge or minimalist account of justice, but one which has been particularly influential in recent times in relation to policy-making, particularly in Britain and America. Probably its most significant exponent is Friedrich A. Hayek, whose thought we will examine in this chapter with an eye also to its policy outcomes, for 'by their fruits you shall know them' is as good a rule in political theory as it is in common morality.

Hayek and Rawls have a good deal in common despite their sharply opposed theories of justice. They are both thinkers of the post-Enlightenment world, assuming a kind of possessive individualism and taking little account of the fact that human beings can only properly be understood as persons-in-relation. Neither has much historical interest, or recognises how deeply

---

[1] It was Ronald Reagan who first spoke of 'the magic of the market'.

people and societies are shaped by traditions slowly evolving over time. Both speak in terms of rights – the right to have one's basic needs met, or the right to freedom of choice. They speak, as Lesslie Newbigin has cogently pointed out, in terms of 'wants' and 'needs', but they relegate questions of purpose to the private realm, and accordingly have no way to adjudicate between needs and wants.[2] Both agree that a modern society must tolerate or welcome a diversity of ideas of the good, but must accept a commonly recognised account of justice. They both eschew religious and metaphysical considerations and appeal to a rather disembodied rationality, but Alasdair MacIntyre is surely right in suggesting that in the absence of a commonly recognised criterion there is no way of resolving the dispute between them. In his view, both are caught up in the predicament of modern secular pluralism.

THE MARKET ORDER IN THE GREAT SOCIETY

Hayek's argument starts from a distinction between two kinds of order. There are contrived orders, devised by human beings to serve their purposes in the light of as much knowledge as is available to them. This is what the Greeks called *taxis*, and illustrated by the line of battle. In a line of battle the individual soldier has forfeited his freedom and is under orders. In a battle the commanders rarely if ever have the information they need to steer the battle towards a successful conclusion – the outcome is frequently more accidental than the victors care to admit.[3] In a *taxis* brave goals are pronounced, but in complex modern societies there is rarely enough relevant knowledge available to ensure that these goals are achieved.

Then Hayek distinguishes 'spontaneous orders', which are organic growths, not the result of human planning and decision-making, or calculated to serve directly human purposes or goals. The Greek term *kosmos* is applied by Hayek to these 'orderly structures which are the product of the action of many

[2] Lesslie Newbigin, 'Whose Justice?'
[3] This theme is explored illuminatingly by Isaiah Berlin in his *The Hedgehog and the Fox*. New York: Mentor Books, 1957.

men but are not the result of human design'.[4] A spontaneous order has no purpose, no *telos*; it has not been brought into being by an outside agency; like Topsy, it has 'just growed'. Nevertheless, a spontaneous order can be very useful to the individuals with their separate goals who operate within it.[5]

The only spontaneous order to which Hayek gives significant attention is the market. It is the central order in the Great Society which he desires. In the market (or other spontaneous orders for that matter) individuals' free pursuit of their own interests and purposes is balanced out and adjusted in an impersonal and mechanical way 'which will be destroyed if some of the actions are determined by another agency on the basis of different knowledge and in the service of different ends'.[6] It is 'an impersonal process which brings about a greater satisfaction of human desires than any deliberate human organization could achieve'.[7] The market order provides the central mechanism whereby we fulfil our own purposes and contribute 'to the satisfaction of needs of which we do not know, but sometimes even to the achievement of ends of which we would disapprove if we knew about them'.[8] Community is not founded on neighbourliness or a shared goal, but on the recognition that the spontaneous orders, particularly the market' best preserve the individual's freedom to pursue personal goods with real opportunities of success. Interestingly, Hayek adopts the Greek term *catallaxy* for a market order. This root has to do with exchange, but he also welcomes the other meanings, 'to admit into community' and 'to turn from enemy into friend'. Theologically the root refers to reconciliation, suggesting perhaps the high moral, social and even spiritual role Hayek allocates to the market.[9] Through the market we respond not only to our own needs, but also to the needs of strangers, who thus enter into an indirect relationship with us. The operation of the market is more than a bartering of goods,

---

[4] F. A. Hayek, *Law, Legislation and Liberty*, vol. I: *Rules and Order*. 2nd ed., London: Routledge, 1982, p. 37.
[5] *Ibid.*, p. 39.   [6] *Ibid.*, p. 51.
[7] F. A. Hayek, *Law, Legislation and Liberty*, vol. II: *The Mirage of Social Justice*. 2nd edn., London: Routledge, 1982, p. 63.
[8] *Ibid.*, pp. 109–110.   [9] *Ibid.*, pp. 108–9.

or an efficient way of running an economy; it is the creation of community, the overcoming of antagonism, the reconciliation of enemies.

The market, thus understood, is the central institution in the Great Society which Hayek desires. This is a large-scale and prosperous society in which people are not bound together by reciprocal obligations, a shared good, or a common goal, but in which each person is set free as far as possible to pursue an individual rather than a shared good. Common goods in a modern society can only be imposed by an overmighty state intent on limiting human freedom. The Great Society is like a hotel rather than a barracks or indeed a family home; each person is free within broad limits to do their own thing and pursue their own purposes. And the boundaries of the state must as far as possible be rolled back to give free play to the catallaxy. Politics 'has become much too important, much too costly and harmful, absorbing much too much mental energy and material resources'; it is increasingly regarded as 'a necessary but incurable evil'.[10] In the Great Society freedom, understood as choice, is maximised; a multitude of ends is being pursued; and regulation is only necessary when ends collide too violently. Community is not founded on neighbourliness, shared goals, solidarity, let alone a common good. Hayek would totally reject Michael Ignatieff's claim that 'a decent and humane society needs a shared language of the good'.[11] The limited agreement that binds the Great Society together is about means rather than ends.[12] Neither the market nor the state provide a forum for dialogue about various understandings of the good, or any kind of arbitration between goods. They are, or ought to be, entirely neutral in such matters, and this neutrality is the basis of freedom. The market serves not to shape or constrain human desires and needs, but to fulfil as far as may be those that already exist. Any attempt to develop a

---

[10] F. A. Hayek, *Law, Legislation and Liberty*, vol. III: *The Political Order of a Free People*. 2nd edn., London: Routledge, 1982, p. 149.
[11] Michael Ignatieff, *The Needs of Strangers*. London: Chatto & Windus, 1984, p. 14.
[12] Hayek, *Mirage*, p. 3.

general consensus about the good and the right is inherently coercive and destructive of freedom.[13]

JUSTICE IN THE GREAT SOCIETY

This is the context in which Hayek develops his account of justice. Even in a Great Society, a congeries of individuals each pursuing a private good, justice exists as an *objective* reality – not, it is true, rooted in the will of a supernatural Being or based upon a rational natural law – but still something to be discovered and recognised rather than made, to which we should conform.[14] Justice in this sense is part of the structure of things, not an arbitrary human construct over which people have control – another indication that, despite his disavowals, there is an ontology lurking in Hayek's scheme.

Hayek does not see justice as the fundamental principle of solidarity, giving shape and purpose to the good society. For him justice is understood as a set of rules or procedures. Just behaviour is following these rules; it has nothing to do with aiming at just goals or attempting to bring about a just situation.[15] These rules are essentially negative; they amount to little more than rules of 'due process' in social life, and especially in market exchanges. They are not 'principles of the good society', but simply guides for individual conduct. Indeed it is doubtful whether for Hayek a just society can mean any more than a society in which most people follow these rules of fair dealing most of the time. It is, he says, meaningless to describe a factual situation as just or unjust.[16] Interpersonal transactions are 'a game' in which the behaviour of the players, but not the result, can be just or unjust, and the behaviour includes the intentions of the players. It is unjust to intend to damage another human being's interests or person, but if the damage is simply the unintended consequence of an impersonal transaction the issue of justice does not arise.[17] And these rules

[13] See John O'Neill, 'Polity, Economy, Neutrality', *Political Studies*, 43 (1995), 414–31.
[14] Hayek, *Mirage*, pp. 15, 60.
[15] Hayek, *Ibid.*, pp. 38–9; *Political Order*, p. 151.   [16] Hayek, *Mirage*, p. 32.
[17] *Ibid.*, p. 70.

are entirely negative: 'the basic values of a great or open society must be negative,' he writes, 'assuring the individual of the right within a known domain to pursue his own aims on the basis of his own knowledge'.[18]

This minimal and negative account of justice leads Hayek to launch a frontal attack on the notion of social justice. Social justice, he says, is a 'humbug', a dishonest notion, intellectually disreputable. It is a profoundly muddled concept which attempts to instil into a Great Society the attitudes and the patterns of behaviour characteristic of a tribal, face-to-face society. It thus becomes profoundly destructive.[19] It inevitably erodes freedom, and 'as long as the belief in "social justice" governs political action, this process must progressively approach nearer and nearer to the totalitarian system'.[20]

I believe [he writes] that 'social justice' will ultimately be recognised as a will-o'-the-wisp which has lured men to abandon many of the values which in the past have inspired the development of civilisation – an attempt to satisfy a craving inherited from the traditions of the small group but which is meaningless in the Great Society of free men.

Unfortunately, this vague desire which has become one of the strongest bonds spurring people of good will to action, not only is bound to be disappointed. This would be sad enough. But, like most attempts to pursue an unattainable goal, the striving for it will also produce highly undesirable consequences, and in particular lead to the destruction of the indispensable environment in which the traditional moral values alone can flourish, namely, personal freedom.[21]

A concern with social justice is, then, according to Hayek, subversive of freedom, socially divisive and ironically 'one of the greatest obstacles to the elimination of poverty'.[22]

THE LIMITS OF JUSTICE

Comment must start with Hayek's narrow understanding of justice. He teaches that strictly only human behaviour can be just or unjust. It does not make sense, he suggests, to speak of a natural calamity, say an earthquake or the death by cancer of a

---

[18] Hayek, *Political Order*, p. 130.   [19] Hayek, *Mirage*, pp. 90, 97.
[20] *Ibid.*, p. 68.   [21] *Ibid.*, p. 67.   [22] *Ibid.*, p. 139.

child, as unjust. It is in fact sometimes not easy to draw a clear
frontier between injustice and misfortune. A theist, for instance,
must wrestle with the question why a just and loving God
permits such disasters to happen, and it seems a fairly basic
human instinct to seek to relate the death of someone one loves
to a moral order of the universe. Most of us struggle at times of
crisis to justify the ways of God to human beings; it is not easy
to work through bereavement without putting it in some framework of meaning. Hayek prescinds from this whole debate. He
is not willing to encourage the common human tendency to
relate what happens to oneself to some broader universe of
meaning. For him we live in a morally pluralist society in which
there is no such thing as moral truth, in which it is meaningless
to say that my cancer is unjust, and where a statement that
cancer is evil is hardly more than an arbitrary emotional
outburst.[23] For Hayek, human conduct which follows a few
relatively simple and direct rules of due process and fairness in
market transactions is just; and unjust behaviour is behaviour
which breaks these rules, and nothing else:

To speak of justice [he writes] always implies that some person or
persons ought, or ought not, to have performed some action; and this
'ought' in turn presupposes the recognition of rules which define a set
of circumstances wherein a certain kind of conduct is prohibited by
them.[24]

A situation can only be unjust if it is the direct result of unjust
action and intention. The outcomes of market transactions
conducted according to proper, fair procedures are not in
themselves either just or unjust. 'Justice is not concerned with
those unintended consequences of a spontaneous order which
have not been deliberately brought about by anybody.'[25]
However great the gap between rich and poor which results
from the operation of the market, one cannot speak about the
distribution as being unjust. Justice is not, then, a criterion of
distribution. Because the operation of the market is impersonal,

---

[23] Judith N. Shklar deals illuminatingly with the distinction between injustice and
misfortune in her *The Faces of Injustice*. This is discussed further in ch. 2 of the present
work.
[24] Hayek, *Mirage*, p. 23.   [25] *Ibid.*, p. 38.

that is losers are not the victims of a conscious intention on the part of winners to do them down, no question of justice can arise.

Raymond Plant has produced a penetrating critique of this position. He argues that issues of justice are not only relevant to how a state of affairs arose but also to how we respond to it. An earthquake or famine may not be the result of unjust intention or behaviour, but issues of justice arise in how we respond to the situation: 'If we can compensate the victims at no comparable cost to ourselves, then to fail to do so when they [the victims of the disaster] bear no responsibility for their condition is where part of the potential injustice lies.'[26]

Let me give an example. A worker, A, is laid off by a business concern, X, as part of a successful effort to improve productivity and profit. As a result of A's unemployment and reduced income, the firm X increases its profits and is able to raise the pay of its remaining employees (particularly the Chief Executive!), and increase its dividend. It seems fair to suggest that the resultant distribution is not just; A is the victim who deserves compensation because his unemployment and poverty is an important factor contributing to the increased prosperity of the remaining workers and the shareholders. This is not to suggest that an intention of the overall exercise was to act unjustly towards A, to do him down. But the end *result* is unjust, and society has an opportunity and a responsibility to do something about it. Many of the outcomes of markets, like this one, are not intended but are foreseeable, and are matters about which something can and should be done if justice is to be maintained.

Hayek dismisses this sort of argument by saying, 'Society has simply become the new deity to which we complain and clamour for redress if it does not fulfil the expectations it has created'.[27] But we may well enquire whether Hayek, in making

---

[26] R. Plant, *Citizenship Rights and Socialism*. Fabian Pamphlet 531, London: Fabian Society, 1988. This argument is developed in various other writings, particularly Kenneth Hoover and R. Plant, *Conservative Capitalism in Britain and the United States*. London: Routledge & Kegan Paul, 1989, and R. Plant, 'The Neo-Liberal Social Vision' in A. J. Elliot and I. Swanson (eds.), *The Renewal of Social Vision*, Occasional Paper, no. 17, Edinburgh: CTPI, 1989, pp. 8–22.

[27] Hayek, *Mirage*, p. 69.

the 'spontaneous order' of the market the central social institution in this way and protecting its outcomes against moral scrutiny, has not himself made the market a 'new deity', beyond question and above justification.

THE JUSTIFICATION OF THE MARKET

The market as Hayek presents it stands beyond good and evil; it is there as a fact of life. And this, he argues, is a positive advantage in a morally pluralistic culture, where there is no value consensus. In theological language, the market is held up as a kind of order of creation, or even an order of redemption. The market blends together the diverse goods of human beings to the general advantage. It does not require or call for assessment against any particular moral standard. Values are available for individuals to choose or reject freely; a Great Society is free from an agreed moral order, and cannot be justified against any specific ethical standard.

Yet the spontaneous order of the market needs legitimacy. It requires to command the allegiance of the citizens. Although the market has no built-in purpose it is a serviceable device for individuals in the pursuit of their private purposes, and more efficacious in this than any alternative arrangement: it 'brings about a greater satisfaction of human desires than any deliberate organization could achieve'.[28] Human beings allow it to continue because it makes possible the satisfaction of their needs; but they also risk failure.[29] For Hayek the belief that success in the market depends primarily on individual effort and merit is a myth (frequently encouraged by governments and educational systems), but it is a *useful* myth, because it appears to give some moral support to the market by suggesting that its outcomes are just. The flip side of this argument is not often noticed: if those who benefit from the market have not earned their benefits by their energy or their intelligence, those who are disadvantaged by the market do not deserve their condition either. On strict Hayekian principles the dangerous

---

[28] *Ibid.*, p. 63.   [29] *Ibid.*, p. 70.

distinction between the 'deserving' and the 'undeserving' poor
has also to be rejected, for the market is recognised to be a
lottery, if a useful one.

For Hayek the justification of the market as an institution that
rewards the deserving and penalises the idle and incompetent is
in fact spurious: 'in the market only the conduct of the players
but not the result can be just'.[30] Hayek is even reluctant to use
'invisible hand' reasoning to suggest that the self-interest of
participants in market transactions is mysteriously transformed
into justice or the common good. Plant's conclusion is fair:

> Does [the market] have a more substantial moral basis? The answer
> to this is clearly no, as Hayek has the courage to admit. It does not
> secure a fair worth of liberty; it does not secure equality. The market
> is neutral and amoral. Success depends on luck as much as anything
> else, the luck of birth, of upbringing, of education, of being in the
> right place at the right time, and certainly not solely upon merit or
> desert.[31]

This of course leaves us with serious problems. The central
institution of the Great Society, and indeed that Society itself,
makes no claim to moral legitimacy. The market is presented
simply as the aptest device for the orderly and efficient running
of a morally fragmented society, where each may pursue
private purposes with the minimum of outside interference.

INDIVIDUALISM AND SOCIETY

Hayek's thought clearly lies behind Margaret Thatcher's
famous statement: 'There is no such thing as society. There are
individual men and women and there are families.'[32] His
critique of tribalism and of what he calls 'teleocratic societies',
bound together by one world-view and with one set of goals
which all citizens are expected to pursue, has much validity. A
good deal of collectivist thought and of Christian social
theology has in fact been naively nostalgic for simple, face-to-
face communities, and has advocated policies some of which

---

[30] *Ibid.*, p. 70.
[31] Hoover and Plant, *Conservative Capitalism*, p. 231. Cf. Hayek, *Mirage*, pp. 93–6.
[32] In an interview in *Woman's Own* (31 Oct. 1987).

can only be applied to complex modern societies at very great cost. But Hayek repeatedly asserts that we have no moral obligations, no moral links, to strangers. In the Great Society there is no 'general obligation to help and sustain one another; indeed such an obligation is incompatible with the Great Society'. Moral obligation 'can exist only towards particular known people – and though in a Great Society it may well be a moral obligation towards people of one's choice, it cannot be enforced under equal rules for all'.[33]

There is some validity in Hayek's criticism of those who believe that a large and complex modern society can be, or ought to be, closely integrated by a shared value system and common beliefs. Yet we ought, according to the gospel, to love and serve our neighbours, and everyone is our neighbour. If we help everyone we come across in need we may become saints, but we are not likely to contribute in a major way to the efficiency of the economy.[34] But to posit a society where people are bound together *only* by involvement in the market and observance of some simple rules of non-interference in other's private space is individualism run wild. Such proposals rest on a severely truncated account of justice and of the moral bonds which hold people together in relationship.

The ideological nature of Hayek's theory of justice is betrayed by the fact that it leaves the wealthy and the powerful undisturbed and unchallenged provided that they obey the simple rules of fair dealing. In fact, they are told, 'we are generally doing most good by pursuing gain'. For

The aim for which the successful entrepreneur wants to use his profits may well be to provide a hospital or an art gallery for his home town. But quite apart from the question of what he wants to do with his profits after he has earned them, he is led to benefit more people by aiming at the largest gain than he could if he concentrated on the satisfaction of the needs of known persons. He is led by the invisible hand of the market to bring the succour of modern conveniences to the poorest homes he does not even know.[35]

---

[33] Hayek, *Mirage*, p. 165, cf. p. 91.
[34] Zenon Bankowski, 'The Law of Love', Inaugural Lecture, The University of Edinburgh, 1994.
[35] Hayek, *Mirage*, p. 145.

Protecting the vulnerable against extreme deprivation may be in the interests of all, but this has nothing to do with justice; the poor have no claim on the rich.[36] Similarly, aid to poorer countries has nothing to do with justice.[37] The rich and the powerful may, if they wish, be comfortable in their selfishness, for through it they are doing good to others at no cost to themselves!

The claim of the neighbour

The issue here is the question, Who is my neighbour? Hayek believes that as we move from a face-to-face society towards the Great Society the moral claims of the neighbour become less as our obligation to act with procedural justice to everyone expands. He does not appear to believe that an ethic of the neighbour is valid in a Great Society. His reply to the lawyer's question is very different from that of Jesus, who by way of answer told the story of the Good Samaritan, which is clearly a concrete application of an ethic of the neighbour to a large, if pre-modern, society composed of strangers and people in socially defined roles.

There is in the Bible a morally challenging enlargement of the understanding of the neighbour and the neighbour's claims. The elemental meaning of the word is that a neighbour is one who lives close by, and is almost certainly someone very like us. People who are basically different, and do not have the same moral claim on us – slaves, aliens, untouchables – may live close by, but they are not neighbours. They might support the life of the neighbourhood, but they are not part of it for they do not belong in the community. Neighbours may squabble, but they stand shoulder to shoulder against the outside world, recognise that they are 'members one of another', and have moral obligations to one another. Neighbours belong together; they are interdependent; they ought to be able to rely on one another.

When the Bible enjoins us to love our neighbour, or to do

[36] Hayek, *Ibid.*, p. 87; *Political Order*, p. 55.   [37] Hayek, *Mirage*, p. 89.

justice to our neighbour, it is often this natural neighbour who is first in question. But the meaning of neighbour quickly expands. In Leviticus 19, for example, after an injunction to love the neighbour who is clearly the fellow Israelite, there follows a command to love the strangers, the marginalised people, as if they were physical and racial neighbours. The excluded people are to be incorporated into the moral community. The stranger is to be treated as a neighbour for two specific reasons: Israel remembers having been strangers in Egypt, the bitterness of exclusion and oppression; and they have found again and again that their God, the God who does justice, has a special care for strangers, the poor and the oppressed.

In the parable of the Good Samaritan,[38] it is the stranger, the despised and hated foreigner, the heretic excluded from the covenant people, the feared Samaritan, who shows himself through his actions to be the neighbour to the Jew, lying wounded and forlorn by the roadside. The stranger acts graciously as a neighbour to the one who needs help. The alien becomes the neighbour. Strangers and enemies are neighbours, with moral claims upon us. In the development from the intimate face-to-face society to the Great Society, where strangers pass to and fro on their legitimate business on the Jericho Road, we are surrounded by increasing categories of neighbours with very specific claims on us, specific needs and specific contributions. Without this moral seasoning, the Great Society becomes callous and inhumane. Those who have the power to help, in Hayek's scheme, pass by on the other side of the road.[39] A Hayekian interpretation of the parable would suggest that the priest and Levite, in refusing to be distracted from going about their business, acted morally. The robbers may be enterprising, but they act unjustly because they break the law. The Samaritan took a personal choice to succour the wounded Jew; but his behaviour is not in any way normative. The smooth working of the Great Society would be seriously

---

[38] Luke 10.25–37.
[39] For a fuller discussion of the theme of the neighbour see Forrester and Skene, *Just Sharing*, pp. 80–9.

impeded if we all went and did likewise![40] Here we have highlighted the tension between the Hayekian moral universe and the Judaeo-Christian tradition.

HAYEK AND THE THEOLOGIANS

Hayek's treatment of spontaneous orders is redolent of the theological notion of orders of creation, which Karl Barth and others believed served to make absolute contemporary manifestations of the state, the family and so forth as fairly unambiguous expressions of God's purposes. Is it possible that, despite his avowed rejection of any metaphysic or theology, there is a kind of lurking cosmology here, which provides an implicit justification of the market, a given, which is also part of a gracious provision for human flourishing? For, if so, the market should be treated with reverence, as an order beyond criticism. Lord Harris of High Cross often speaks of 'the miracle of the market';[41] other economists of like persuasion describe how 'miraculously' Adam Smith's invisible hand ensures efficient outcomes.[42] Such a wonderful order is beyond criticism; we interfere with it at our peril. The proper approach is one of humility and awe: 'The fundamental attitude of true individualism', Hayek writes, 'is one of humility toward the processes by which mankind has achieved things which have not been designed or understood by any individual and are therefore greater than individual minds.'[43]

Thus quasi-religious sanctions are placed in the way of any serious critique or reform of the market. 'We interfere with markets at our peril,' writes Gordon Hughes, 'since market forces may be compared to Canute's tide so that attempts to resist their effects may be both costly and ineffective.'[44]

[40] I am indebted to Dr Graham Blount and to a paper on the interpretation of the parable of the Good Samaritan by my colleague Dr J. I. H. McDonald for many of these points.

[41] For instance, expounding Hayek, in Michael Alison and David L. Edwards (eds.), *Christianity and Conservatism*. London: Hodder & Stoughton, 1990, p. 184.

[42] Gordon A. Hughes in Hughes *et al.*, *The Economics of Hard Choices: Justice and the Market*. Occasional Paper, no 21, Edinburgh, CTPI, 1991, p. 3.

[43] Friedrich A. Hayek, *Individualism and Economic Order*. Chicago: University of Chicago Press, 1948, p. 32.

[44] Hughes, *Economics of Hard Choices*, p. 1.

Hayek shares with most other contemporary theorists of justice an attempt to set aside explicitly metaphysical and theological considerations, and an affirmation of secular pluralism. He carefully eschews theology as a dangerous distraction from the kind of thinking about society which he regards as necessary. He protests against the concept of social justice as a 'superstition' which 'has become almost the new religion of our time (and in which many of the ministers of the old religion have found their refuge)'.[45] To this he adds the occasional jibe at 'a large section of the clergy of all Christian denominations, who, while increasingly losing their faith in a supernatural revelation, appear to have sought a refuge and a consolation in a new "social" religion which substitutes a temporal for a celestial promise of justice, and who hope that they can thus continue their striving to do good.'[46]

But although Hayek has no time for theologians, or indeed for religion, there are theologians and believers who like Hayek. Just as some theologians have attempted to baptise Rawls, so there are a few contemporary theologians who see Hayek's position as at least compatible with Christian theology.

G. Walker, writing from a conservative theological position, argues that Hayek's conclusions could well be rooted in biblical Christianity. He questions whether there is as sharp a tension between the market order and the Judaeo-Christian moral tradition as Hayek himself supposes. Christians may see in the workings of the market the beneficent hand of God: 'the spontaneous mechanisms of the market may be a mercy of God, a mechanism providentially suited to man's imperfect nature', and capable of channelling sinfulness in a beneficent direction. The market and contemporary Christianity need one another to provide support and interpretation.[47] In the United States some other extremely conservative theologians take a similar line.

But there are more active politicians with a Christian

---

[45] Hayek, *Law, Legislation and Liberty*, p. xvi.
[46] Hayek, *Mirage*, p. 66.
[47] G. Walker, *The Ethics of F. A. Hayek*. Lanham, Md.: University Press of America, 1986, esp. pp. 108–15.

commitment who endorse Hayek's line. The most prominent
British personality who appears to give unqualified support to a
Hayekian position and defends it from time to time on a
Christian basis is Margaret Thatcher. Thatcherism's remarkably unqualified espousal of a Hayekian position distinguishes it
sharply from the Christian Democracy which it sees as its
equivalent in the rest of Western Europe. Christian Democracy
has its ideological roots in the soil of official Roman Catholic
social teaching and therefore takes it for granted that the state
and the community have a responsibility to protect the weak
and the poor against the outcomes of the market. This reflects a
very un-Hayekian understanding of how sin and power operate
through the market to the disadvantage of those who are in
control of few resources.

But most Christian thinkers who support Hayek do so with
considerable reservations. Brian Griffiths, an evangelical Christian who is a distinguished British economist and was a close
advisor of Margaret Thatcher, for instance, cannot accept
Hayek's extreme individualism and, in particular, his rejection
of the possibility that we have moral responsibilities for
others.[48] As a Christian, Griffiths believes that Hayek's account
of justice is far too narrow, and he affirms that the market
economy can only operate acceptably in a moral framework
which has been decisively shaped by Christianity. Hayek's
account of justice is too narrow; for a Christian justice must be
more than the rules of the game. Christianity therefore 'puts
certain limits on the market place, not on the basis that they are
politically necessary to secure greater freedom in the market
economy, but that they are right and desirable in themselves'.[49]
For a Christian, Griffiths affirms, a concern for the poor is not
optional or pragmatic: 'It is legitimately a function of government acting on behalf of society as a whole and comparable to
its mandate to maintain law and order.'[50] Griffiths's intellectual
endeavour is 'to rescue the market economy from capitalist

[48] Brian Griffiths, *The Creation of Wealth*. London: Hodder & Stoughton, 1984, pp. 8off.
[49] Brian Griffiths, *Morality and the Market Place*. London: Hodder & Stoughton, 1982,
p. 9.
[50] *Ibid.*, p. 36.

ideology' – and that means a very broad rejection of a Hayekian viewpoint, and the taming of the market so that it may serve Christian ends. The market, he says, can only be defended 'if it is defended within the bounds of Christian justice'.[51]

I doubt whether Brian Griffiths realises just how radical are the implications of that last, key comment. If we hearken not to the politicians, the intellectuals and the wealthy but to the hungry and the weak and the poor, the homeless and the wretched we hear a cry of protest against the injustice of the outcomes of the market. The other side of Hayek's argument that the winners in market transactions do not merit or deserve their success is that these victims and losers do not deserve their plight, and ought in justice to be delivered from it. The market of itself can neither define nor deliver justice. It is a good servant, but a bad master. To be just, and indeed to be efficient, markets require outside regulation. The market must be harnessed to serve the ends of justice.

HAYEKIAN JUSTICE AND PUBLIC POLICY

There is no need to argue that the ideas of justice that we have been discussing in this chapter have had a profound and continuing impact on public policy in Britain, in the United States (often in the variant advocated by Milton Friedman), and in many other countries around the world, not least those of the former Soviet Union and its previous satellites in Eastern Europe. The central emphasis in Hayek's thought on the virtues of the market, allied with a suspicion of the state, have seemed to be ideas whose time has come.

In the aftermath of the Second World War there was in western countries an extraordinary confidence in the general beneficence and effectiveness of state power. This was mirrored in the new regimes in the former colonial countries, as those who had struggled for freedom took over power and often then

---

[51] *Ibid.*, p. 39. Useful discussions of Griffiths's views are Ronald H. Preston, *The Future of Christian Ethics*. London: SCM, 1989, ch. 9, and John Atherton, *Christianity and the Market*. London: SPCK, 1992, ch. 4.

showed that they would use it much as had the former imperial nation. And the Marxist states, believing in the dictatorship of the proletariat, regarded political power as an indispensable instrument for the transition to communism. In the same decades, there continued to be a pervasive and deep-seated distrust of the market, partly ideological and partly arising out of memories of the sufferings of many during the Depression of the 1930s. Keynesian or socialist ways of regulating the market were widely seen as techniques for ensuring that such widespread unemployment, poverty and demoralisation should never return, and government, it was commonly believed, could safely be allowed to oversee such measures. As government had led the allied nations to victory in the Second World War, so it could confidently be trusted to play the leading role in achieving a just post-war settlement.

In recent decades the pendulum has swung, and the old distrust of the market has been replaced with a no less extreme suspicion of the state and all its works. This has been most marked in the United States, where there is a long tradition of suspicion of government, but it spread in the 1960s and 1970s from Western Europe and the United States to most of the rest of the world.

Robert E. Lane demonstrated empirically in the mid-1980s that Americans had a decided preference for market justice over political justice, and that they had more confidence that the market would lead to acceptable outcomes than that the political system can indeed promote justice and the common good. The market, but not the government, was generally believed to be 'fair and wise'; people believed that they were more likely to receive fair treatment and their just deserts from the market than from the political system. Benefits received from government were not seen as fair or just, but rather as the outcome of partisan rivalries in which electoral advantage and group self-interest play a far greater role than any considerations of justice, fairness or desert. The market was perceived as embodying a basic harmony of interests, so that everyone gains something from it, whereas the democratic state assumes an irresolvable conflict of interests, with the distribution of benefits

and liabilities at the discretion of the winners in power struggles, rather than reflecting any effective principles of justice or
fairness. Thus in the 1980s and 1990s in the States, and in many
other countries as well, Hayekian accounts of justice can be said
to articulate a deeply and widely held view, if not a consensus,[52]
and Rawlsian views, which give a greater place to the state as a
dispenser of justice and are less sanguine about the market's
capacity to operate justly, can apparently rely only on a
minority opinion except, perhaps, among intellectuals.[53]

This swing of public opinion, which is repeated widely
around the globe, has encouraged and enabled the extension of
market processes and Hayek-style understandings of justice into
more and more sectors of life and areas of public policy. The
record of such developments is mixed. Whereas the market
supported by Hayekian theories has shown itself to be effective
in wealth creation in various contexts, and to encourage
economic vitality, there are other areas where it produces far
more mixed, or positively harmful, results.

In classical social and economic thought the market and its
procedures were assumed to be concerned with only part of life,
if a very important part. Adam Smith, it may be remembered,
wrote *The Wealth of Nations* (1776), which has not inaptly been
seen as a manifesto for the free market and for market values;
but earlier he had written *The Theory of Moral Sentiments* (1759),
which emphasised other values such as sympathy and disinter-
estedness which he believed to be necessary for a healthy
society and, indeed, on the strength of which the vitality and
efficiency of the market ultimately depends. The moral and
social order within which a market operated was crucial to its
effectiveness; and that moral order operates on different and
sometimes contrasting principles from those properly operative
in the market sphere. A. O. Hirschman, Adam Seligman and
others have pointed out that for Adam Smith the need for the

---

52 But notice that the popular view rejects Hayek's suggestion that market outcomes
   are largely a matter of luck or accident; it is important if people are to have
   confidence in the market that they should believe that its outcomes bear some
   relation to desert.
53 Robert E. Lane, 'Market Justice, Political Justice', *American Political Science Review*,
   80:2 (June 1986), pp. 383–402.

'sympathy, complacency and approbation' of others was more powerful than avarice and ambition as a driving force for economic activity and the pursuit of wealth.[54] The need for appreciation, for a recognition of one's worth, and the sentiment of benevolence also set limits to the sphere of self-interest. Were these limits to be eroded, avarice and acquisitiveness became destructive of civil society which was understood as 'a realm of solidarity held together by the force of moral sentiments and natural affections'.[55]

What has happened in societies where the thought of Hayek and his like has become dominant is what Habermas calls 'the colonization of life-forms' – market forces and market values have invaded one area after another, replacing existing values and procedures with market values and market procedures. In some cases this has been extremely harmful, because market forces can be destructive if dominant in spheres of life in which they do not properly belong. Michael Walzer argued in an important book that there are various 'spheres' of life, in each of which there are different criteria of justice which are appropriate.[56] What is happening widely today is that market criteria which have their place in economic activity are invading other spheres of life, often destroying values and structures which are necessary for the long-term health of the economy and the market, to say nothing of the flourishing of society as a whole.

The case of health care

A case in point is the provision of health care. Obviously there is an economic dimension to health care, and market forces have a place. But are the provision of health care and the relation between physician and patient simply or mainly eco-

[54] Adam Seligman, *The Idea of Civil Society*. New York: Free Press, 1992, p. 27; citing A. O. Hirschman, *The Passions and the Interests*. Princeton: Princeton University Press, 1977, p. 109.

[55] Seligman, *Idea of Civil Society*, p. 33.

[56] Michael L. Walzer, *Spheres of Justice*. New York: Basic Books, 1983. Walzer is, of course, aware that the different criteria of justice appropriate to the various spheres must have *something* in common if they are indeed forms of justice.

nomic matters? Acrimonious debates are going on about these matters in most countries, the issues being posed including the cost-efficiency of health care delivery and health care as an area where most people expect to find justice and not infrequently find the opposite. Alastair Campbell has recently argued that health is an aspect of freedom, and injustice in health care provision is experienced as oppression, the freedom of the weaker members of society being taken away by the more powerful.[57] If he is right that health care provision is as much a matter of freedom as of justice, he has posed a difficulty for Hayekians who give priority to freedom and argue that the market is the most effective provider of care and market outcomes even in health have nothing to do with justice.

Right-wing thinkers like Hayek also launch a powerful attack on the traditional idea of a *profession* such as medicine being a group of disinterested people primarily devoted altruistically to the care of their patients rather than the pursuit of their own interests or the lining of their own pockets. Professionals, the argument goes, are as selfish as anyone else, and the fact that a profession has a monopoly of a certain kind of provision gives them extensive powers of enrichment at the expense of the public. George Bernard Shaw was right, they claim, when he suggested that all professions are conspiracies against the laity.[58] To the patient this pretence may not, they suggest, in fact matter as much as one might suppose, because Adam Smith's famous words are as true of doctors as of other occupations: 'It is not from the benevolence of the butcher, the brewer or the baker that we expect our dinner, but from their regard to their own self-interest.' The remainder of the quotation is not at all true of doctor-patient relations: 'We never talk to them of our own necessities but of their advantages'![59] And here lies the nub of the problem: unless we can talk to doctors in the confidence that they will put *our* interests first we cannot have the trust that is essential to the professional relationship. If

[57] Alastair V. Campbell, *Health as Liberation: Medicine, Theology and the Quest for Justice.* Cleveland: Pilgrim Press, 1995, p. 1.
[58] G. B. Shaw, *The Doctor's Dilemma*, Act I.
[59] Adam Smith, *The Wealth of Nations.* London: Dent, 1910, p. 13.

the market is allowed to pervade the caring professions, true caring is corroded.

It is not that doctors and other professionals are exempt from the selfishness of other human beings; indeed all the empirical evidence goes against this and confirms the existence of original sin! The British Medical Association initially strongly resisted the introduction of the National Health Service basically because it was feared that it would hurt doctors' purses, and the American Medical Association today opposes any measures of 'socialized medicine' with considerable vehemence. But as long as a professional ethos and an ethic of care are honoured there is an in-built restraint to the acquisitiveness of physicians and to the total capitulation of the health care system to market forces. Long traditions of public service, of care and of professional values can quickly be corroded by market forces and by the assumption that the best way to care for one's patient is indirectly, as a kind of by-product of making as much money as possible.

When the market colonises the health care system, patients become customers, symptoms rather than people are treated, there is an emphasis on productivity rather than care, the system becomes increasingly adversarial – patient and doctor seeing one another as potential opponents in court, and the practice of medicine is seen as a *battle* against disease, in which defeat is unthinkable, rather than the care of a sick person.[60] Medical care is commodified and becomes enormously expensive. As one American physician writes, 'One reason for this is our demand for the best. We want the best health care available, and, fortunately, many of us can get it. In general, American health care is the most technologically advanced health care in the world. But the price for getting the best care is very high, and it goes up every year.'[61] But is this expense really necessary? Alastair Campbell writes:

Many studies have revealed the wastefulness – and at times the

---

[60] On this see particularly William F. May, 'Adversarialism in Medicine' in *The End of Professionalism?* Occasional Paper, no. 6, Edinburgh: CTPI, 1985, pp. 3–18.
[61] William A. Fintel and Gerald R. McDermott, *A Medical and Spiritual Guide to Living with Cancer*. Dallas: Word Publishing, 1993, p. 115.

dangerousness – of this domination of technology over health care
. . . Rates of surgery and use of expensive equipment are much higher
in the United States than in other countries, to no obvious advantage
and probably with higher risk to patients.[62]

America spends proportionately far more on health care
than any other developed nation, yet its comparative health
record is not good.[63] The real victims are the poor. Some
thirty million Americans have no health insurance at all. Many
of them are in employment, but fall in the gap between
government programmes and private health insurance; they
earn too much to qualify for Medicaid or Medicare and do
not earn enough to pay private insurance premiums.[64]
Women and children, the poor and ethnic minorities are, of
course, particularly hard hit. Indeed, 'the more a person needs
ready access to medical services, the less likely it is to be
available'.[65]

Thus the power of what someone has called the modern
'medical industrial complex' in the health market makes it by
no means an even playing field. The stress is on competition to
make money; professional self-interest and acquisitiveness are
assumed, encouraged and endorsed; and the victims are many.
Injustice causes suffering and death even within an extraordinarily expensive health care system.

It would be wrong to suggest that these or similar problems
do not occur in health care systems which have been less
deeply penetrated by market forces and Hayekian principles
than the American. In the British National Health Service
(NHS), for instance, there is a very serious problem of
inequalities in health care provision, which is a major contributor to the fact that poorer people in Britain have less
good health care within the NHS than richer people, and
their life expectancy and general level of health are markedly

---

[62] Campbell, *Health as Liberation*, p. 72.
[63] 'Among OECD [Organization for Economic Cooperation and Development]
countries, the United States ranks nineteenth in infant mortality rates, sixteenth in
life expectancy for women, and twenty-first in life expectancy for men.' Campbell,
Health as Liberation, p. 68.
[64] Fintel and McDermott, *Medical and Spiritual Guide*, p. 125.
[65] Campbell, *Health as Liberation*, pp. 68–75 (69).

inferior.[66] An internal market is being gradually extended within the NHS despite strong resistance. But for all its problems, the NHS is both very much cheaper than the US health care system, delivers better overall results in standards of health, and does not discriminate against poor people. The injustices are recognised as problems that must be tackled.

On a Rawlsian or a Christian basis the issues I have outlined in the previous paragraphs in relation to health care are essentially questions of justice. Once they are recognised as such, something must be done about them. For Hayek, in contrast, they are simply matters of market outcomes. The market, if left to its own operation, will provide the best quality of health care, effective, cheap and customer/patient oriented. Questions of justice do not arise.

The evidence in the area of health care does not seem to support the Hayekian view. I would suggest that in this area there is certainly a place for market considerations in, for example, ensuring that competition provides value for money in drugs, and that the market principle of 'consumer sovereignty' entitles the patient to full knowledge of diagnosis and treatment. But it also appears that when market considerations penetrate deeply into a health care system they corrode its central values and result in serious injustices, even if, on Hayekian grounds, they are not recognised as such.

---

[66] See, for instance, Peter Townsend and Nick Davidson, *Inequalities in Health: The Black Report*. Harmondsworth: Penguin, 1982; Alison J. Elliot (ed.), *Inequalities in Health in the 1980s*. Occasional Paper, no. 13, Edinburgh: CTPI, 1988, and *The Market and Health Care*. Occasional Paper, no. 19, Edinburgh: CTPI, 1990. The economist Julian Le Grand has pioneered studies in inequalities in health care in Britain since the publication of his *Strategy of Equality*. London: Allen & Unwin, 1982.

CHAPTER 7

Communication, gender and justice

If it is in fact the 'first principle of society', the quality that holds a decent community together, it is not at all surprising that justice is commonly understood as relational, that is, as having to do with the ties which bind people together, the links of responsibility and rights and affection that make a number of people into a community. These relationships and ties are forms of communication; for community to exist, communication must take place, and the quality and nature of that communication determines whether there is justice in the community or not.

As we have seen in the previous two chapters, a great deal of thought about society starts with the individual, or is individualistic through and through. Society, for individualist thought, is primarily a device for safeguarding individuals and assisting them in the fulfilment of their personal purposes; a just society is one that performs these functions well. There have been strenuous protests against the individualistic rationalism which is characteristic of most post-Enlightenment social thought, particularly from those thinkers who are labelled 'communitarian' – Alasdair MacIntyre, Charles Taylor, Michael Sandel, Stanley Hauerwas and others. The main focus of this chapter, however, will be not on the communitarians, but on Jürgen Habermas, a major and extraordinarily prolific thinker who affirms and endeavours to continue what MacIntyre has called 'the Enlightenment Project' and rejects the communitarians' critique of liberalism, while taking with the utmost seriousness the fact that human beings are communicators and can only be understood in relationships and in community. Communicative action and solidarity are indeed the foundations of his account of justice, the principles of which he believes to be latent in the processes of communication which bind people together.

We will also discuss the most effective and yet sympathetic challenge to Habermas's thought, that which comes from feminist thinkers who argue that Habermas's account of justice is based almost entirely on male experience and neglects or undervalues whole dimensions of justice and of morality which are important to women and commonly figure in women's experience, but are also necessary for a society if it is to flourish and manifest a rich and humane understanding of justice. A healthy, inclusive community, they argue, needs a broader account of justice than that offered by Habermas. And some of their emphases are impressively close to dimensions of justice which have been stressed in the Christian tradition but seriously neglected in most modern western social thought.

Although Habermas has shown rather little interest in theology and religion, an increasing number of theologians have been fascinated by him, and some of them, as we shall see, have been proposing an even broader and more inclusive sense of community and solidarity than Habermas envisages, requiring a correspondingly broader account of justice to sustain it. I shall discuss their contribution, and give some attention to both the communitarian and the post-modernist critiques of Habermas's thought. Just as some theologians have attempted to 'baptise' Rawls and Hayek, so some have seen in Habermas a thinker who can provide an account of community and of justice which is congenial to Christian insights and may be recruited into Christian thought about society as were Aristotle, Kant, or Hegel in the past. Habermas's social thought appeals to many Christians because, although he largely rejects theology and eschews religious presuppositions, his theory of communicative action has many resonances with Christian understandings of community.

This chapter, then, is concerned with the understandings of justice which emerge from Habermas's vast intellectual project and the feminist critique. As before, I will attempt some theological assessment and will also ask about the implications for policy-making and practice of Habermas's theory of justice.

HABERMAS: A CRITICAL THEORY OF JUSTICE

Habermas's thought emerges from the 'critical theory' of the Frankfurt School of scholars whose central endeavour has been to update and reconsider crucial Marxist insights. He is by far the most prominent contemporary representative of the school, which in the past boasted of luminaries such as Theodor Adorno, Walter Benjamin, Max Horkheimer, Eric Fromm and Herbert Marcuse, while for a time the theologian Paul Tillich was also involved. The Judaeo-Christian tradition, Hegel and the Marxist heritage (which last is now somewhat difficult to detect in his work) have given Habermas a strong emancipatory interest. A central function of critical theory is to expose structures of domination and exploitation, often elaborately concealed, for what they are. Domination and oppression wherever they may be found are to be removed. Thus Habermas's critical theory is more than an academic exercise;[1] it is intended to eventuate in action for radical social change.

Habermas stands in the tradition of Hegel and of Marx; this distinguishes him from Rawls and Hayek, who are more heirs of Kant and Hume. Hegel and Marx 'philosophise out of dissatisfaction, out of the "experience" that the world is not as it ought to be'. The task for them is not the discovery of the order of justice in the world and then conforming to it; the world has to be changed, transformed, revolutionised if justice is to be recognised and realised. Then Marx breaks free from Hegel in rejecting the belief that thought and ideas are the primary agents of this transformation, which is necessary before the world can be understood and justice grasped and actualised.[2] For Habermas and the other critical theorists, Marx

---

[1] Although Habermas has been honest enough to admit that his major project *The Theory of Communicative Action* became 'hopelessly academic'. Cited in David Schlosberg, 'Communicative Action in Practice: Intersubjectivity and New Social Movements', *Political Studies*, 43:2 (June 1995), 291–311 (292).

[2] N. Lobkowicz, *Theory and Practice: History of a Concept from Aristotle to Marx*. Notre Dame: University of Notre Dame Press, 1967, pp. 340–1.

provides the basic resources for a liberating critical theory, but did not in fact succeed in constructing such a theory adequate to his own time, while mechanical applications of Marxist insights to the present day are unhelpful and unilluminating.[3] What is needed, and what Habermas endeavours to provide, is a critical theory which actually engages with the experiences and structures of oppression of today, which are in many ways different from those of the past.

Justice and modernity

Hence Habermas embarks on a massive critical analysis of modernity, while still wishing to affirm and press forward the Enlightenment Project. The answer to the problems of the present day for him is to mine more deeply than before into certain seams of the Enlightenment heritage; the disease of modern enlightened rationality can only be healed by homeopathy. Modernity, according to Habermas, has deep-seated and intractable problems. These include the fragmentation that comes from no longer having a shared, broad common vision of the good, which is at least from time to time capable of constraining the forces of oppression. Habermas is not blind to the fact that the modern 'enlightened' world has been plagued by conflict, cruelty, oppression and suffering to a quite unprecedented degree. The tolerant liberal university showed itself singularly ineffective in resisting Hitler or in naming and exposing the evil of the Holocaust. The idealistic programmes of socialism and the welfare state now show clear signs of exhaustion, and there is deep concern as to whether modern society has adequate resources to enable it to respond to the challenges of today. The modern world has communication networks of unparalleled effectiveness, but seems to have little of substance to communicate. And modern communication does little to create community, but much to act as an opiate of the people.

I do not have the space to do more than outline Habermas's

---

[3] On the emancipatory interest in Habermas's thought see especially Thomas McCarthy, *The Critical Theory of Jürgen Habermas*. London: Hutchinson, 1978, pp. 75ff.

sophisticated, perceptive and immense on-going critique of modernity. 'Distorted communication' lies at the heart of his diagnosis of the malaise of our time; and proper communication is the essential remedy.[4] There is no going back to a pre-Enlightenment age of innocence; we must find the resources for dealing with today's problems today, rather than searching for answers in a tired tradition. Religious insights are to be excluded on principle: 'With the historical transition from traditional to modern society . . . ', he writes, 'religious and metaphysical world-views lose their capacity to provide consensual justification of norms of social interaction and the autonomous individual becomes the centre of the moral universe'.[5] Modernity must provide its own way of generating and validating norms of conduct both private and public, and this can only be some form of discussion seeking a consensus:[6] modernity 'must create its normativity out of itself'.[7] In the public sphere no one should have recourse to dogmas or traditional wisdom and all differences of opinion should be settled by the force of rational argument.[8]

There is, on the face of it, a problem here, not dissimilar to that which we encountered in relation to Rawls's 'overlapping consensus'. It is this: if appeals to the tradition, to dogma, or to metaphysical truths are ruled out, and moral truth is to be grounded only on what most people accept or believe, or can be persuaded uncoercively to accept, is there any way of achieving a critical distance from the conventional wisdom of a particular society or culture? On what grounds can we say that Hitler, or Stalin for that matter, were wrong and evil in their policies and their behaviour? Is there any way of escaping from relativism, or

---

[4] One of the ironies of the situation is that Habermas who puts such immense stress on the importance of communication is himself a poor communicator! The response that the issues with which he deals are so complex that they cannot be simplified without trivialisation I find unconvincing.

[5] Ciran Cronin in Translator's Introduction to J. Habermas, *Justification and Application: Remarks on Discourse Ethics*. Cambridge, Mass.: MIT, 1993, p. xii.

[6] J. Habermas, *The Philosophical Discourse of Modernity*. Cambridge, Mass.: MIT, 1987, p. 7.

[7] Habermas, *ibid.*, p. 16, cited in Stephen K. White, *The Recent Work of Jürgen Habermas: Reason, Justice and Modernity*. Cambridge: Cambridge University Press, 1988, p. 91.

[8] Thompson and Held, *Habermas*, p. 4.

from an affirmation of the infallibility of the majority? Indeed, is the attempt to develop an ethics which is largely independent of tradition and of metaphysics not doomed to failure?

Consensual justice

Habermas responds to such difficulties by suggesting that in a pluralist situation in which no overarching vision of the good is possible, and probably not desirable either, it is necessary to focus on justice. His theory concentrates on the procedures to be adopted in seeking justice rather than on the substantive content of justice. If one sets up an effective procedure for 'making sense together', for reaching consensus, this will be the way of achieving concrete just outcomes. Habermas believes that implicit in any serious communication is a search for agreement or consensus on what is good and what is true; he presents a consensus theory of truth and a consensus theory of justice.[9] Pettit's question whether in Habermas's view a statement secures rational consensus because it is true, or it is true because it secures rational consensus, applies to justice as well; and in neither case is it clearly answered, so that we are left uncertain whether Habermas believes that justice has some objective grounding (as in the first reading of Rawls) or is simply what commands general assent (as in the second reading of Rawls).[10]

For many years Habermas has claimed that in the structure of language 'autonomy and responsibility are posited for us. Our first sentence expresses unequivocally the intention of universal and unconstrained consensus.'[11] Speech is seeking agreed understanding rather than an effort to express ourselves. 'Reaching understanding,' he writes, 'is the inherent *telos* of human speech.'[12] But the discourse which seeks consensus is only

---

[9] Philip Pettit, 'Habermas on Truth and Justice' in G. H. R. Parkinson (ed.), *Marx and Marxisms*. Cambridge: Cambridge University Press, 1982, pp. 207–28.

[10] Pettit, 'Habermas on Truth and Justice', p. 213.

[11] J. Habermas, *Knowledge and Human Interests*. Cambridge: Polity, 1986, p. 314, cited in William Outhwaite, *Habermas: A Critical Introduction*. Stanford: Stanford University Press, 1994, p. 38.

[12] J. Habermas, *The Theory of Communicative Action I: Reason and the Rationalisation of Society*. Boston: Beacon, 1984, p. 287.

authentic if it is uncoerced, if, that is, it approximates to what Habermas calls the 'ideal speech situation', in which no one is inhibited by fear or threat or status from sharing fully in the search for agreement and in which each participant may introduce any considerations desired. 'Participants alone,' Cronin writes, 'are ultimately competent to adjudicate claims concerning their needs and interests, and only a consensus achieved in argumentation that sufficiently approximates to the conditions of the ideal speech situation can legitimately claim to be based on rational considerations, and hence to be valid.'[13] In the ideal speech situation there is no intimidation, no pressure, no 'pulling rank'; only the force of the better argument is recognised. Participants do not seek to use or manipulate one another; they do not talk at or for one another, but to and with one another. Discourse under Hitler or Stalin was the very opposite of the ideal speech situation; violence, coercion and fear inhibited the honesty and openness to the truth and to one another which are necessary if truth and justice are to be brought into the open and the obscurantist interests of power are to be transcended.

On the face of it the ideal speech situation has similarities with Rawls's Original Position. But the differences are of the greatest importance. One enters the Original Position by passing through a Veil of Ignorance; in the ideal speech situation the more knowledge of interests, of constraints, of possibilities and of feelings the better; indeed without such information the discussion cannot effectively proceed; productive discourse is only possible between real people, with relationships and histories, and knowledge of their society and its problems. Only so can one expect a rational outcome of their discussion.[14]

Procedural justice

Unlike Rawls, Habermas does not believe that we can predict the outcome of real discussions about justice among those who will be potentially affected:

[13] Cronin in Habermas, *Justification and Application*, p. xviii.
[14] See Benhabib, *Situating the Self*, pp. 73, 169.

Participants alone are ultimately competent to adjudicate claims concerning their needs and interests, and only a consensus achieved in argumentation that sufficiently approximates to the conditions of the ideal speech situation can legitimately claim to be based on rational considerations and thus to be valid. Accordingly the discourse theory of ethics demands that we go beyond theoretical speculations concerning justice and enter into real processes of argumentation under sufficiently propitious conditions.[15]

What we have then is a *procedure* for enabling people to discover what justice means in particular circumstances, rather than a full-blown theory of justice such as Rawls proposes. From Habermas one receives a general account of how to work out what justice is in specific contexts, but hardly anything about what justice demands in a particular situation. 'The most that can be expected from a "philosophical ethics"', he writes, 'is a clarification of what justice is, in the sense of universally valid procedural criteria appropriate to the judging of the justness of proposed norms; it cannot go further and tell us with the same certainty *what justice demands*, in the sense of picking out determinate norms for guiding action.'[16] The way to uncover the demands of justice is to follow the procedures of discourse ethics in real situations.

Habermas carefully eschews the individualism characteristic of Rawls and others. The determination of the nature and the demands of justice is a communal activity. In the ideal speech situation people listen to one another and discuss justice and its demands without the assumption that each person puts individual interests, present and future, first. The ideal speech situation is a communal context, and the community that is involved in the discussion is the widest possible, for everyone who might have an interest, or something to say, should be in principle a participant.

This suggests perhaps that Habermas's account of justice is not as lacking in substantive content as many have believed. Pettit is right in saying that 'Habermas does have substantive opinions on the nature of justice'. But these opinions have, as it

---

[15] Cronin, in Habermas, *Justification and Application*, p. xviii.
[16] White, *Recent Works of Jürgen Habermas*, p. 50, cf. p. 73.

were, to be teased out of him. For Pettit these views can be summed up as 'the just system is that which impartially and maximally satisfies people's real needs'.[17] This does not seem on the face of it to present a developed theory of justice, or to take adequate account of the social nature of human beings; but Habermas's community of discourse in the ideal speech situation is in a real sense a model of what justice means. Justice necessarily involves the kind of participation and dialogue that is presupposed in the ideal speech situation.[18] A just society is one in which there is the minimum of coercion and the maximum of attentiveness to what each person and group has to contribute and to say, a society where manipulation and ideological control are systematically discountenanced, where people are able to relate freely and openly to one another, where people learn to 'speak the truth in love'.

Such implications are not spelled out precisely by Habermas, in contrast with the way in which Rawls details the decisions which must be made in the original condition, and how they should be embodied in the social order. But they are clearly implicit in the position Habermas develops, and thereby give to his thought a somewhat optimistic air. Despite his determination not to pre-empt the outcome of concrete discussions about the demands of justice in particular situations, he is strangely confident for one who comes from the Marxist tradition that it is possible here and now to overcome the distortions of ideology and interest.[19] A theologian might echo Anselm in suggesting that he has not yet considered the gravity of sin and its pervasive distortion of human judgements.

Thus Habermas, like Rawls, produces a largely procedural account of justice, outlining the way in which justice may be found. There is perhaps implied in his argument more about the nature and content of justice than might appear on the surface, but he has a marked respect for the concrete situation

---

[17] Pettit, 'Habermas on Truth and Justice', p. 228.
[18] See Reynaud de la Bat Smit, *The Justice of God and the Formation of Society*. Unpublished PhD thesis, Durham: University of Durham, 1993, esp. p. 176.
[19] This point is argued very effectively by Pettit, 'Habermas on Truth and Justice', pp. 207–28.

and the need to leave the actual decision to the participants –
not surprising for one who stands in a tradition of suspecting
'pure' theory as a disguise for interest, and believing in praxis.
He lacks the pervasive individualism of Rawls, and sees social
life as a co-operative enterprise. In some ways he is in fact
closer to the communitarians than is Rawls, but, for a vestigial
Marxist, he places surprisingly little stress on history and rejects
the communitarians' emphasis on the inevitability of arguing
within the resources offered us by a specific tradition because,
they claim, there is no objective and independent standpoint,
no reasoning that is not shaped by tradition.

Habermas, more markedly than the later Rawls, is a universalist; his accounts of truth and of justice claim to be valid
everywhere and to be founded on something that orthodox
Marxists deny – unchanging elements in human language and,
ultimately, a universal community of discourse. For him, as for
Plato, justice is not a principle or principles (as with Rawls),[20]
or a simple set of procedures governing a part of social life (as
with Hayek), but a way of structuring the good society. Justice
must lie at the heart of any true relating, community or social
organisation. He sees justice as a form of social order, the
central processes of a society, in which barriers to communication and community have been largely eroded so that authentic
forms of co-operative endeavour and sharing are increasingly
enabled.

Habermas has, it is true, a universalistic and rationalistic
perspective, but he has also a far more critical stance towards
modern society than either Rawls or Hayek. The essential
problem with modern society as he sees it is exactly what Hayek
discerns as its distinctive excellence – that modern society is
impersonal and individuals are set free from so many ties of
relationship, reciprocity and responsibility. His 'discourse
ethics' points in the direction of participation, equality and
community. And he proposes a thoroughgoing hermeneutic of
suspicion of social structures.

---

[20] Although in broad terms he accepts that justice is fairness.

The psychological grounding of discourse ethics

Just as Hayek's account of justice assumes the classical self-interested economic man if it is to work, and Rawls builds into his original condition key assumptions about the psychology and behaviour of the decision-makers behind the Veil of Ignorance, so Habermas sees the need to ground his discourse ethics on an understanding of human nature and psychology if it is to operate effectively. Discourse between the gullible, or the cowed, or the dementing is hardly likely to lead to anything approaching an ideal speech situation, or to just outcomes. Habermas turns for confirmation or illustration of his belief that the search for a consensus and the ideal speech situation are latent whenever we enter seriously into discussion of Chomsky's work on the development of language, for support for his belief that the ideal speech situation is a developmental climax to Piaget's research into how children develop the ability to think conceptually, and for exemplification of his conviction that the discourse ethics of the ideal speech situation will produce just outcomes to Lawrence Kohlberg's studies of the stages of moral reasoning.

Kohlberg and his associates based their work on careful empirical studies of the development of moral consciousness among young people – mainly boys – in the United States, but they claimed that these studies produced a more or less universal pattern of human moral development.[21] Kohlberg's schema consisted of six stages of moral development in three levels:

I – Preconventional Level. Here the child responds to punishments and rewards or the physical power of the person who commands.

1　The Punishment and Obedience Orientation: here it is the consequences of actions rather than any idea of the meaning or value of these consequences that determines moral behaviour.

2　The Instrumental Relativist Orientation: right action is what satisfies one's own needs, or occasionally the needs of others. Simple ideas of fairness and reciprocity are present, but 'human relations are viewed like those of the market place'.

---

[21] But see the devastating examination of the methodology of these studies by Brian Barry in his *Justice as Impartiality*, pp. 237–46, 259–66. My concern, however, is not with methodological issues but with the use Habermas makes of Kohlberg's results.

II – Conventional Level. Here the stress is on loyalty to the group, family, or nation, and conformity to the standards of the group.

3 The 'Good-boy-nice-girl' Orientation: Good behaviour is what pleases others, and there is a tendency to conform to stereotypes.

4 Law and Order Orientation: Here authority, fixed rules and maintaining the social order are the most important emphases.

III – Post-conventional, Autonomous or Principled Level. Here there is an effort to discover and follow moral principles which have a general validity and are not simply based on the norms of one's group.

5 Social Contract Legalistic Orientation: There is a tendency to stress rights and to base moral action on a properly achieved social consensus.

6 Universal Ethical Principle Orientation: conscience decides what is right in the light of universal ethical principles like the Golden Rule or the categorical imperative, which are freely chosen and reflect logical comprehensiveness, universality and consistency.[22]

Kohlberg gave evidence that most adults never advance beyond stage four; somewhat upwards of 20 per cent reach stage five; and only between 5 per cent and 10 per cent reach stage six. Habermas attempts to apply these stages to *social* development, suggesting that ancient societies were in the conventional stage, partly because they were in the grip of mythical world-views, while in modernity there is a gradual and still far from complete movement into the post-conventional stage.

Kohlberg's empirical work is certainly important for our understanding of the moral development of children in the West, but his schema is so replete with unexamined value assumptions that it has to be treated with considerable caution. He says that as a matter of fact the stages are the same in all cultures and societies, and people progress through them in the same order, but his attempts to suggest that he is not presenting a movement from worse to best, that his schema is not highly prescriptive, do not carry conviction. Religion and mythical world-views appear only in the early stages in Habermas's appropriation of Kohlberg, whom he regarded as 'a heuristic

---

[22] I have adapted this outline of Kohlberg's stages from McCarthy, *Critical Theory*, pp. 250–1. There is a tabular form in Outhwaite, *Habermas*, pp. 52–3.

guide and encouragement',[23] and religion is seen entirely as an *obstacle* to true maturity. The schema is shot through with the dogmas and assumptions of modernity, and involves a singular arrogance in the understanding of non-western and pre-modern societies and cultures. I find it hard to see how it can be regarded as providing objective empirical support for Habermas's account of justice and for discourse ethics. As so often in work of this kind, the normative conclusions are in fact in the work from the beginning and pervade and shape it. Perhaps a theologian should do no more than point to the text about the need to become as a little child if one is to enter the Kingdom of Heaven, as a reminder that mature, sophisticated and enlightened people and societies may still have much to learn from the simple and direct vision of the child, or indeed of ancient societies.

FEMINISTS ON HABERMAS AND JUSTICE

It is not hard to see what some feminists find attractive in Habermas's thought. He attempts to deal with real people, not abstract stereotypes like those who gather behind the Veil of Ignorance in Rawls's Original Position. Habermas's people have interests, feelings and relationships. These things matter in discourse to determine justice in a particular situation; the views of daughters and mothers, of sons and fathers, need to be taken into account. The ideal speech situation, Habermas teaches, is implied as the goal of these normal people's discourse, not something that is imposed from outside. His stress on communicative action excludes from the start an artificial individualism; his actors are people-in-relationship; and his understanding of community is far more than a device for securing individual ends: it is an essential component of what it is to be human. Unlike the communitarians, Habermas does not treat traditions with something approaching reverence, which makes him more acceptable to those who see all the

---

[23] J. Habermas, *Communication and the Evolution of Society*. Boston: Beacon Press, 1979, p. 205, cited in William C. Placher, *Unapologetic Theology: A Christian Voice in a Pluralistic Conversation*. Louisville: Westminster/John Knox, 1989, p. 80.

major traditions as irretrievably patriarchal. His belief that there is a need for radical social transformation is also congenial to feminists, even if they sometimes might wish to differ from the kinds of transformation that Habermas would espouse, or from some of the emphases in his critique of modernity. His stress that we face particular other people in specific situations and that the just way of responding and acting cannot always be determined in advance by reference to a comprehensive set of principles tunes in with some prominent feminist ideas.

And yet, despite all this, feminist theorists detect major flaws in Habermas's account of justice which make it too narrow and too thin. Even those who are most sympathetic to Habermas's scheme believe it needs substantial enrichment and broadening if it is to be serviceable, acceptable and effective. Some feminists suspect that ultimately Habermas's theory does little more than 'reflect the prejudices of a contemporary adult white male Central European of bourgeois education'.[24] Habermas, of course, claims that his discourse ethics reflects *our* deepest intuitions and expectations; but the feminists raise the question who 'our' refers to: are women included, or is it in fact based upon male insights and experiences exclusively? Does Habermas also merit Susan Moller Okin's charge that, despite the fact that this is concealed more than it was in the past, 'major contemporary Anglo-Saxon theories of justice are to a great extent about men with wives at home'?[25]

Such suspicions are encouraged by the eagerness with which Habermas enlists Kohlberg on his side. As Carol Gilligan, who had been one of Kohlberg's assistants, points out in her classic book, *In a Different Voice: Psychological Theory and Women's Development*, Kohlberg and Piaget before him devoted almost all their attention to the moral development of boys. Gilligan argues that in Piaget's 1932 account of the development of moral judgement in the child, girls are an aside and it is assumed that 'the child' is male, but in Kohlberg's research 'females simply do not exist'. Kohlberg's six stages in the development of moral

---

[24] J. Habermas, 'Moral und Sittlichkeit: Hegels Kantkritik in Lichte der Diskersethic', *Merkar*, 39:12 (Dec. 1985), 1042, cited in Outhwaite, *Habermas*, p. 55.
[25] Okin, *Justice, Gender and the Family*, p. 110.

judgement from childhood to maturity are based upon his study over a time span of over twenty years of eighty-four boys. Kohlberg claims universality for his stages, but the groups not included in his sample appear rarely to reach the higher levels of moral development.

Prominent among those who appear to be deficient in moral development when measured by Kohlberg's scale are women, whose judgements seem to exemplify the third stage of his six-stage sequence. At this stage morality is conceived in interpersonal terms and goodness is equated with helping and pleasing others. This conception of goodness is considered . . . to be functional in the lives of mature women insofar as their lives take place in the home.[26]

Thus Habermas buys into a body of theory based on research into male subjects, and not unexpectedly reflecting male experience and male assumptions and leading to male conclusions. It is assumed, and believed to have been demonstrated, that women's characteristic virtues and experiences are most effectively deployed in the family and the private sphere; in public, their inadequacy will be made manifest. Habermas has many good things to say about the divide between the public and the private spheres, about what he calls 'systems' and 'lifeworlds', but Kohlberg traps him into confining women effectively to the lifeworld, to the private and domestic sphere.[27] If women stray into the systems in the public sphere, the inadequacies of their moral development will become obvious; to survive in such arenas (I use the term advisedly) they must adapt to male models of behaviour. Habermas draws a hard and fast boundary between system and lifeworld and develops an interesting theory of the 'colonisation' of lifeworlds by alien systems, resulting in such developments as a 'hollowing out' of the family as outside influences from the systems become more and

---

[26] Carol Gilligan, *In a Different Voice: Psychological Theory and Women's Development.* 2nd ed., Cambridge, Mass.: Harvard University Press, 1993, p. 18.

[27] The distinction between 'lifeworld' and 'system' reminds me of certain formulations of Luther's theory of the 'Two Kingdoms', and it has the same problems. When different norms are operative in different spheres, and there is little clear critical relation between them, all sorts of iniquities can be justified as necessary according to the norms of a particular sphere. This is why Luther on politics sometimes sounds rather like Machiavelli.

more influential, and often destructive, in family life. The
market and the bureaucracy 'colonise' the family and introduce
their own, very different, values.[28] Habermas sees little possibility of any kind of mutual interchange between lifeworld and
systems. And he has been accused of failing to analyse male
dominance in both lifeworld and systems.[29]

The family becomes a lifeworld in which standards of justice
are not applicable; instead, care, affection and sympathy, altruism and generosity find their proper place in the family. When
justice considerations invade or colonise, the effect is corrosive of
these other virtues. Nor is the family commonly seen as a sphere
of justice, where relationships should be just, and where suc-
ceeding generations learn what justice is and why it is important.
Habermas seems little interested in the possibility that there may
be substantive injustices woven into the fabric of the modern
family and, by him almost as much as by Rawls, the need for a
pedagogy of justice and a discipline of justice in the family and
elsewhere is overlooked.[30] Susan Moller Okin is surely right in
suggesting that just families are necessary if they are to socialise
and prepare children to be citizens in a just society, and that an
adequate account of justice cannot be achieved without a
thorough critique of the public/domestic divide.[31]

How, then, should we respond to the gap that is generally
believed to exist between a universalising justice which finds its
domain only in large-scale structures and is impersonal, impartial and general in all its operations and an ethic of care,
altruism and generosity which seems to find its natural home in
the family and in face-to-face relations and is frequently
considered inapplicable in the public realm? The problem
becomes particularly acute when we discover that there are
certain important kinds of care, generosity and mercy which

---

[28] Outhwaite, *Habermas*, p. 9.

[29] On this see especially Nancy Fraser, 'What's Critical about Critical Theory? The
Case of Habermas and Gender' in Seyla Benhabib and Drucilla Cornell (eds.),
Feminism as Critique: Essays on the Politics of Gender in Late Capitalist Societies. Cambridge:
Polity, 1987, pp. 31–56.

[30] This is strange for one who is indebted to Piaget and Kohlberg for accounts of moral
development. But for them it is clearly implied that after a certain stage the family
actually inhibits moral development.

[31] Okin, *Justice, Gender and the Family*, pp. 19, 25ff., 111.

are more appropriately delivered impersonally by large-scale organisations; strangers have needs, some of which can only be properly met if they are allowed to remain strangers.

The feminists have, I think, demonstrated that the separation of justice and care has encouraged the impoverishment and rigidifying of the idea of justice, and has allowed deep injustices to be perpetuated in small-scale structures because these are believed to be outwith the domain of justice and to live by a different, and probably higher, morality of care and love. Susan Okin believes that a thoroughgoing espousal of a Rawlsian approach would ensure that 'one is not forced to choose between an ethic of justice and an ethic of sympathy or care, nor between an ethic that emphasises universality and one that takes account of difference'.[32] And Carol Gilligan concludes:

[T]hrough the tension between the universality of rights and the particularity of responsibility, between the abstract concept of justice as fairness and the more contextual understanding of care in relationships, these ethics keep one another alive and inform each other at crucial points. In this sense, the concept of morality sustains a dialectical tension between justice and care, aspiring always toward the ideal of a world more caring and more just . . . [33]

Here we are dealing in theological terms with the relation of love and justice, a theme to which I shall return in Part IV of this book. Meanwhile we are indebted to the feminists for a timely reminder that, despite the difficulties, justice and care belong together. A justice without care is hard and impersonal, and a care without justice is sentimental and sometimes becomes the kindness that kills.[34]

HABERMASIAN JUSTICE AND PUBLIC POLICY

Habermas and the other critical theorists consistently declare that their thinking is rooted in practice and seeks practical

---

[32] Okin, 'Reason and Feeling in Thinking about Justice', 238.

[33] Gilligan, 'Do the Social Sciences have an Adequate Theory of Moral Development?', p. 47.

[34] See Lawrence A. Blum, 'Gilligan and Kohlberg: Implications for Moral Theory', *Ethics*, 98 (April 1988), 427–91; Benhabib, *Situating the Self*, esp. pp. 180–9; Okin, *Justice, Gender and the Family*, pp. 170–86.

outcomes. Their critique of modern social institutions and processes is directed towards human emancipation, and they believe that theory and practice may not be separated. With Rawls and Hayek it was not hard to see the kind of policies their theories support and to recognise that their discourse was substantially intended to guide or warn those responsible for the making and implementation of policy. With Habermas and his allies it is not altogether clear what they have to say to policy-makers, and whether they can pass beyond diagnosis to prescription, or indeed whom they are addressing. Marx and the orthodox Marxists believed: that thought flowed out of, and back to, transformative action; that significant change could only come through revolution; that the proletariat was the agent of universal emancipation; and that their critiques and theories were intended to be weapons in the struggle.

Habermas and the other critical theorists have constantly reaffirmed the unity of theory and practice, but their theorising has become increasingly remote from any identifiable field of practice. They talk a great deal about relevance and the need for radical change, and the necessity to be concrete in addressing specific issues, but in reality they seem unable to carry through their own programme. 'They present a revolutionary theory in an age which, on their account, is non-revolutionary'.[35] They seem to assume that no one is listening to them, except perhaps other intellectuals and theorists. Adorno, in melancholy mood, even saw his thought as addressed to the future, not to today; it consisted of messages in 'bottles thrown into the sea' for future readers whose identity and whose role must of necessity be unknown![36] And this vagueness about both the audience and the function of their thought leads them in a rather non-Marxist and universalising direction: they are addressing humankind and expecting little specific practical response. They fall 'back on a concept of critique which they, themselves, in other contexts, rejected: an

---

[35] D. Held, *Introduction to Critical Theory*. Berkeley: University of California Press, 1980, p. 399.
[36] Cited in Stephen T. Leonard, *Critical Theory in Political Practice*. Princeton: Princeton University Press, 1990, p. 44.

ahistorical essence becomes the criterion for the evaluation of the present'.[37]

Alternatively, they seek some group that might be the replacement of the proletariat as the agent of social transformation. Thus Habermas has devoted considerable attention to what he calls 'new social movements', but so far without identifying the new revolutionary class or group that is necessary if his theory is to be effectively channelled into action. As a consequence, critical theory has been able to make remarkably few linkages with actual movements for social change, despite the fact that it affirms that its truth or validity is to be assessed not only in abstract terms but in application and practice.

Critical theory, then, does not ally itself to a class, or party, or group which it sees as the agent of emancipation and its most appropriate partner in practical discourse. Despite its Marxist roots, it was consistently antagonistic to the communist dictatorships of Eastern Europe, and it has not been embraced by European social democrats as the kind of theoretical underpinning that they need for their policies. As a result it has become rather introspective and academic in the negative sense of that term, dangerously insulated from the mutual interrogation of theory and practice that it explicitly requires, neither tailored to illumine specific practices, nor open to the possibility of testing in practice. David Schlosberg's comment is apt: 'For a social theory supposedly defined by its practical intent, critical theory has made remarkably few connections to political practice.'[38]

While acknowledging that critical theory is seldom seen as a resource by those who make policy for states and large-scale institutions and is not focused on the kind of policy issues that are at the centre of attention in theories of justice such as those of Rawls and Hayek, however, there are policy-makers and implementers of policy, particularly at the intermediate and grassroots levels, who turn to Habermas for guidance and illumination. Stephen Leonard sees Dependency Theory, Paulo Freire's Pedagogy of the Oppressed, liberation theology and

[37] Held, *Introduction to Critical Theory*, p. 371.
[38] Schlosberg, 'Communicative Action', p. 291.

feminist theory as exemplary instances of putting a Habermasian understanding of justice into practice.[39] Indeed he argues
that such practice can purify and enrich theory: 'the more
questionable features of the "critical theory" of Marx, the
Frankfurt School, Habermas and Foucault, must be abandoned
in favour of the kind of "critical theory in practice"' which one
finds in these movements.[40]

John Forester, in a series of writings, has explored with others
the practical outworking of critical theory in various spheres of
public life, particularly planning. He is concerned with 'planning for people in a precariously democratic but strongly
capitalistic society [in which] the structure of the economy
organises autonomy and independence for some people, powerlessness and dependency for others'.[41] In such a context,
planners are concerned not just for technical issues but for
'decent outcomes', for social welfare and social justice. Their
task is not to apply or enforce from above, as it were, a theory
or a policy, or even a substantial set of principles of justice such
as those provided by Rawls or Hayek. It is necessary, he says, to
remember that 'planners work on problems, with people'.[42]

Habermas's procedural account of justice encourages the
planner to enter into discourse with those who will be affected
by the plans and the decisions. Forester accordingly advocates a
thoroughly participative, democratic way of planning, in which
planners in fact encourage democratic politics at the grass-roots
and see themselves as the servants of people rather than the
agents of a bureaucracy where decisions are handed down from
above after perhaps perfunctory and formal consultation, or no
consultation at all. '[T]he day-to-day work of planning is
fundamentally communicative',[43] Forester argues, and the
planner must learn 'the practical and critical work of listening'[44] and of taking people seriously – in other words, the

---

[39] See Leonard, *Critical Theory*.　　　[40] *Ibid.*, p. xxiii.
[41] John Forester, *Planning in the Face of Power*. Berkeley: University of California Press,
1989, p. 3. See also John Forester, *Critical Theory, Public Policy and Planning Practice:
Toward a Critical Pragmatism*. Albany: State University of New York Press, 1993; and
John Forester (ed.), *Critical Theory and Public Life*. Cambridge, Mass.: MIT, 1985.
[42] Forester, *Planning in the Face of Power*, p. 4.　　　[43] *Ibid.*, p. 11.
[44] *Ibid.*, p. 6.

planner must be aware of the constraints which make truthful communication difficult and must strive to approximate to something like the ideal speech situation.

Planners who not only hear words but also listen to people carefully and critically are more likely, in dialogue with the people to whom they are attentive, to develop understandings of what justice means in a particular context. In dialogue and in listening, relationship and community are built up and we discover together what justice means in a particular situation:

Developing the ability to listen critically is a political necessity. Listening well is a skilled performance. It is political action, not simply a matter of a friendly smile and good intentions. Without real listening, not simply hearing, we cannot have a shared, critical and evolving political life together. In listening we may still better understand, explain, and cut through the pervasive "can't", the subtle ideological distortions we so often face, including, of course, our own misunderstandings of who we are and may yet be. Listening well, we can act to nurture dialogue and criticism, to make genuine presence possible, to question and explore all that we may yet do and yet become.[45]

Thus in the practice of planning, Habermas's discourse ethics and his pure procedural account of justice can be shown to 'work', and only so can people be brought together and held together in a just community, because for Habermas the *telos* of speech and interaction is reaching understanding rather than asserting control.

David Schlosberg applies communicative action to other types of social process and social institution. Conflict resolution programmes in San Francisco are directed towards a just outcome from conflict situations through what is called 'active listening', aimed at deeper understanding: 'As one participant put it, "The panel makes sure each disputant understands what the other is saying. Once there's mutual understanding, the first hints of conciliation usually begin to emerge." '[46] The success rate is remarkably high: 'For the two programmes examined . . . in San Francisco and Santa Cruz, once people agree to

[45] *Ibid.*, p. 118.
[46] Schlosberg, 'Communicative Action in Practice', 300.

participate disputes are conciliated in a mutually agreeable manner in over 95 per cent of the cases.'[47]

Thus the procedures of justice that Habermas proposes can provide a model for actual ways of achieving just outcomes from conflict situations. Schlosberg's other case, of non-violent action in social agitation, suggests that these methods may be appropriate in wider circles than in face-to-face relationships. Leonard's examples see the approach of communicative action for justice as effective in broad social movements, mainly of critique and protest. Many of the same principles could apply to legislation, policy-making, administration and the judiciary at the level of the state. Is it too much to suggest that in democratic politics political parties should listen attentively to what their opponents are saying, and that administration should be a participative affair? At this point Habermas and the principle of subsidiarity in Roman Catholic social teaching point in the same direction. But just as the act of communication has implicit in it the *telos* of consensus and community, so Habermas's account of justice holds up the utopian hope of a broad community in which people attend to one another's feelings and listen to what they are saying and what they are afraid to say. Justice is what holds people freely together in community; lurking in Habermas's account of the procedures of justice is the hope of a reconciled community in which relationships are just and loving.

THE POST-MODERNIST CHALLENGE

The post-modernists, particularly as represented by Jean-François Lyotard, are deeply suspicious of the Habermas project, as of any feminist approach that is seeking a universal norm of justice. Habermas and his like, they suggest, for all their talk of an emancipatory interest, are committed to the realisation of a consensus which in actuality cannot but be coercive. Lyotard suggests that the reality is that one person or group imposes the account of justice that suits them on others

[47] *Ibid.*, 301.

'terroristically' (to borrow the characteristic term that Lyotard uses to shock people into awareness); coercion is of the essence of any universalising project.

'Consensus', Lyotard writes, 'has become an outmoded and suspect value. But justice as a value is neither outmoded nor suspect. We must thus arrive at an idea and practice of justice that is not linked to that of consensus.'[48] For Lyotard the search for agreement is inherently coercive and therefore unjust; justice, in contrast, is allowing everyone to do their own thing free from pressure to conform to others' views and expectations; he 'objects to anything being required if there is to be justice . . . The just outcome, for him, is always a kind of accident.'[49] Negatively, the post-modernists claim to have demystified all previous accounts of justice by revealing the power-play that goes on below the surface, so that what has been labelled 'just' has frequently, if not always, been a way of dignifying and legitimating processes which oppress, exclude or discipline people. The wolf of injustice has been decked out as the lamb of justice.[50]

There is a valid and important insight here, reflecting views presented earlier by Reinhold Niebuhr and others who showed how easily and subtly justice degenerates into injustice, and how powerful groups assert the right to define what justice is and use notions of justice to disguise their own oppressions. But there is also a problem, which is this: if all principles and norms are inescapably oppressive and justice is everyone doing their own thing, we may understand society as a bunch of little temporary groups engaged in a variety of activities in a situation of great freedom, but we have no means of generating the kind of norms of justice which are necessary for policy-makers in the larger community. Nor are we capable of deciding that the freely chosen activities of any group, however destructive to themselves or others, are unjust and unaccep-

---

[48] Jean-François Lyotard, *The Post-modern Condition: A Report on Knowledge*. Minneapolis: University of Minnesota Press, 1984, p. 66.

[49] Stanley Raffel, *Habermas, Lyotard and the Concept of Justice*. London: Macmillan, 1992, p. 7.

[50] Stephen K. White, *Political Theory and Postmodernism*. Cambridge: Cambridge University Press, 1991, pp. 115–16.

table; there are no boundaries to the diversity that should be tolerated, nurtured and celebrated. The kind of policy-making with which this book is concerned is rejected as by its very nature oppressive, and justice is no more than a way of celebrating and protecting a diverse pluralism. Only those who seek to discern and apply limits are unjust. Accordingly I see Lyotard as little more than a *reductio ad absurdum* of the stress of Habermas and others on the need for the maximum possible amount of freedom and participation in the search for the principles of justice which should guide the community in the arrangement of its affairs.

HABERMAS AND THEOLOGY

Habermas, more emphatically even than Rawls or Hayek, believes that religion and theology have become redundant in the public realm. Christianity, although in his view as in Hegel's the most 'rational' of the religions, is no longer viable after the fatal wounds inflicted on it in bruising encounters with science and with secular morality. The world religions have left an enduringly relevant deposit of a universalistic morality, but no longer themselves have a raison d'être.[51] Habermas sees their theologies as weak and inadequate for the demands of the modern age.[52] 'Post-metaphysical thought,' he writes, 'does not challenge any specific theological assertions; rather it asserts their meaninglessness. It wants to prove that, in the basic conceptual system in which the Judaeo-Christian tradition is dogmatised (and hence rationalised), theologically meaningful statements cannot be asserted.'[53] Religion cannot any longer provide a basis for ethics because it depends on outdated world-views and patterns of authority, and its utopian content and interest in liberation and reconciliation have been absorbed by

---

[51] Charles Davis, 'Pluralism, Privacy, and the Internal Self' in Browning and Fiorenza, *Habermas*, pp. 2–72 (157).

[52] Rudolph J. Siebert, *From Critical Theory to Communicative Political Theology*. New York: Peter Lang, 1987, p. 87.

[53] J. Habermas, *Philosophical-Political Profiles*. Cambridge, Mass.: MIT, 1983, cited in A. James Reimer (ed.), *The Influence of the Frankfurt School on Contemporary Theology*. Lampeter: Mellen Press, 1992, p. 232.

philosophy. Religion may survive in private, but it deserves no place in public debate because religion is no longer plausible and religious beliefs are subjective and arbitrary, not subject to public review.[54] In short, religion no longer can shape an understanding of justice for the modern age, nor share in the delivery of justice. It is up to an openly criticisable secular rationality to present a viable account of justice and of the way to justice. In doing this it 'cannot incorporate the full meaning of what classical ethical theories once conceived as cosmic justice in terms of salvation. The solidarity on which discourse ethics builds remains within the bounds of earthly justice.'[55] And yet, he can also say: 'Justice is inconceivable without at least an element of reconciliation.'[56]

Habermas's repudiation of religion and theology can best be understood in the light of the earlier, rather tortured but deeply significant, discussions of the issue within the Frankfurt School. In 1937 Walter Benjamin wrote in an article: 'The work of the past is not closed for the historical materialist.' Horkheimer responded rather tartly, recognising a theology lurking just below the surface: 'Past injustice has occurred and is ... Those who were slain in it are truly slain.' And in another place, a few years earlier he wrote:

What happened to those human beings who have perished does not have any part in the future. They will never be called forth to be blessed in eternity. Nature and society have done their work on them, and the idea of the Last Judgement in which the infinite yearning of the oppressed and the dead is taken up once again is only a remnant from primitive thought which denied the negligible role of the human species in natural history and humanised the universe.

And then a note of wistful pathos enters into Horkheimer's text:

All these desires for eternity and above all for the entry of universal justice and goodness are what is common between the materialist

---

[54] Francis Schüssler Fiorenza, 'The Church as a Community of Interpretation' in Browning and Fiorenza, *Habermas*, pp. 66–91 (73).

[55] J. Habermas, 'Justice and Solidarity: On the Discussion Concerning Stage 6' in Thomas E. Wren (ed.), *The Moral Domain: Essays in the Ongoing Discussion between Philosophy and the Social Sciences*. Cambridge, Mass.: MIT, 1990, pp. 224–52 (247).

[56] *Ibid.*, p. 246.

thinker and the religious point of view, as opposed to the indifference of the positivist view. However, while the religious thinker is comforted by the thought that this desire is fulfilled all the same, the materialist is permeated with the feeling of the limitless abandonment of humanity, the single true answer to the hope for the impossible.[57]

But it was the same Horkheimer who had taken umbrage at Benjamin's 'religious' thought, who later said that 'behind every genuine human action stands theology . . . a politics which, even when highly unreflected, does not preserve a theological moment in itself is, no matter how skilful, in the last analysis, mere business.'[58] According to Habermas, Horkheimer's intellectual project was that of 'salvaging the truth in religion', but paradoxically Horkheimer also held that 'one cannot secularise religion without giving it up'. He believed that 'it is in vain to strive for unconditional meaning without God'. Habermas continues:

Once the rationality of the remorse experienced by a religiously tutored conscience is rejected by a secularised world, its place is taken by the moral sentiment of compassion. When Horkheimer expressly defines the good tautologically as the attempt to abolish evil, he has in view a solidarity with the suffering of vulnerable and forsaken creatures provoked by outrage against concrete injustices . . . *solidarity and justice are two sides of the same coin*; hence, the ethics of compassion does not dispute the legitimacy of the morality of justice but merely frees it from the rigidity of the ethics of conscience.[59]

Horkheimer is haunted by the necessity and the possibility of a universal solidarity and compassion which transcend even death itself, and an objective and transcendent foundation for justice. Habermas is far more equable. He sums up his response to Horkheimer's adage that to seek to salvage an unconditional meaning without God is doomed to futility thus:

Philosophy cannot provide a substitute for the consolation whereby religion invests unavoidable suffering and unrecompensed injustice,

---

[57] These citations are taken from H. Peukert, 'The Church as a Community of Interpretation' in Reimer, *Influence of the Frankfurt School*, pp. 233–4.

[58] Cited in Davis, *Theology and Political Society*, p. 18. Cf. pp. 134ff.

[59] Habermas, *Justification and Application*, p. 134. The whole essay 'To Seek to Salvage an Unconditional Meaning Without God is a Futile Undertaking: Reflections on a Remark of Max Horkheimer' is relevant.

the contingencies of need, loneliness, sickness and death, with new significance and teaches us to bear them. But even today philosophy can explicate the moral point of view from which we can judge something impartially as just or unjust; to this extent, communicative reason is by no means equally indifferent to morality and immorality.[60]

THE THEOLOGIANS AND HABERMAS

Even if Habermas believes theology has now become irrelevant, philosophy having, as it were, sucked dry the theological orange and thrown away the pulp, there are theologians who take Habermas very seriously and argue either that there is a theology latent in Habermas's position, or that a sound and relevant public fundamental theology can be constructed on Habermasian foundations. The argument that there is a theology lurking in Habermas's thought starts from Habermas's recognition that 'solidarity and justice are two sides of the same coin', and that many of his axiomatic convictions about the importance of truth and justice, and people and community are in fact derived from a Judaeo-Christian faith which he, and many modern people, no longer share as a faith. He also recognises a 'homesickness in the midst of exile', and a longing for a kind of messianic age which he expresses in the hope of the perfect community of the ideal speech situation.[61]

A group of theologians, mostly students of Johann Baptist Metz, have taken the ideal speech situation and the Habermasian emphasis on solidarity as an opening into discourse that is necessarily theological.[62] Helmut Peukert believes that communicative action is ultimately incoherent unless it operates within a theological horizon. To posit the ideal speech situation, he

---

[60] *Ibid.*, p. 146.
[61] See Siebert, *From Critical Theory*, p. 88.
[62] In addition to Peukert's writings noted below, see Siebert, *From Critical Theory*, and *The Critical Theory of Religion: The Frankfurt School*. Berlin: Mouton, 1985; De la Bat Smit, *The Justice of God and the Formation of Society*; Edmund Arens, 'Towards a Theological Theory of Communicative Action', *Media Development*, 28:4 (1981), 12–16; Davis, *Theology and Political Society*, esp. ch. 4; Browning and Fiorenza, *Habermas*.

argues, implies a universal community of communication: 'in principle, in any communicative act the entire human species is implied as the final horizon of the communication community'.[63] Universal solidarity involving mutual acceptance of partners in communication, and attention to the other, is the only way forward. This principled universal solidarity, according to Peukert and his associates, raises four questions for which theology offers distinctive resources. What of the dead, of the victims of injustice and oppression, of those who in the past have been excluded and forgotten, and on whose past suffering our present flourishing depends? Is there a hope for future generations and for the victims of today who will die without having done more than greet justice and community from afar? Can a hope for justice be sustained when it appears to be denied by experience and empirical evidence at every turn, unless it is based upon a faith which is embodied in an actual community which encompasses past and future generations as well as people of today? And can such solidarity be found except in the church, which is, Peukert believes, at least in principle capable of realising itself as a universal community of emancipation, acceptance, love and justice – a communion, that is, of the sort that discourse ethics requires if it is to be fully coherent?

This discussion has taken us into matters to which I shall return later and deal with more systematically (see Part IV). Meanwhile, it may be noted that just as the feminists who are most sympathetic to the approach of Habermas to the question of justice believe that his substantive conclusions need supplementation and enrichment, so the theologians who are attracted to his position believe that it is not fully coherent unless it is placed within a theological horizon.

---

[63] H. Peukert, 'Fundamental Theology and Communicative Praxis' in Reimer, *Influence of the Frankfurt School*, p. 230. Peukert's major book is *Science, Action and Fundamental Theology: Toward a Theology of Communicative Action*. Cambridge, Mass.: MIT, 1984. See also his 'Universal Solidarity as Goal of Communication', *Media Development*, 28:4 (1981), pp. 10–12.

PART IV

Theological fragments

We have seen in earlier chapters of this book some ways in which contemporary pluralism raises problems for policy-makers and practitioners. It is often experienced not so much as healthy diversity, but as fragmentation of a sort which seems to obscure the necessary guidelines and norms. We found people of integrity and insight complaining about 'moral vacuums', about the problems which arise when nobody knows what justice is, about sudden and inadequately justified reversals of ideology. At the theoretical level we found a diversity of incompatible world-views and theories of justice on offer, and we noted that attempts to base theory and policy on a consensus are fragile because consensus seems today to be rather thin and temporary. But even if we agree that something richer and more robust than a Rawlsian consensus is needed at the heart of things if we are to have a healthy social life, it is difficult to see how the religious beliefs of a minority, however strongly held, can be constructively deployed for the good of society as a whole.

CHAPTER 8

Lively and truthful survivals?

FAITH AND JUSTICE

In a seminal essay, Father John Langan asks what Christian faith may contribute to our understanding of justice. The two answers which are most attractive and simple are both of doubtful usefulness for Christians involved in the practice of working for justice in a modern pluralistic society.

The first of these answers is 'everything': true justice is the justice of God who calls all people to live together in justice and peace. Apart from what God reveals there is no understanding of justice; Christians alone truly know what justice is and what the God of justice demands. This view faces two major difficulties. First, in a pluralistic society a purely theological and Christian view is hardly likely to find general acceptance. Secondly, a theological view of justice is likely to be so general that it requires some kind of ethical or theoretical mediation if it is to bear on the specific issues of justice today. Alternatively, it may make absolute the norms and structures of a past age. Those who believe that the Decalogue or the Sermon on the Mount provide norms for the day-to-day operation of the Chase Manhattan Bank are liable not to be taken seriously; at the end of the day they tend to find themselves marginalised and without influence on the shaping of policy. Nevertheless, faith may help to motivate and support people in their vocations, as they strive to live and work well amid the perplexities of modernity.

The second answer to the question as to the contribution of the Christian faith to our understanding of justice is 'nothing'.

Policy-making and political theory rest on philosophy and the facts of the case; theology has nothing relevant to offer. Moral guidance for the understanding of justice is to be found in the natural law, which is in principle accessible not only to people of faith but also to all rational beings. Some who give this answer believe that Christian faith relates only to questions of individual salvation, while others regard politics as the field for practical reason and human prudence, independent of any distinctively theological insights. Justice understood through reason rather than revelation is a virtue necessary for the achieving of the essentially secular ends of the temporal city. And as this city today is religiously plural, appeals to a specific faith tradition are likely to be divisive and ineffective. Here theology speaks the language of the world as a condition of securing a hearing. But it may also encourage the practice of the virtue of justice.[1]

The first view certainly requires qualification. It would be arrogant for believers to suggest that they know everything about justice. More modestly, they might suggest that they have some insights into the nature and the demands of justice which they have a responsibility to share in the public forum. These insights are not simply plucked out of the tradition or directly revealed; they emerge from the subtle and complex interplay between theology and practice. The second view, in suggesting that theology has nothing to add, is only tenable for those who believe that Christian truth can be translated without remainder into the language of philosophy or 'the language of the world'. It can reinforce a generally accepted and recognised 'common morality'; but in a situation of moral fragmentation its appropriateness is not so obvious.

John Langan also gives an illuminating account of ways in which in the past the theological ideas of Augustine and Ambrose influenced philosophical understandings of justice, in modifying with charity the vindictive character of justice, in the transformation of the circumstances of justice by Christian faith, and in Augustine's redefinition of justice in terms of love. But

[1] John Langan, 'What Jerusalem Says to Athens' in John C. Haughey (ed.), *The Faith that Does Justice*. New York: Paulist, 1977, pp. 152–80 (153–5).

can such fertilisation and dialogue continue today, in the conditions of post-modernity? Not, I think, if Alasdair MacIntyre's account of the modern condition is in any way plausible.

MORAL FRAGMENTATION

MacIntyre has argued that modern moral discourse and practice 'can only be understood as a series of fragmented survivals from an older past', so that many central moral problems are today insoluble with the resources of modernity, since these are simply fragments detached from the original context which gave them meaning and efficacy. MacIntyre suggests that modern deontological ethics is haunted by the ghost of older understandings of divine law and the divine command which have no place in the metaphysics of modernity. Teleological ethics is similarly dependent on metaphysical conceptions which have no home in the modern world. In such a situation coherent moral discourse becomes impossibly difficult, and philosophical resolutions of moral questions are perpetually elusive. What we need, he continues, is the skills that anthropologists use in other cultures, identifying survivals and unintelligibilities which are often not noted as such by those within these cultures. Only so may we understand what is happening in the moral domain, which is today so volatile and lacking in coherence and rationale.

Modern society, for MacIntyre, is morally fragmented since there are no generally accepted criteria for the resolution of moral disputes and conflicts, no moral framework.[2] The moral fragments that survive today were embedded and embodied in various traditions and practices which are, for the most part, dismissed as irrelevant survivals among deviant minorities and are discredited by modernity. We cannot understand moral standards properly, MacIntyre believes, without situating these fragments in the context of the traditions of moral enquiry from which they have come. Only if we take seriously the traditions of moral enquiry may we be able to make progress towards resolv-

[2] Alasdair MacIntyre, *After Virtue*, pp. 104–5.

ing key issues of today. Lesslie Newbigin makes a similar point even more baldly: there is, he suggests, 'no possibility of achieving an agreed definition of justice within the conceptual framework of secular liberalism.'[3] We have seen something of the kind of difficulties MacIntyre and Newbigin highlight in earlier chapters.

Disputes which appear to be irresolvable about justice and goodness represent not only academic difficulties but also major problems for practitioners 'on the ground', as it were. Politics and policy-making then become, in MacIntyre's telling phrase, 'civil war carried on by other means',[4] an arena in which interest groups compete for control, using ideas as weapons rather than constraints and as justifications for volatile policy changes which in fact are little influenced by overarching moral considerations, or the ideological pendulum swings from one extreme to another without the reasons for the change being clear or generally acceptable. A lasting and grounded moral consensus of the sort Rawls's theory of justice requires looks more and more like a will-o'-the-wisp.

Indeed the modern public forum seems inhospitable to serious moral discourse. Questions of the common good, of the nature of community and its goals, of what it means for human beings to flourish together in relationship are rarely entertained. Moral choices are commonly regarded as private matters, and there is a pervasive scepticism about the possibilities of determining ends and norms for a society. Political discourse is relegated to the realm of what Max Weber called 'instrumental rationality' – the means to ends which are either arbitrary choices or imposed from above by the powerful. In such an impoverished public forum it is not surprising that no place at the table is reserved for theology, and that theologians are uncertain how best to contribute.

PUBLIC THEOLOGY

Attempts at the present time to produce some grand theology of justice seem doomed to failure. This is in part because social

---

[3] Lesslie Newbigin, 'Whose Justice?', 310.   [4] MacIntyre, *After Virtue*, p. 236.

theology is in a good deal of methodological disarray at present. The middle axiom approach of J. H. Oldham and William Temple was ecumenically popular in the 1930s and 1940s, but does not seem to 'work' effectively today. It appears to require a higher degree of religiously sympathetic consensus than now exists; it is pervasively elitist and 'top-down'; and the progression from doctrine through ethical principles and middle axioms to application often filters out theological content from the end product. It has also been criticised for relying on a rather old-fashioned understanding of value-free social analysis.[5]

The modern development of 'public theology' in the United States, associated with names such as Max Stackhouse, David Tracy, M. J. and K. R. Himes, Robert Benne and Ronald Thiemann, seems to be modelled on the 'public philosophy' advocated by Walter Lippmann a generation ago, and like it attempts to restore and shape a consensual politics. It is subject to the danger of being public in the sense of (to use a slogan popular in the 1960s) 'letting the world set the agenda', or allowing the specific public addressed to determine the shape of the message. In the case of Lutherans like Robert Benne and Ronald Thiemann, the idea of public theology is somewhat entwined with the doctrine of the two kingdoms, so that there is a danger of a different word, a different theology, being addressed to the temporal realm other than the word that is addressed to the church.[6]

'Public theologians' differ in how far they attempt to restore a consensual politics, attempting to renew a rich and lively understanding of the common good, or alternatively accept or even celebrate modern secular pluralism. Some see their contribution in terms of a repristination of natural law and a

---

[5] I have discussed the middle axiom approach in ch. 2 of my *Beliefs, Values and Policies*.
[6] Max Stackhouse, *Public Theology and Political Economy*. Grand Rapids: Eerdmans, 1987; Robert Benne, *The Ethic of Democratic Capitalism: A Moral Reassessment*. Philadelphia: Fortress, 1981, and *The Paradoxical Vision: A Public Theology for the Twenty-first Century*. Minneapolis: Fortress, 1995; David Tracy, *The Analogical Imagination: Christian Theology and the Culture of Pluralism*. New York: Crossroad, 1981; Ronald Thiemann, *Constructing a Public Theology*; M. J. Himes and Kenneth R. Himes, *Fullness of Faith: The Public Significance of Theology*. New York: Paulist, 1993.

public philosophy which claims to express rational and universal insights rather than the specifics of any religious system;
others regard the task as demonstrating the continuing relevance and truthfulness of Christian symbols and doctrines to
the issues with which people struggle in the public domain. A
leading exemplar of the public, natural law philosophers was
the liberal Roman Catholic John Courtney Murray who saw his
task as the renewal of the public philosophy of the nation,
drawing on the resources of natural law thinking in the catholic
tradition. An outstanding proponent of the second group is
Ronald Thiemann who is intent on offering the distinctive
insights of the Christian tradition as a contribution to public
conversation about the good of society. But probably the
outstanding English-speaking 'public theologian' of this century
was Reinhold Niebuhr, whose countless and deeply influential
theological fragments arose from his constant profound political
and theological engagement.

Liberation theology, despite many premature obituaries, is
very much alive. But it has surely learnt the dangers of tying
theology too closely and unambiguously to one particular form
of ideology, theory or social analysis. It is now beginning to
recognise the need for a variety of dialogue partners in the task
of proclaiming good news to the poor and speaking for the
dumb, and from the beginning it has recognised the central
importance of serious critical theological work in the service of
the poor and of justice.

My own conviction is that all serious theology must be public
theology, and that the most committed and probing theology is
also the most publicly relevant, the most capable of injecting
'theological fragments' into public debate. Karl Barth, I think,
hit the nail on the head in 1932:

I believe that it is expected of the Church and its theology . . . that it
should keep precisely to the rhythm of its own relevant concerns, and
thus consider well what are the real needs of the day by which its own
programme should be directed . . . I believe, in fact that, quite apart
from its ethical applications, a better Church dogmatics might well be
finally a more significant and solid contribution even to such questions
and tasks as that of German liberation than most of the well-meant

stuff which even so many theologians feel in dilettante fashion that they can and should supply in relation to these questions and tasks.[7]

Out of Barth's ponderous work on dogmatics, how many theological fragments were injected into public debate on a whole range of issues! Yet Barth felt that at the time of crisis he had failed. He wrote 'to German theologians in prisoner of war camps' in 1945:

I shall therefore openly confess that, if I did reproach myself for anything when I look back to the years I spent in Germany [1921–35], it is that, out of sheer concentration on my churchly and theological task . . . I failed . . . to give a warning, not just implicitly, but explicitly, not merely privately but also publicly . . . against the tendencies . . . in the Church and the world about me.[8]

Despite this sense of inadequacy, this feeling that he could and should have done more, Barth's theological project as a whole was in a real sense a response to the issues and the crises of the day – as was the theology of Augustine of Hippo, Reinhold Niebuhr and many another.

FRAGMENTATION AS PREDICAMENT AND AS OPPORTUNITY

Whatever one may think of MacIntyre's rather apocalyptic scenario at the level of academic discourse, it corresponds in general terms to the confusing experience of practitioners in many fields today, as we have seen in the chapters on criminal justice and on poverty. Practitioners often feel that they are making do with fragments of moral insight, and fragments which are often in unacknowledged conflict with other fragments. And they frequently recognise that the fragments which are most important for them as insights into reality, as in some sense *true*, are derived from a tradition which was and is nurtured in a community of shared faith to which they may or may not belong, and which is now a minority view in society.

[7] Karl Barth, *Church Dogmatics*, vol. i, *The Doctrine of the Word of God (Prolegomena to Church Dogmatics)*, Part i. Edinburgh: T. & T. Clark, 1975, p. xvi.
[8] Cited in Eberhard Bethge, *Dietrich Bonhoeffer: A Biography*. London: Collins, 1970, p. 92.

A theologian should not, I think, be ashamed of offering in public debate 'fragments' of insight. Systematic, carefully developed theories, after all, can sometimes conceal practices which are inhumane and brutalising; ideologies can serve as the emperor's new clothes, so that the theologian's task, as a little child, is to cry out, 'But the emperor's got no clothes on!'; a fragment of truth reveals that to which most people have allowed themselves to be blinded. Truth telling in a fragmentary way becomes even more important when the scheme to conceal the emperor's nakedness is something that is hurting people and destroying community.

Such a fragmentary theology assumes that in this life we never see save 'in a mirror dimly', and only at the end 'face to face.'[9] This might make us cautious about regarding theology as some grand, coherent theory rather than a series of illuminating fragments which sustain the life of the community of faith which nurtures them, and claim also to be in some sense 'public truth'.

The Danish theologian Kierkegaard was a resolute opponent of the grand theorists and systematisers of his day, of whom Hegel was the chief. 'In relation to their systems,' Kierkegaard wrote, 'most systematisers are like a man who builds an enormous castle and lives in a shack close by; they do not live in their own enormous systematic buildings. But spiritually that is a decisive objection. Spiritually speaking a man's thought must be the building in which he lives – otherwise everything is topsy-turvy.'[10] Kierkegaard's suspicion of systems and grand theories was well grounded. He knew that the castle of theory often serves in its magnificence to conceal what is actually going on, to disguise an often unpalatable reality, and even to legitimate awful practices. He understood thought, and above all thought about God, as something which must be dwelt in, which must relate to experience, and which must expose untruth and injustice wherever they are found. The castle of theory needs to be cut down to size, demystified as it were, so

[9] I Cor. 13.12.
[10] Alexander Dru (ed.), *The Journals of Søren Kierkegaard*. London: Oxford University Press, 1938, p. 583. Cf. p. 582.

that humans can live and flourish there. Accordingly, Kierkegaard saw his role as a theologian as like that of Socrates,
asking questions, exposing falsehood, and, gadfly-like, stinging
people into awareness of the truth. He wrote in parables and
epigrams and meditations which were deliberately unsyste-
matic. He wrote *Philosophical Fragments*, followed by an immense
volume, playfully entitled *Concluding Unscientific Postscript*. And in
communicating so, Kierkegaard perhaps gives us clues as to
effective theological communication in the modern, or post-
modern, age at a time of moral fragmentation.

Kierkegaard was well aware that fragments often fit together,
or are derived from larger systematic wholes. He knew that
theological fragments have their home in a community of
shared faith, the church which, if it is true to its calling, does
not wistfully look back to an unrecoverable past, but looks
forward with expectation to God's future, and meanwhile offers
its fragments as a contribution to the common store and seeks
to embody its insights in its life.

When a fragment is recognised as in some sense true, one
should expect an interest in its provenance, in its embeddedness
in a broader truth. Thus Alasdair MacIntyre's intellectual and
spiritual pilgrimage has led him from despair with modernity,
back to a rediscovery of Augustine and Aquinas, and ultimately
to a revalidation of the moral law. MacIntyre's own position is
now close to his account of Augustine's view:

To direct our love . . . toward that form is something we are only able
to achieve when our love is directed toward a life which perfectly
embodies that form in its actions, the life of Jesus Christ. The
peculiarities of that life alone can evoke from us a response of love
which is both love directed toward that particular person and toward
the form of justice. And Jesus points us toward that immutable form
of justice in God which we first directly apprehended within our own
minds, but toward a clearer apprehension of which we continually
move, as we come to love God more and more, as he is revealed in
Jesus Christ . . . [11]

And MacIntyre goes further, in suggesting that this immersion

---

[11] MacIntyre, *Whose Justice?*, p. 154.

in the love of Jesus and of justice leads to the reaffirmation and fulfilment of morality:

> The self-revelation of God in the events of the scriptural history and the gratuitous grace through which the revelation is appropriated, so that an individual can come to recognise his or her place within that same history, enable such individuals to recognise also that prudence, justice, temperateness and courage are genuine virtues, that the apprehension of the moral law was not illusory, and that the moral life up to this point requires to be corrected in order to be completed but not displaced.[12]

In the three chapters of this section I am concerned with bringing together 'theological fragments' which have been illuminating, instructive or provocative in grappling with policy issues 'on the ground', reflecting on them, and on their embeddedness in the structure of Christian faith, and enquiring whether this gives clues as to a constructive theological contribution in the public realm today.

Are there theological fragments which might be recognised as public truth and serve to give some coherence and integrity to the system, even in 'the desolation of reality that overtakes human beings in a post-religious age that has grown too wise to swallow the shallow illusions of the Enlightenment' (John Gray)? And might these fragments perhaps be the aptest way of confessing the faith, and the greatest support for living in truth, in the public realm today?

---

[12] Alasdair MacIntyre, *Three Rival Versions of Moral Enquiry*. Notre Dame: University of Notre Dame Press, 1990, p. 140. I am grateful for these points to an unpublished paper, 'Theological Reflections on the Philosophy of Alasdair MacIntyre', by Professor David Fergusson (1995).

CHAPTER 9

Love, justice and justification

Christians believe in a God of justice and of love; and more, they teach that God *is* justice as God is love. In our experience of God we encounter both love and justice and learn what they are. Christians therefore claim, however tentatively and provisionally, to know what justice is because God reveals himself as justice and as love. The insights into justice which arise from revelation, in worship and in experience, are often fragmentary and frequently hard to relate to conventional accounts of what it is. But because they believe these insights are true, Christians down the ages have sought to relate them to the accounts of justice which prevail in the public realm and have struggled with questions of how and when justice may be realised.

In this chapter I discuss the question of the relationship between the justice that is known in justification and the justice that should be acknowledged and applied in daily life and in public policy. Can the justice of God that is known and celebrated in Christian worship be confined to some ritual or sacred dimension of life, or is it simply a matter of the relation between God and the individual soul? What is the relation between God's justice and the relative justice which seems to be the best that can be hoped for in a fallen world? What is the relation between justice and love? Is Christian theology capable of suggesting an enrichment and enlargement of the understanding of justice which might make it more serviceable as, in Rawls's terms, 'the first virtue of social institutions, as truth is of systems of thought'?[1]

---

[1] Rawls, *Theory of Justice*, p. 3.

JUSTIFICATION

Theological fragments can emerge as radically new readings of the Bible, or as the rebirth of earlier readings which have been forgotten. These are sometimes capable of exposing the inadequacy of the conventional wisdom of the age, and can lead to a re-ordering of understanding and of practice. And experience of crisis, personal or collective, often stimulates such radical rereadings.

Perhaps the most significant such theological fragment to emerge at the start of modern times in relation to a Christian account of justice was Martin Luther's rereading of the Epistle to the Romans while he was in inner turmoil about his inability to live up to the standard of what he then believed to be God's justice. Luther described the turning-point in this crisis of his life and faith:

I greatly longed to understand Paul's Epistle to the Romans and nothing stood in the way but that one expression, 'the justice of God', because I took it to mean that justice whereby God is just and deals justly in punishing the unjust. My situation was that, although an impeccable monk, I stood before God as a sinner troubled in conscience, and I had no confidence that my merit would assuage him. Therefore I did not love a just and angry God, but rather hated and murmured against him. Yet I clung to the dear Paul and had a great yearning to know what he meant.

Night and day I pondered until I saw the connection between the justice of God and the statement that 'the just shall live by his faith'. Then I grasped that *the justice of God is that righteousness by which through grace and sheer mercy God justifies us through faith.* Thereupon I felt myself to be reborn and to have gone through open doors into paradise. The whole of Scripture took on a new meaning, and whereas before the 'justice of God' had filled me with hate, now it became to me inexpressibly sweet in greater love. This passage of Paul became to me a gate to heaven . . .

If you have a true faith that Christ is your Saviour, then at once you have a gracious God, for faith leads you in and opens up God's heart and will, that you should see pure grace and overflowing love. This it is to behold God in faith that you should look upon his fatherly, friendly heart, in which there is no anger nor ungraciousness. He who sees God as angry does not see him rightly but looks only on a curtain, as if a dark cloud had been drawn across his face.[2]

The just God *is* the loving God, Luther discovered; God's justice cannot be separated from his love. God is not two-faced; even his discipline and his wrath are ultimately expressions of his love. Justice is a manifestation of grace and forgiveness, which is clearly shown in the strange fact that God justifies the ungodly. Justification by faith implies that we cannot claim to have earned God's favour by what we have done, or what we are, or by our piety and devotion. We stand before God putting our trust in God's faithfulness and grace, in the conviction that God cares for us and accepts us just as we are. God's justice is displayed most clearly in God's grace and love, in his acceptance as just of those who are still sinners, still offenders. God's justice is expressed in God's acceptance and care for sinners, for the excluded, the forgotten and the marginalised. Justice is thus integral to the being of the Triune God, bound together in the giving and receiving of love.

Christians believe that we learn what justice truly is from God, and out of our experience of God's dealings with us we discover both what it is and what it demands. In the experience of being justified is revealed the true justice of God, which is justice itself. 'The essential characteristics . . . which distinguish the God of the Jewish and Christian scriptures,' writes Alasdair MacIntyre, ' . . . are that He is just and that he cannot possibly not be'.[3]

Justice is thus a central theme of the biblical witness, which presents a distinctive account of justice as integral to the being of God. Some of these insights have penetrated deeply into western thought and culture, justifying Gustavo Gutierrez's statement that 'justice and right cannot be emptied of the content bestowed on them by the Bible.'[4] This biblical tradition has in the past deeply shaped the western understanding of

[2] Cited in Ronald Bainton, *Here I Stand: A Life of Martin Luther.* New York: Abingdon-Cokesbury Press, 1950, p. 65 (italics mine).
[3] Alasdair MacIntyre, 'Which God Ought We to Obey and Why?', *Faith and Philosophy,* 3:4 (1986), 361.
[4] G. Gutierrez, *Power of the Poor in History*, p. 211.

justice, and vestiges of this are to be found widely, so that one may argue, for example, that Rawls's Difference Principle commends itself because it is historically rooted in the biblical understanding of justice, and Rawls finds it in the overlapping consensus because values and attitudes have down the centuries been deeply influenced by the Judaeo-Christian scriptures.

SOCIAL JUSTICE

In the Judaeo-Christian tradition, justice is understood in relational terms. It is about the proper structure of relationships between God and people, and among human beings. The biblical understanding of justice is thus primarily and pervasively social. Justice is not a virtue or quality which an individual can have in isolation, as it were. It is rather a quality of relationship, it has to do with the links of obligation, responsibility and care that bind people together in society.[5]

God's righteousness is shown particularly in the covenant where he takes the initiative of binding himself to his people in love and grace.[6] The covenant is not a contract in which God's grace is conditional on the goodness or faithfulness of his people, for he is constantly faithful to it. Even God's wrath is understood as an attempt to bring Israel back to loyalty to the covenant, loyalty expressed by both divine and human justice. Thus justice is not in any way to be opposed to grace, mercy and forgiveness. Within the covenant God's people experience his grace and justice as care, discipline and protection.

This concept of covenant has been transposed significantly into the modern public sphere to illumine the proper relation between physician and patient. While there is a necessary element of contract in professional relationships, William May suggests that covenants 'have a gratuitous, growing edge to them', for 'the biblical notion of covenant obliges the more

---

[5] A theologically based concept of 'relational justice' has been developed very interestingly by the Jubilee Centre in Cambridge. See M. Schluter and D. Lee, *The R-Factor*. London: Hodder & Stoughton, 1993, and J. Burnside and Nicola Baker (eds.), *Relational Justice: Repairing the Breach*. Winchester: Waterside Press, 1994.

[6] On this see especially James D. G. Dunn, 'The Justice of God: A Renewed Perspective on Justification by Faith', *Journal of Theological Studies*, 43:1 (1992), 1–22.

powerful to accept some responsibility for the more vulnerable and powerless of the two partners. It does not permit a free rein to self-interest, subject only to the capacity of the weaker partner to protect himself or herself through knowledge, shrewdness and purchasing power.' Furthermore, a decent society founded on covenant principles recognises obligations of care and justice towards those who cannot, for one reason or another, contribute directly to social production and would be declared redundant in a society founded simply on the basis of contract. As May writes:

[T]he Mount Sinai covenant requires the Israelites to accept responsibility for the widow, the orphan, the stranger, and the poor in their midst. Still earlier, the covenant with Noah set forth a responsibility for the nonhuman creation. And Jesus later insisted that God will measure his people by their treatment of the sick, the imprisoned, the hungry, and the thirsty; God joins himself to the needy and makes their cause his own. Contractualism, on the contrary, builds few constraints upon action other than those that prudent self-interest and explicit legislation impose.[7]

God's people are expected to reflect the divine justice in the quality of their dealings with their neighbours. Human justice is response to the divine justice, and modelled upon it. The horizontal and the vertical relationships are interdependent. Justice is, as Luther discovered, a quality of relationships rather than an abstract principle, or a divine edict, against which human actions and human persons are to be measured. And in being justified we are set free to respond to our neighbours and to take them and their needs seriously for their own sake rather than using acts of charity, and all our dealings with our neighbours, as ways of earning our justification and salvation. We are set free to serve.

James Dunn has argued that while justification can bring peace to the individual soul, as Luther and many others have found in their own experience, it is essentially social and is concerned with the breaking down of barriers that keep people apart and hostile to one another and with right and loving

---

[7] See William F. May, *The Physician's Covenant: Images of the Healer in Medical Ethics.* Philadelphia: Westminster Press, 1983, pp. 120, 124.

relations between people. 'Justification by faith', he writes, 'is a banner raised by Paul against any and all such presumption of privileged status before God by virtue of race, culture or nationality, against any and all attempts to preserve such spurious distinctions by practices that exclude and divide.'[8] Justice is thus constitutive of community, and of a very special kind of community in which pride, arrogance, privilege and oppression are minimised, and in which there is a central stress on reconciliation.[9] Within a community justice demands a special concern for the disadvantaged and the marginalised, for the orphan, the stranger, the widow and the poor. A just community must seek strenuously to include them fully within its life.

TWO KINGDOMS

Many Christians, and to a considerable extent Martin Luther himself, have tended to understand justification as an intensely private and individual matter – a new relationship with God which gives the believer peace and enables a reaching out to the neighbour in love and service. Or, alternatively, justification is understood as something confined effectively to the 'spiritual realm', the church, without impinging on secular or temporal activities, where a very different understanding of justice holds sway. Thus there emerges the possibility that the justice of God that we encounter in justification may be radically different from the 'worldly justice' which is operative in the realm of politics and policy-making.

The classical Lutheran account of the two realms suggests that God operates in two different ways in dealing with the powers of this world and with people as citizens in their secular vocations on the one hand, and in proclaiming the gospel through the church on the other. God's 'proper work' is the justification of the sinner and the preaching of the gospel of

[8] James D. G. Dunn, 'Justification/Justice', Unpublished paper, 1988, and 'The Justice of God'.

[9] See Markus Barth, 'Jews and Gentiles: The Social Character of Justification in Paul', *Journal of Ecumenical Studies*, 5 (1968), 241–67.

God's unconditional love. God's 'strange work', or *opus alienum,* is a very different expression of his love through the maintenance of order and the meeting of human needs through the various vocations or callings. As Carl Braaten describes it:

This doctrine of the two kingdoms marks out the identity of the church within the global horizon of the politics of God and the divine governance of this world. This doctrine draws a distinction between the two ways of God's working in the world, two strategies which God uses to deal with the powers of evil and the reality of sin, two approaches to human beings, to mobilise them for active co-operation in two distinctly different types of institutions. One is created as an instrument of governance seeking justice through the administration of law and the preservation of order, and the other is an instrument of the Gospel and its sacraments announcing and mediating an ultimate and everlasting salvation which only Christ can give in an act of unconditional love and personal sacrifice.[10]

These two realms are the spheres of the law and of the gospel, and Lutherans believe that they should not be confused; they have separate and distinct remits and, although they are both areas where God's sovereignty holds sway, God expresses his authority in very different ways in the two realms.

'The confusion of law and gospel', writes Robert Benne, 'is a very serious threat to the Christian mission in the world. If the law is mistaken for the gospel, the gospel loses its character as grace offered freely to all.'[11] Benne then goes on to explore some ways in which the gospel is made law in present times. This, he argues, is responsible for the characteristic 'sentimentalism in mainline Protestantism's public theology', betrayed in a tendency towards pacifism in international relations and an expectation that the state through its welfare activities will express compassion and *agape,* that forgiveness should characterise the criminal justice system, and that people in their secular callings should express altruism rather than self-interest.

The problem with all this [he concludes] is that the 'gospel ethic' is not fit for the challenges of the world. The cross reminds us of that. The world cannot be directly run by gospel love or the Christian

---

[10] Carl E. Braaten, *Principles of Lutheran Theology.* Philadelphia: Fortress, 1983, p. 135, cited in Benne, *Paradoxical Vision,* p. 80.

[11] Benne, *Paradoxical Vision,* p. 93.

virtues that are elicited by it. The world is run under the law, the 'left-hand kingdom of God'. The law must and does account for the fallenness of the world. It demands and coerces. It holds persons responsible. It judges. It aims at the better amid a welter of worsts. Responsible policies are trade-offs between what justice demands and what is possible in an intransigent world; irresponsible policies are often those that are mistakenly shaped by the assumption that love can become a direct principle for public ethics.[12]

There is much good sense in this position. But there are grave problems as well. It has often been interpreted to suggest that the gospel has no word to address to the public sphere, and does not qualify or illumine the sway of the law there. Benne himself quotes a Lutheran jurist as saying that public life 'should remain untouched by the proclamation of the gospel, completely untouched', and a distinguished Lutheran theologian of last century, Christian Luthardt, as saying

The gospel has absolutely nothing to do with outward existence but only with eternal life . . . It is not the vocation of Jesus Christ or of the gospel to change the orders of secular life and establish them anew . . . Christianity wants to change the person's heart, not his external situation.[13]

Under Hitler such an interpretation of the Two-Kingdoms theory was used to justify a church policy of non-interference in the political realm which in fact became collusion with Nazism. Benne and other contemporary Lutherans wish to distance themselves from this kind of danger, which they believe rests on a misunderstanding of Luther's teaching.[14]

But Luther does himself suggest that the principles which should guide actors in the public realm have nothing to do with the gospel, and that theologians in this area should give way to the Aristotle whom Luther labelled, in relation to his influence on theology, 'this damned, conceited rascally heathen'! Reason, prudence and the great thinkers of the past give the necessary guidance in politics, Luther declared:

God made the secular government subject to reason because it is to

[12] *Ibid.*, pp. 95–6.   [13] *Ibid.*, p. 79.
[14] From the radical wing the most interesting reconsideration of the two-kingdoms theory is Ulrich Duchrow, *Two Kingdoms: The Use and Misuse of a Lutheran Theological Concept.* Geneva: Lutheran World Federation, 1977.

have no jurisdiction over the welfare of souls or things of eternal value, but only over bodily and temporal goods, which God places under man's dominion. For this reason, nothing is taught in the Gospel about how it is to be maintained and regulated, except that the Gospel bids people honour it and not oppose it. Therefore the heathen can speak and teach about this very well, as they have done. And, to tell the truth, they are far more skilful in such matters than the Christians . . . Whoever wants to learn and become wise in secular government, let him read the heathen books and writings.[15]

Rulers and policy-makers, following such guidance, nonetheless act as representatives of God, masks for God's strange work of justice in the world. The injunctions of the gospel – say those in the Sermon on the Mount – apply only in the spiritual and personal realm. Thus even when a ruler resorts to violence, he is a 'veil' of God, and in Luther's words, 'The hand that wields this sword and slays with it is then no more man's hand but God's, who hangs, tortures, beheads, slays and fights. All these are His works and His judgements.'[16] Even tyrants, it would seem, are representatives of God, who are as such not to be questioned or brought to account. The public realm is effectively freed from theological scrutiny and does not require enrichment by theological insights, which are not relevant to its distinct task. In Robert Benne's view there is 'a general presumption against direct action' and, although the church can call on the state to be faithful to the law, law is not integral to the gospel, the church not having a privileged insight into the law.[17]

It is not surprising that the Lutheran position that there is no clear relation between the justice we experience in justification and the justice which is applicable in worldly affairs came under strong criticism in the 1930s, particularly from Karl Barth and his associates. The issue was highlighted by the German Church Struggle and the passivity amounting to

[15] Martin Luther in Jaroslav Pelikan and H. T. Lehman (eds.), *American Edition of Martin Luther's Works*. St Louis: Concordia, and Philadelphia: Muhlenberg Press, 1955ff., vol. XIII, p. 198.
[16] Martin Luther, 'Whether Soldiers, too, can be Saved'. *Works of Martin Luther: The Philadelphia Edition*. Philadelphia: Muhlenberg Press, 1931. vol. V, p. 36.
[17] Benne, *Paradoxical Vision*, p. 217.

collusion with, or even enthusiastic support of, Nazism on the part of some prominent Lutheran theologians and church leaders.

In a little book on *Justification and Justice*, Barth posed the question directly:

Is there a connection between the justification of the sinner through faith alone, completed once for all by God through Jesus Christ, and the problem of justice, the problem of human law? Is there an inward and vital connection by means of which in any sense human justice (or law), as well as divine justification, becomes a concern of Christian faith and Christian responsibility, and therefore also a matter which concerns the Christian Church?[18]

Barth answers his own question with a resounding 'Yes!' Thought about human and worldly justice must be vitally connected with the truth of divine justification; gospel and law are not separate spheres, but the gospel is prior to the law, and the law must be read as an expression of the gospel and in the light of the gospel. In face of Hitler it was essential to affirm this; otherwise there was no *theological* ground for questioning and opposing the Nazi parody of justice. But it is not only in such times of crisis that this must be affirmed; only so, Barth believed, may the church affirm the sovereignty of Christ over the whole of life and contribute distinctively to the search for true justice and its embodiment in policy and practice.

LOVE AND JUSTICE

Another important theological dualism which can serve either to clarify the understanding of justice or to obscure the public relevance of Christian notions of justice is that between love and justice. In the Christian tradition love and justice are not regarded as identical, although they are closely related. And much energy has been devoted to exploring the nature of the relationship.

An influential modern account of the relation of love and justice was developed by the American theologian, Reinhold Niebuhr, particularly in his major works, *Moral Man and Immoral*

[18] Karl Barth, *Church and State* [Rechtfertigung und Recht]. London: SCM, 1939, p. 1.

Society (1932), *An Interpretation of Christian Ethics* (1935), and his Edinburgh Gifford Lectures, *The Nature and Destiny of Man* (1941).

Reinhold Niebuhr is of special interest for our present purposes because his thought, more than that of any other theologian in the English-speaking world in the twentieth century, was an acknowledged influence on politicians and policy-makers. His impact went well beyond the bounds of the church, and an influential group of foreign policy-makers and theorists, among whom Professor Hans Morgenthau was probably the best known, were popularly dubbed 'Atheists for Niebuhr'.

Niebuhr developed a formidable reputation for 'discerning the signs of the times' in a continuous stream, sometimes amounting to a flood, of sermons, manifestos, essays, public statements and, above all, magazine and newspaper articles, particularly in his own journal *Christianity and Crisis*. These 'theological fragments' brought a brilliant analytical mind to bear on current events, a mind that was engaged simultaneously in a rigorous on-going dialogue with the Christian tradition and a struggle to discern the deeper significance of what was happening in the world. Niebuhr's 'fragments' alone would have earned him a formidable reputation, but fortunately he was able to lay out in systematic form at least the outlines of the quarry from which his fragments of insight came. *Moral Man and Immoral Society* is both a significant and influential work in political theory and a challenge to theology to take seriously the ambiguities, ironies and limitations of social ethics. In *An Interpretation of Christian Ethics* Niebuhr declares war on what he believes to be the naive idealism of liberal Christianity, which proclaims an absolute ethic in sunny times but at times of crisis capitulates to the spirit of the age, and on the cynicism about earthly possibilities which he identifies with conservative 'orthodoxy'. His Christian ethics, he believes, steers a middle course, walking boldly and wisely among the tragedies, ironies and relativities of political and economic life. His Gifford Lectures, *The Nature and Destiny of Man*, delivered in 1939 as the Second World War began, represented a sustained systematic theological statement which showed, in the words of his friend John C. Bennett, 'that Reinhold Niebuhr is not merely a brilliant diagnostician but that he is also a great constructive theologian'.[19]

Niebuhr believed that his discernment of what was happening and its significance was rooted in the kind of theology and theological ethics that he outlined in his major books. Because he believed that this theology was in a real sense *true*, it provided a privileged access to insight into other aspects of reality. Christianity, he taught, provided a far more satisfactory account of the human condition, its limits and its possibilities, than any of the alternative views on offer. Its rivals, like the forms of theology he rejected, always tipped over either into cynicism and hopelessness, so that politics resolved itself into nothing more than the attempt to circumscribe sinfulness and evil as narrowly as possible, or into a frothy and ungrounded optimism which believed that absolute ideals could be realised in a fallen, broken world, and at the end of the day actually caused damage and suffering and led to disillusion and despair. Christianity, correctly understood, provides the best insights into reality, the surest basis for 'discerning the signs of the times', and the most effective guidance for prudent and responsible action in the public realm.

Niebuhr's robust Christian realism, he believed, gave a better insight into the heights and depths of human nature than any of its rivals. 'All the known facts of history', he declared with characteristic sweeping boldness, 'verify the interpretation of human destiny implied in New Testament eschatology'.[20] The truthfulness of the gospel is confirmed by the events of history; and the same gospel provides the most effective lens for understanding and interpreting what is happening in our day. Niebuhr dug deep into the tradition of Christian theology and found there, alongside a deep conviction about the fallenness of the human condition, a realistic appraisal of the possibilities and limits of the political realm.

Central to Niebuhr's theological and ethical concern was the

---

[19] Cited from Bennett's review in Ronald H. Stone, *Professor Reinhold Niebuhr: A Mentor to the Twentieth Century*. Louisville: Westminster/John Knox, 1992, p. 153.
[20] Reinhold Niebuhr, *The Nature and Destiny of Man*. 1 vol., London: Nisbet, 194-3, vol. II, p. 330.

relation between love and justice. This was for him a continuing and pervasive issue, and as John Bennett said, 'There is no more fruitful analysis in all his ethical writings than his discussion of this problem.'[21] Niebuhr drew a sharp and important distinction between love and justice, but he believed that they were necessary complements to one another.

Love he understood in terms of *agape*, altruistic, self-sacrificial concern for the other, subordinating one's own interests to those of others. This kind of love was supremely exemplified in Jesus' life and teaching, culminating in the cross. It can operate as a relevant possibility in face-to-face relations, in family life and in small groups and, to some extent, within the church. Yet his own brother, Richard, suggested that his early distinction between 'immoral society' and 'moral man', who was in personal relations capable of altruistic love, was too simple. Reinhold, he argued, was 'still too romantic about human nature in the individual':

I am convinced that there is quite as much hypocrisy in this idealisation of our personal relationships as there is in our collective behaviour. Take such a thing as brotherly love. I hate to look at my brotherly love for you to see how it is compounded with personal pride . . . and with selfish ambition . . . Therefore I must dissent from the whole argument that 'individuals (as individuals) have a moral code . . . which makes the actions of collective man an outrage to their own conscience'. They have a code which makes their own actions an outrage to their own conscience.[22]

But, while affirming that *agape* was a relevant ideal in face-to-face relationships, Reinhold Niebuhr understood it in the light of the cross and was increasingly willing to concede that the human predicament involved the difficulty even in intimate relationships of expressing altruistic love.

In politics love remains as the 'impossible possibility'; attempts to operate altruistically and lovingly in fact lead to harmful results in collectivities and in politics. Here justice, 'the approximation of brotherhood under the conditions of sin',

[21] Cited in D. B. Robertson (ed.), *Love and Justice: Selections from the Shorter Writings of Reinhold Niebuhr*. Philadelphia: Westminster, 1957, p. 11.
[22] Letter cited in R. W. Fox, *Reinhold Niebuhr*. New York: Pantheon, 1985, pp. 144–5.

must be the guide. 'The struggle for justice,' Niebuhr wrote, 'is as profound a revelation of the possibilities and limits of historical existence as the quest for truth. In some respects it is even more revealing, because it engages all human vitalities and powers more obviously than the intellectual quest.'[23]

Notice that Niebuhr spoke of the 'struggle' for justice; he was in no doubt that relative justice is the fruit of temporary settlements of competing claims. Justice is the adjustment and balancing of rights and interests; it is essentially a compromise. And while justice is not unrelated to love, Niebuhr made a sharp distinction between absolute justice, which human beings find impossible to achieve, and the relative and temporary approximations to justice which result from the effective balancing of conflicting interests and give for a time an acceptable degree of justice in the social and economic orders. Policy can never hope to achieve more than such relative justice; the direct pursuit of absolute justice, like the pursuit of love, leads to tyranny and disaster.

Nonetheless, justice 'cannot exist without love and remain justice. For without the "grace" of love justice always degenerates into something less than justice.'[24] Love, as it were, gives the clue to the inner nature of justice; and justice without love becomes distorted into something diabolic and tyrannical. 'Love,' Niebuhr wrote, 'is both the fulfilment and the negation of all achievements of justice in history'.[25] No system of justice is so perfect that it can dispense with 'the refinements which voluntary and uncoerced human kindness and tenderness between individuals add to it.'[26] The task of the policy-maker is thus to seek always better approximations to justice by adjustments to group interests, but without attempting to eliminate these interests or replace them with some ideal of pure altruism. Thus the search for justice involves 'tragic choices'; it is an

---

[23] Niebuhr, *Nature and Destiny of Man*, vol. II, p. 244.
[24] D. B. Robertson, *Love and Justice*, p. 28.
[25] Niebuhr, *Nature and Destiny*, vol. II, p. 246.
[26] Reinhold Niebuhr, *An Interpretation of Christian Ethics*. New York: Meridien, 1951, p. 181.

arena of on-going struggle and conflict in which no final resolution is possible in a sinful world.

Niebuhr's 'Christian realism' is also important for his sensitive awareness of the manifold ways in which ideas of justice are used to conceal interests, or are distorted into being covers for collective selfishness, imparting to it a savour of morality and idealism, or become in fact no more than weapons in social conflict.

Niebuhr's thought had considerable influence on several generations of politicians and political theorists. His theological fragments became recognised counters in secular discourse on politics and international relations. The story that Roosevelt would ring him from the White House and ask 'What's the word of God for today, Reinie?' is certainly untrue, but it points to the fact that he had a massive intellectual impact on active politicians and other practitioners. Alan Paton spoke for many when he wrote of Reinhold Niebuhr, 'I think him to be the wisest man I ever knew, with an understanding of human nature and of human society that no one has equalled in our century.'[27]

And yet, Niebuhr's realism, especially in the hands of theologically unsympathetic devotees, could easily deteriorate into an accommodation with the status quo and a cynical assumption that politics was simply the struggle between self-interested groups and justice no more than temporary and fragile equilibrium between conflicting interests. It proved easy for this understanding of justice to free itself from any kind of theological control, so that love as the impossible but relevant ideal disappeared over the horizon and justice became, as Thrasymachus had argued in Plato's *Republic*, the interest of the stronger.

JUSTICE AND CHARITY

There are those who would hold justice and love more closely and unambiguously together than Reinhold Niebuhr found he

---

[27] Cited in Stone, *Professor Niebuhr*, p. 133.

could. Paul Tillich, for example, held that the truest form of justice was dynamic 'transforming or creative justice'.[28] Tillich is emphatic in declaring that 'justice is just because of the love which is implicit in it'.[29] It is impossible to evacuate the love from justice without transforming it into injustice. Justice is a form of love. There is here, as Niebuhr well knew, a problem. It really is not possible to conceive of a polity run on the principles of love alone. In collectivities larger than the family – and even there, much of the time – we have to deal with justice as a form of love. But a society or a polity in which the understanding of justice has been narrowed, in which justice is not in some obvious sense an expression of love, is impoverished and easily becomes inhumane.

The twentieth-century mystic, Simone Weil, argued that justice and love, understood as charity, are identical. In the parable of the sheep and the goats Jesus declares those who give aid to the needy to be just.

The Gospel [Weil suggested] makes no distinction between the love of neighbour and justice . . . We have invented the distinction between justice and charity. It is easy to understand why. Our notion of justice dispenses him who possesses from the obligation of giving. If he gives all the same, he thinks he has a right to be pleased with himself. He thinks he has done a good work. As for him who receives, it depends on the way he interprets the notion whether he is exempted from all gratitude or whether it obliges him to offer servile thanks.[30]

Weil was aware of the problems that arise from the inequality of giver and receiver. Those who give must respect as equals those who receive and affirm their equal worth; in a sense the transfer is merely restoring or moving towards the proper situation of equality. She wrote:

The supernatural virtue of justice consists of behaving exactly as though there were equality when one is the stronger in an unequal relationship. Exactly, in every respect, including the slightest details, of accent and attitude, for a detail may be enough to place the weaker

---

[28] P. Tillich, *Love, Power and Justice*. New York: Oxford University Press, 1960, p. 64.

[29] *Ibid.*, p. 15. Cf. pp. 57, 71.

[30] Simone Weil, *Waiting on God*. London: Collins, 1959, p. 96, cited in Diogenes Allen and Eric O. Springsted (eds.), *Spirit, Nature and Community: Issues in the Thought of Simone Weil*. Albany: State University of New York Press, 1994, p. 114.

party in the condition of matter, which on this occasion naturally belongs to him, just as the slightest shock causes water that has remained liquid below freezing point to solidify.[31]

Both parties acknowledge the claim of justice and affirm the equal worth of one another.

Weil's argument is helpful in responding to the cry for justice, not charity, from the needy of the world. The problem is that the word charity has been devalued and emptied of its meaning as it is used to describe patronising and voluntary handouts from their superfluity on the part of the prosperous. For Weil an understanding of charity as *agape* lies at the heart of the notion of justice, and in an unequal and needy world the demand of justice is to move promptly and decisively towards structures and relationships of justice.

The word 'charity' has been debased in modern usage; its true sense as love/justice needs to be recovered lest our account of charity is inherently patronising and assumes inequality, and our notion of justice becomes narrow and hard: 'Love is not love without a passion for justice', writes Miranda, and 'The love that the Bible knows is love-justice.'[32] Paul Ricoeur is right to say that 'We show little or no understanding of love when we make charity the counterpart and supplement of, or the substitute for, justice; love is co-extensive with justice . . . justice is the efficacious, institutional and social realisation of love.'[33] Miranda is persuasive when he argues that with great frequency terms in the Bible which denote the doing of justice have been mistranslated as almsgiving, and God's demand for justice has been diluted into a request for voluntary and meritorious disbursements from the surplus of the rich which systematically create a false relationship between giver and receiver and do not impinge in any way upon the structures of injustice in society. The issue is not 'charity' (in its modern sense) but rather justice as restitution and restoration of God's

[31] Weil, *Waiting on God*, pp. 100–1, in Allen and Springsted, *Spirit, Nature and Community*, p. 143.

[32] Miranda, *Marx and the Bible*, p. 62.

[33] Cited in J. Miguez Bonino, *Toward a Christian Political Ethics*. London: SCM, 1983, p. 114.

just ordering. Oppression or demeaning of the poor and structural injustice are denials of the covenant relationship with God.

A FEMINIST ACCOUNT OF LOVE AND JUSTICE

Feminist theorists and theologians have in recent times provided an important critical and constructive critique of traditional accounts of love and justice. To select a particularly perceptive example, Linda Woodhead has argued that the male theologians themselves have narrowed and impoverished the understanding of agapeistic love.[34] She suggests that most recent writing by male theologians on love describes it as something like 'self-sacrificing equal regard which is indifferent to the value of its object'. Love is a one-way flow, freely and generously offered to one who merely receives it; as soon as it becomes two-way, a mutual relationship, it loses its agapeistic quality. Christian love has been understood increasingly in terms of 'equal regard' – a universalising term suggesting a cool, rational and detached attitude: no fiery eroticism here! Indeed, as soon as emotional involvement enters, it is suggested that the relationship degenerates into something less than *agape*. 'Yet many women', writes Woodhead, 'want to deny the similarity between agape and regard. They want to define agape as something much warmer, deeply concerned and emotionally attached, a maximal rather than a minimal beneficence.' Accordingly, some women prefer to speak of 'liking' or 'attention' rather than 'regard' as characterising a loving relationship. This is more self-involving for the person doing the liking, and challenges the one liked to be worthy of the liking. The boundaries between the two parties are eroded; their autonomy is threatened. This may be seen as undesirable by proponents of the (male) account of *agape* as equal regard; but 'it seems more like a promise to many women. They believe that their humanity is enriched rather than diminished by contact with others at a profound level.' Women, Linda Wood-

---

[34] Linda Woodhead, 'Love and Justice', *Studies in Christian Ethics*, 5:1 (1992), 44–61.

head suggests, are more likely than men to see human beings as social beings, whose identity is to be understood in terms of relationship. She quotes Helen Oppenheimer:

Maybe the time has come to rehabilitate *liking* as not just respectable but excellent; as a central element in what we ought to mean when we talk about [Christian] love.[35]

The command to love your neighbour is concrete and specific; it cannot be reduced to an equal regard that is universal and impartial. Women, because they have usually been more aware of the ties of family and of neighbour, of specific forms of neighbour-love, have tended to be suspicious of the suggestion that one should love everyone equally, as of the belief that 'regard' is an adequate rendering of love.

Woodhead also questions the common linkage (which we have encountered in the thought of Reinhold Niebuhr) between *agape* and self-sacrifice. 'Self-sacrifice for its own sake,' she writes, 'can make people into monsters rather than angels.' Virginia Woolf's account of 'the angel in the house' is apropos:

If there was a chicken, she took the leg; if there was a draught, she sat in it – in short she was so constituted that she never had a mind or a wish of her own, but preferred to sympathise always with the minds and wishes of others.[36]

Women have increasingly tended to realise the evil and destructive consequences of the demand for self-abnegation and self-sacrificial love, which can erode the self-acceptance which enables authentic love.

Woodhead also challenges the call to be indifferent to the value of the loved one since this denies value to people in their uniqueness. God's love is concrete and specific; God even shows partiality in loving. But, as Helen Oppenheimer writes:

'Partiality' ought not to scare us. It is no more and no less than the acknowledgement of individual mattering, the love that appreciates and minds about particular people for their own sakes . . . What is wrong with 'taking sides' is not the good we do to one side, but the hurt we may do to the other. If we find ourselves neglecting, or spoiling, or abusing, we need to be more even-handed and partiality

[35] Helen Oppenheimer, *The Hope of Happiness*. London: SCM, 1983, p. 94.
[36] Cited from Ann Loades, *Searching for Lost Coins*. London: SPCK, 1987, p. 24.

becomes a vice; but the august partiality of God is taking hold of the special character of each creature as uniquely significant.[37]

Neighbour-love, Woodhead suggests, would better be thought of as 'an active desire for the well-being of the neighbour, and for communion with him or her, based on a recognition of the neighbour's unique worth'.[38] Such love is affective, it involves affection and liking, strives for the good of the neighbour, and hopes that loving will be mutual.

At the conclusion of her important and constructive reconsideration of the Christian concept of love, Linda Woodhead turns to consider justice. Unfortunately she does not ask how her account of love might shape the understanding of justice and influence just policy-making, on Tillich's assumption that 'justice is just because of the love which is implicit in it'.[39] Rather she operates with a Niebuhrian understanding of justice as the balancing of competing interests and rights, backed up by coercion, and suggests, quite correctly, that this may have little to do with love. Christians, she says,

should not be concerned with another person's rights, but with their well-being. They should not be concerned with what is fair, only what the situation demands. Did the man who fell among thieves have a right to be helped? Is it fair to give the same wages to men who have worked all day and those who have worked one hour? These considerations are alien to Christian love.[40]

Justice can restrain sin and improve the lot of categories of people, she suggests. It should not be despised. But '[i]t is love and not justice which is the banner under which both Christians and feminists should serve'.[41]

But this is a counsel of despair. It removes love from the impersonal public realm, failing to recognise that there are ways of loving one's neighbour which require that the neighbour remains a stranger if the neighbour's dignity is to be affirmed. Decent welfare provision, for example, is inconceivable with an account of justice which is simply the balancing of conflicting claims and rights, rather than an expression of a

---

[37] Oppenheimer, *Hope of Happiness, p. 120.*   [38] Woodhead, 'Love and Justice', 56.
[39] Tillich, *Love, Power and Justice,* p. 15.   [40] Woodhead, 'Love and Justice', 60–1.
[41] *Ibid.,* 61.

justice which is shaped by love.[42] It is not enough to say that love cannot be commanded or institutionalised, for we are in fact commanded to love our neighbours and our enemies, and this command seems to be addressed to nations and collectivities as well as individuals. After all, in the story of the sheep and goats, it is the nations, not individuals, which are called to account for whether they have responded justly and lovingly to the needs of their neighbours.[43] Feminists' accounts of love such as the one I have discussed can prove important resources for the refreshment and enrichment of contemporary understandings of justice and should not be confined to face-to-face relations and domestic life.

JESUS THE JUST ONE

'What does the Lord require of you?' enquires the prophet Micah, and replies famously that the demand of the Lord is that we do justice, and love kindness, and walk humbly with our God.[44] Here we have a fitting reminder that in the foundational documents of Judaeo-Christian faith the call for justice has a central place, and justice is understood in a broad and remarkably specific way. Justice is given its distinctive content in this passage by being linked with *ḥesed*, steadfast love or loving kindness, and with humble walking with the God of justice and of love. Justice here is something to be *done*, not simply or primarily a matter for reflection. In the Beatitudes in their Matthean version, the frail little band of disciples hear that those who hunger and thirst after justice (*dikaiosunē*) are blessed, and will be satisfied.[45] Justice here is something about which we should be passionate, something for which we should hunger and thirst. And those people who are passionate about justice are seldom those who live in 'the culture of contentment', but rather the victims, the oppressed, the forgotten and the excluded – the poor and the poor in spirit as well, those who are persecuted for justice's sake, and those who take their stand alongside those who suffer from injustice. Perhaps the theolo-

---

[42] An important exploration of these issues is Michael Ignatieff, *The Needs of Strangers*.
[43] Matt. 25.31–46.   [44] Mic. 6.8 (RSV).   [45] Matt. 5.6.

gian's task here is not so much to take part in elegant academic games, moving conceptual counters on a board, as to articulate the cry of the oppressed, and speak for the dumb.

For the biblical witness emphasises again and again that justice is the vindication of the poor and the oppressed. Here we are not dealing with the blindfold figure of justice with scales in hand, but with a proactive understanding of justice as healing, reconciling, setting things aright. The word translated 'justice' in the servant song from Isaiah 42.1–4 adapted from the Septuagint in Matthew's gospel as an interpretation of the significance of Jesus is not *dikaiosunē* but *krisis*. The Servant of Jahweh comes in judgement, to do justice as the vindication of the weak and the poor, for whom Jesus had a special care:

> Behold, my servant whom I have chosen,
> my beloved with whom my soul is well pleased.
> I will put my Spirit upon him,
> and he shall proclaim justice to the Gentiles.
> He will not wrangle or cry aloud,
> nor will any one hear his voice in the streets;
> he will not break a bruised reed
> or quench a smouldering wick,
> till he brings justice to victory;
> and in his name will the Gentiles hope.[46]

The bruised reed and the smouldering wick will be vindicated and protected. And this justice is for the Gentiles, not just for Israel.

Then note the future tenses: we are dealing here with hope, with a vindication and a restoration which lie in the future. But meanwhile, disciples and others are enjoined to 'seek first the Kingdom of God and his justice [*dikaiosunē*]'.[47] The justice of God is embodied in a system, in the Rule of God, in a structured ordering of things and people and relationships. This Kingdom both is and is not yet; it is for its full coming that we hope. We have reliable clues to its nature and can discern

---

[46] Matt. 12.18–21. Miranda comments on this passage: 'In Christ's works of justice on behalf of the poor and helpless, Matthew sees – as does John – the definitive realisation of Judgement: "till he has led *mishpaṭ* to victory".' *Marx and the Bible*, p. 129.

[47] Matt. 6.33.

earnests of its coming, particularly in the life and death of Jesus, and in our experience of the God of Justice. Here we see the justice of God embodied and expressed in action, in teaching and in suffering.[48] As Lesslie Newbigin suggests, 'At the centre of the Christian understanding of justice there stands the cross, not a symbol but a historic deed in which the justice of God was manifested in his covenant faithfulness right through to the point where the just died for the unjust.'[49] In the Book of Acts Jesus is proclaimed as the Just One.[50] Paul declares that Jesus has become our justice.[51] But here we see through a glass darkly, and only at the end, face to face. The Kingdom and its justice is something that we seek, trusting in the promise that those who seek shall find. And meanwhile, it is in constant tension with our temporal systems, particularly in what they do to the bruised reed and the flickering wick.

Here we have no more than a fragmentary, if distinctive, account of justice which suggests that we should look forward in hope to a just order which will be given in its fullness by God. Although now we can only know it in part, it stands in tension with the injustices of present orders and makes it impossible for us to adopt the kind of realism which gives finality to the present situation and ceases to hope for the justice which will be given by God, and is at present experienced and glimpsed in part. This justice constrains our doing of injustice and vindicates the victims. Faith, to adapt the terminology of the Letter to the Hebrews, gives substance to our hope for justice.

JUSTICE EMBODIED IN POLICY AND PRACTICE

It is not hard to show how Christian notions about justice have interacted historically with other accounts of justice, often challenging, sometimes accommodating, frequently legitimating alternative views of justice. John Langan has shown how Ambrose and Augustine altered the understanding of justice to

---

[48] See John C. Haughey, 'Jesus as the Justice of God' in Haughey, *The Faith that Does Justice*. New York: Paulist Press, 1977, pp. 264–90.
[49] Newbigin, 'Whose Justice?', 310.
[50] Acts 3.14, 7.52.   [51] I Cor. 1.30.

be found in classical political thought, in particular by modifying the retributive and vindictive character of justice by charity or love and by redefining justice in terms of love. For Ambrose, and his disciple Augustine, charity becomes the central dimension of justice; justice is a form, if partial and incomplete, of love. The Church is to be 'the form of justice' both in the way it structures its own life and in the guidance it gives to 'the world'. The promotion of justice is not simply to be seen as a political matter, but also 'as a partial realisation of the fullness of the communion of love given and received in the Kingdom of God'.[52] Christian faith accordingly is directed towards a community of love which goes beyond the relative justice that is possible in the earthly city, striving towards the transcendent justice of the heavenly city. Meanwhile even the best human arrangements are no more than vestiges of the true justice of the City of God.[53]

In similar fashion, Aquinas reconceptualised justice in the light of the mercy and the love of God. His teaching is summarised by Carl J. Friedrich:

[T]ruth and justice coincide, because the all-pervading reason of God as He deals with the world is implemented by the idea that God's justice is by His mercy (*misericordia*). Such mercy makes Him remove another's misery, and therefore all God's acts are both just and merciful. Thus man's justice to be true virtue ought likewise to be tempered by mercy, by compassion and sympathy.[54]

This is not the place to trace down the ages the interaction between Christian ideas of love and justice and other understandings of justice. This is a process that still goes on today. But does this dialogue affect policy and practice? By way of conclusion, an example of how this may take place is given in Rowan Williams's Assize Sermon delivered before the judges of the Wales and Chester Circuit on 'Administering Justice'. He suggests that since doing justice means giving to everyone their due, justice must reflect what people truly are and their deserts.

---

[52] Langan, 'What Jerusalem Says to Athens' in Haughey, *The Faith that Does Justice*, p. 172.
[53] See Carl J. Friedrich, *Transcendent Justice: The Religious Dimension of Constitutionalism.* Durham, N.C.: Duke University Press, 1964, pp. 10–20.
[54] Friedrich, *Transcendent Justice*, p. 31.

Thus, Williams writes, 'the practice of the law in a humane society, however dull and routine, goes on reminding us that human beings deserve the truth, deserve the attention of grace: that we cannot live humanly, in self-awareness, without truthful and graceful relation with each other – without proper compassion, in fact, since that is what truthful and loving attention offers'. This means we must see one another as God sees us; we only see our neighbour clearly when we look towards God; thus 'the vision of God is the cornerstone of justice'. Williams continues:

Ultimately, all that can be said by the Christian about justice rests on the doctrine of God, not simply as the God whose truthful love is directed towards us, but as the God whose very life is 'justice', in the sense that Father, Son and Holy Spirit reflect back to each other perfectly and fully the reality that each one is, 'give glory' to each other . . . So the Uxbridge Magistrates Court and its local equivalents point us towards the contemplation of the Holy Trinity, and that contemplation, with all that it says about truth and reciprocity, grounds, for the Christian, the vision of a just society. Administering justice is a ministry of the truth of God's life to our imaginations, whether we know it or not.[55]

[55] Rowan Williams, *A Ray of Darkness*. Cambridge, Mass.: Cowley Publications, 1995, pp. 210–12.

CHAPTER 10

Justice and community

In earlier chapters I have argued that it is right to see justice as the first virtue of social institutions, but that ideas like fairness are too narrow to fulfil what is legitimately expected of justice. Justice is essential for a healthy social life; it is what binds people together in community, recognising a nexus of mutual obligations and responsibilities for one another. An acceptable degree of justice is necessary if people are to live together in harmony; a sense of systematic injustice leads to suspicion, hostility and, ultimately, divisive conflict.

I have also suggested that many contemporary accounts of justice are too narrow, or based on too fragile foundations, to serve the purpose of framing an acceptable and decent social order. To borrow a comment of Aristotle, 'they speak of a part of justice only'.[1] It is striking, for example, how reluctant most modern theorists of justice are to speak in terms of desert. All those to whom I give detailed attention in this book resile from taking any serious account of desert. Nozick replaces the concept of desert with the quite different concept of entitlement.[2] This is one indication that a gulf has opened between social and criminal justice, as if they were founded upon quite different principles and did not interact closely. Most modern theories of justice need enriching, broadening, deepening and sometimes qualifying if they are to serve their broad general purpose of shaping and monitoring the social order.

---

[1] Aristotle, *Politics*, 1281 a 10.
[2] Robert Nozick, *Anarchy, State, and Utopia*. Oxford: Blackwell, 1974, pp. 150–3. Cf. John Horton and Susan Mendus, *After MacIntyre*. Notre Dame: University of Notre Dame Press, 1994, pp. 37–41.

Accordingly in this chapter I will explore three 'theological fragments', which suggest ways of enlarging the understanding of justice – justice as generosity, justice as forgiveness or mercy, and the church as a community which has the task of embodying and proclaiming the divine justice.

JUSTICE AS GENEROSITY

There is an ancient conviction that generosity is either a part of justice, or at least a virtue to be closely associated with justice. On the one hand, Cicero spoke of 'charity, which may also be called kindness or generosity' as 'close akin' to justice.[3] On the other hand, some modern thinkers, for example J. R. Lucas, suggest that generosity is in fact opposed to justice.[4] It certainly is, if justice is understood as fairness, or giving each what is due in some arithmetical sense. Hume distinguishes generosity as a supererogatory virtue expressed in individual acts of altruism and benevolence, from justice and fidelity which are systemic and necessary for a well-ordered society. Individual acts of generosity, he suggests, may well conflict with the principles of justice and be harmful to society as a whole.[5] But generosity can also open conventional understandings of justice to something broader and richer which is in fact a truer justice and important for healthy social life.

Generosity in pre-modern times was usually assumed to be an aristocratic virtue, characteristic of one who had a lively sense of the worth of his or her position in society and the responsibilities that went with it. Generosity therefore did not so much challenge an existing social order as make it more acceptable. It is certainly true that justice as generosity can confirm and legitimate social orders which are inherently unjust, denuding justice of its dynamic and critical quality, and leaving the power structures of society unchanged. This is the

---

[3] Cicero, *De Officiis*, Bk. I, s. 7, cited in Alan Ryan (ed.), *Justice*. Oxford: Oxford University Press, 1993, p. 41.
[4] J. R. Lucas, *On Justice*. Oxford: Oxford University Press, 1980, pp. 2, 172, 182.
[5] David Hume, *Enquiries Concerning Human Understanding and Concerning the Principles of Morals*, Appendix III, cited in Ryan, *Justice*, pp. 46–7.

voluntary generosity of the prosperous and powerful which is inherently patronising and which strengthens the social hierarchy by applying palliatives to distress.

Yet the generosity that I wish to commend is often the generosity of the poor, of the victim, of the weak, who are willing to set aside their claims to total reparation or complete restitution, generously to forego the right to fairness. It is often quite impossible to make fair restitution. The land of North America cannot be returned *in toto* to the surviving Native Americans, nor can the victims of torture and death squads be brought back to life. If the oppressors are willing to say, 'I am sorry', and to make what restitution is possible, even if it is largely token and symbolic, then creative justice becomes possible through the generosity of the victim. That kind of generosity is necessary if justice is not to become cold, hard and impersonal, and ultimately destructive.

In chapter 3, in arguing that fairness is not enough, I offered an example of a social worker in a residential institution for young adults with learning difficulties. For her and her colleagues to have operated always strictly according to the criteria of fairness would in fact have made it impossible to run the institution in a fully human way, drawing out the gifts of each resident, gently curbing aggression, and affirming the worth and significance of each person and their contribution to the community.

Thus generosity is a way of broadening and deepening the understanding of justice. It leads to 'a more imaginative kind of reciprocity, a capacity to think of oneself in the other man's shoes, and see how the situation would look if roles were reversed . . . Reciprocity, then, points not only to consistent morality but to Golden Rule morality.'[6] Generosity is necessary if the position of the weak, the handicapped and non-citizens is to be secured. It underlies any decent and humane welfare provision and is the only way of overcoming social division. Generosity, of course, cannot be the only principle of social justice; it must be as it were in joint harness with fairness. But a

[6] Dorothy Emmet, *The Moral Prism*. London: Macmillan, 1979, p. 118.

concern for fairness without a dimension of generosity is inadequate and can become destructive. Generosity, like mercy, brings out the true nature of justice. True justice is more than fairness; it expresses a generosity which sometimes conflicts with rights or desert or fairness both in relation to oneself and others. Generous justice can sometimes mean giving people more than their due. Grudging and demeaning welfare benefits, policies which marginalise an underclass, and the refusal to recognise that human beings who are not citizens or cannot contribute significantly to the common good still have a moral claim on us can all be presented as 'fair', but they are not just because they lack generosity.

Thus justice as fairness, impartiality, or desert should be put in the broad frame of justice as generosity. A broad, loving and generous understanding of justice is necessary for healthy community life. A community depends on people who do not always claim their rights, who are generous and who are more than fair. This is not to deny that fairness is of central importance in the way a community is run. A community in which everyone is demanding fairness for themselves is quite different from a community in which the stress is upon fairness for others.

Christians believe that the justice of God which they encounter in practice, in experience and in worship is such a generous justice. Much in the teaching of Jesus concerns the just generosity or the generous justice of God. In the familiar parable of the labourers in the marketplace, each of the workers received the same pay, independently of how long they had worked, or of their desert.[7] Those who have laboured through the heat of the day complain that they have been unjustly, unfairly treated. And so they have. The parable builds on the justice expressed in the laws requiring that a worker should be paid fairly on the day of his work, a further principle which expands the notion of justice.[8] The existing law protects the poor worker and ensures that the worker receives what is due. The parable suggests that the generosity of the house-

---

[7] Matt. 20.1–16.   [8] Lev. 19.13; Deut. 24.14–15.

holder goes beyond what was contracted for all save those who had worked through the heat of the day. It is a creative justice which responds to the misfortune and need, rather than the work, of those who have stood unhired in the marketplace. Their humanity and their need is recognised and responded to. But those who have worked all day grumble at the unfairness of the householder in failing to divide his recompense in terms of desert.

Can generosity find a place in public policy? There are, of course, vast problems here, which theologically are rooted in the fallenness of the human condition. Generosity can conflict with incentives, encourage dependency, lead to waste and prodigality, and so forth. Generous people can easily be exploited, and generosity can sometimes be a subtle type of manipulative selfishness. It is not at all easy – although it is, at least in some situations, possible – for a group or a collectivity to be generous. The Marshall Plan, providing aid from the United States to help rebuild the economies of the European countries, was such a generous gesture. It is, of course, impossible to conceive a society in which social policy is based upon such an extraordinary principle. Yet a society which rejects or neglects the principle that people are of equal worth and have claims to justice 'as people', not just as citizens, or workers, or consumers, is in danger of becoming inhumane because it despises and mistreats the non-achievers, the handicapped and the poor. Fairness and just deserts in themselves are not an adequate account of justice for a decent public policy. For generosity is, as Piaget recognised, a kind of refinement of justice.[9] Society needs generous justice even in its public policy.

MERCY AND FORGIVENESS

Mercy and forgiveness are a kind of generosity; and like generosity they are often supposed to be opposed to justice, or a way of tempering the harsh demands of justice. Guilty offenders

[9] See Carol Gilligan, 'Do the Social Sciences have an Adequate Theory of Moral Development?' in Haan *et al.*, *Social Science as Moral Inquiry*, p. 36, and Gilligan, *In a Different Voice*, p. 172.

who should receive their just deserts are pardoned instead; the justly condemned are shown mercy. Mercy and forgiveness are often assumed to be ways of evading justice rather than doing justice. And it is often felt that forgiveness and mercy are ways of tolerating or even encouraging sin and offence, compromising with evil, or obscuring the gravity of offence.

Forgiveness and mercy are not identical, but they are closely associated with one another. Forgiveness, according to Jean Hampton, 'is a change of heart towards a wrongdoer that arises out of our decision to see him as morally decent rather than bad'. And it is also the setting aside of an offence. Mercy, in contrast, 'is the suspension or mitigation of a punishment which would otherwise be deserved as retribution, and which is granted out of pity and compassion for the wrongdoer'.[10] Both mercy and forgiveness, she suggests, are gifts or gracious acts to which the offender never has a right. But in some contexts it would be outrageous for the punisher to withhold mercy and forgiveness. She sees mercy and forgiveness as closely associated with justice, indeed as indispensable components of an adequate account of justice. Her dialogue partner, Jeffrie Murphy, however, has difficulty in reconciling the demands of justice with those of compassion. For him, justice is impersonal, impartial and blindfold, and concentrates on dealing with the offence, while mercy and forgiveness are compassionate, humane and focused on the offender as a person.[11] Mercy and forgiveness on the one hand and justice on the other, for Murphy, pull in opposite directions.

In the Christian tradition, however, forgiveness and mercy are integral parts of the divine justice, which should be reflected in systems of justice and patterns of just behaviour. If criminal justice is, as I have suggested, a system of discipline, it has to be understood as directed to its *telos* of reconciliation, healing and the restoration of community through forgiveness and mercy. One can only understand justice properly in the light of its *telos*, which is indeed an integral part of what justice means. If God is

[10] Jean Hampton in Jeffrie G. Murphy and Jean Hampton, *Forgiveness and Mercy*. Cambridge: Cambridge University Press, 1988, p. 158.
[11] *Ibid.*, p. 162.

like a loving parent, we must recognise that such a parent can and should forgive and have mercy upon disobedient children, and can do this without a sentimental condoning of offence.[12] So Pope John Paul II can write: 'True mercy is, so to speak, the most profound source of justice.' He continues:

Christ emphasises so insistently the need to forgive others that when Peter asked him how many times he should forgive his neighbour he answered with the symbolic number of 'seventy times seven', meaning that he must be able to forgive everyone every time. It is obvious that such a generous requirement of forgiveness does not cancel out the objective requirements of justice. Properly understood, justice constitutes, so to speak, the goal of forgiveness. In no passage of the gospel message does forgiveness, or mercy as its source, mean indulgence toward evil, toward scandals, toward injury or insult.[13]

Not only are justice and mercy integral to the justice of God, but also the Judaeo-Christian tradition is full of injunctions to forgive without limit and to have mercy as essential components of doing true justice. Mercy, forgiveness and reconciliation are at the heart of God's justice, which provides a model for human justice.

This theme is contained famously in Portia's speech in *The Merchant of Venice*:

> The quality of mercy is not strain'd;
> It droppeth as the gentle rain from heaven
> Upon the place beneath: it is twice blessed;
> It blesseth him that gives and him that takes:
> 'Tis mightiest in the mightiest; it becomes
> The throned monarch better than his crown;
> His sceptre shows the force of temporal power,
> The attribute to awe and majesty,
> Wherein doth sit the dread and fear of kings;
> But mercy is above this sceptr'd sway,
> It is enthroned in the hearts of kings,
> It is an attribute to God himself,
> And earthly power does then show likest God's

---

[12] See Thomas Talbott, 'Punishment, Forgiveness and Divine Justice', *Religious Studies*, 29 (1993), 151–68 (164).

[13] John Paul II, 'Dives in Misericordia', *Origins*, 10:26 (11 Dec. 1980), 414, cited in L. Gregory Jones, *Embodying Forgiveness: A Theological Analysis*. Grand Rapids: Eerdmans, 1995, p. 89.

When mercy seasons justice. Therefore, Jew,
Though justice be thy plea, consider this,
That in the course of justice none of us
Should see salvation; we do pray for mercy;
And that same prayer doth teach us all to render
The deeds of mercy.[14]

Here a classic passage from a more Christian age affirms that true justice is in God and is known by us through God's dealings with us. Mercy, which shades into forgiveness, brings out the true flavour of justice, a justice which is like the divine justice. Hence justice is not vindictive, unrelenting or mechanical. It is not a machine-like, balanced retribution, the *lex talionis* of the blindfold, impersonal figure of Justitia, with scales and sword in hand. Nor is it cheap grace, which veils the gravity of offence and sin. At the heart of justice we find mercy, forgiveness and love – more than fairness or equity. Portia is appealing beyond the faithfulness to contracts and to due process that Shylock claims, beyond fairness, to something deeper, more creative, proactive, personal and healing.

The Merchant of Venice is now generally admitted to be an anti-Semitic play, with Shylock as a stereotype intended to represent a hard retributive notion of justice assumed to be that of the Hebrew Scriptures. This is, of course, a massive distortion, for it is clear that an understanding of God's justice as an expression of his love, forgiveness and mercy is to be found in both testaments, and in both it is presented as a model for the covenant people to emulate and embody in their structures of law.

Jeffrie Murphy attempts to limit the impact of Portia's speech by pointing out that the case is one of private or civil law, in which the litigant has a right but not an obligation to enforce the letter of the law. This right may be waived to make space for mercy. A judge in a criminal case, however, has an *obligation* to impose a just punishment; if the judge is merciful or compassionate it is suggested that he is culpable for not fulfilling the duties of his office.[15] This distinction is an important

---

[14] *The Merchant of Venice*, Act IV, Scene I.
[15] Murphy and Hampton, *Forgiveness and Mercy*, pp. 175–6.

reminder that mercy and forgiveness do not ignore or cover up offence, and are not incompatible with penalty and with repentance; indeed they address offence in the most serious of ways. But it is too simple to suggest that mercy and forgiveness have no bearing upon criminal offence, or that Portia's speech or the theology of justice that lies behind it are relevant only to a certain class of case. Shakespeare chose his words carefully; he spoke of mercy *seasoning* justice, not tempering or modifying or tampering with it. Seasoning is part of what it seasons, and seasoning brings out the authentic flavour of the dish. Justice seasoned with mercy declares itself to be in the last analysis gracious.

Something like this account of justice was publicly affirmed by the leading judges of Scotland and England when in March 1996 they resisted the attempt of the Home Secretary, Michael Howard, to lay down draconian sentences for certain types of offence. The judges suggested that to deprive them of the discretion to season justice with mercy would in fact result in injustice. Justice that is not adapted to the situation of offender and victim and of society, justice that is a mechanical process that never takes risks for the sake of the healing of relationships, is less than justice.

Carol Gilligan is perceptive in her analysis of *The Merchant of Venice,* suggesting that Shakespeare uses a male actor playing Portia, a woman disguised as a man, to bring into 'the masculine citadel of justice the feminine plea for mercy'. Portia in fact demonstrates the absurdity and harmfulness of the mechanical application of the 'male' theory of justice, and the need for constant exceptions. 'Portia, in calling for mercy, argues for that resolution in which no one is hurt, and, as the men are forgiven for their failure to keep both their rings and their word, Antonio in turn foregoes his "right" to ruin Shylock.'[16]

A similar point is made in a different way by Roberto Unger who, as part of his critique of a contractarian basis for society, suggests that *The Merchant of Venice* contrasts the generous, merciful justice of Belmont with the contractarian and imper-

---

[16] Gilligan, *In a Different Voice,* p. 105.

sonal justice of Venice; Belmont should inject its humane and divine values into the Venetian understanding and practice of justice.[17] But surely the main thrust of the play is to suggest that God's justice is justice enriched with mercy and forgiveness, and that human justice should reflect this?

Forgiveness in politics

'The discoverer of the role of forgiveness in the realm of human affairs', declared Hannah Arendt, 'was Jesus of Nazareth.' Forgiveness, as the faculty of being able to undo the effects of action, is essential if people are to be free agents and able to make fresh starts, if the entail of past errors is to be erased, if the vicious circle of vengeance is to be overcome. Jesus, she writes, denied that only God had the power to forgive sins, and insisted that there was a duty laid upon disciples to forgive without limit. She affirms that Christianity teaches that 'only love can forgive because only love is fully receptive to *who* somebody is, to the point of being always willing to forgive him whatever he may have done', and accordingly there is a problem in speaking about such loving forgiveness in the public sphere. But what love is in face-to-face relations, respect is in the larger domain of human affairs: 'Respect, . . . because it concerns only the person, is quite sufficient to prompt forgiving of what a person did, for the sake of the person.' But surely the manifestation of love in the public realm is justice rather than 'respect', and therefore we must speak of justice savoured with mercy and forgiveness?[18]

It is true that 'one cannot do other people's forgiving for them'.[19] Nor may a detached observer tell victims that they should forgive. We have been reminded by the Kairos Document of 1986 by South African theologians opposed to apartheid that the time and the situation must be right for

---

[17] See the important discussion of Unger's thought in Okin, *Justice, Gender and the Family*, pp. 117–24.

[18] Hannah Arendt, *The Human Condition*. Chicago: University of Chicago Press, 1958, pp. 236–243.

[19] Peter Hinchliff, *Holiness and Politics*. London: Darton, Longman & Todd, 1982, p. 198.

forgiveness if it is not to be something cheap and superficial. God, as victim, offers forgiveness: 'On the cross Christ "bears" our guilt, but this is not expiation. What happens there is the absorption of violence, the redefinition of power, and the establishment of the possibility of forgiveness.'[20] Human victims can mediate the divine forgiveness, and this forgiveness heals and establishes justice. Donald Shriver in his remarkable book *An Ethic for Enemies: Forgiveness in Politics* argues that Black Americans have shown a remarkable openness to the possibility of forgiving their oppressors. Since Emancipation, if not before, the culture of a significant proportion of Black Americans, so deeply shaped by Christian faith, has given them 'a predisposition toward, an ingrained *gift* for, injecting forgiveness into their political relations with the white majority of this country'.[21] And in contemporary South Africa it is not only Nelson Mandela but also multitudes of ordinary Blacks who show a quite extraordinarily magnanimous willingness to forgive, which provides the essential conditions for building a just nation. Kenneth Kaunda and Desmond Tutu both speak of forgiveness as the only way of overcoming 'the entail of the past', and Kaunda believes there is a special African gift for forgiveness. Graham Blount affirms in his fine treatment of forgiveness that the forgiveness which comes ultimately from the representative victim can only be conveyed in solidarity with the victims. Yet if forgiveness is to be effective in politics it must be possible for governments, which are not victims, to speak a word of forgiveness. Only examples such as those deployed by Blount or by Shriver can demonstrate that this is possible, healing and creative of community and of justice.[22] Especially in situations where the entail of history cannot be undone, where it is impossible for past injuries to be cured or full restitution to be made, justice can only be established through forgiveness and this forgiveness is itself a component of

[20] Timothy Gorringe, *God's Just Vengeance: Crime, Violence and the Rhetoric of Salvation.* Cambridge: Cambridge University Press, 1996, p. 247.

[21] Donald Shriver, *An Ethic for Enemies: Forgiveness in Politics.* New York: Oxford University Press, 1995, p. 177.

[22] Graham Blount, 'Forgive us our Debts', Unpublished PhD thesis, University of Edinburgh, 1995.

justice. It is as hard for collectivities to repent as it is for them to forgive, and there are not many instances of either happening. But without repentance and forgiveness the way to justice is closed. Haddon Willmer puts the point well:

Forgiveness in politics cannot be an easy-going acceptance of what is, a whitewashing tolerance. It has to be a practicable policy in which what is wrong is reckoned with, but forgivingly rather than punitively. Forgiveness is not reconciliation on any terms but takes form in the agreement to work together a political system which expresses the will to forgive, is sustained by forgiveness and encourages and enables men [*sic*] to enter into it. Forgiveness in politics must be a quality of events, institutions, processes and participants.[23]

Christian forgiveness in secular life

Despite Arendt's confidence that forgiveness as taught by Jesus can and should be operative in the public sphere, there remain problems of transposition from one sphere to the other which have been addressed by a number of recent writers. Marilyn McCord Adams argues that forgiveness is particularly 'at home' in a Christian context, for Christianity 'deems forgiveness possible and good, because the Creator, Governor, and Redeemer of the world . . . is generous, gracious, and loving'.[24] Christian faith, she argues, decisively shapes the understanding of forgiveness and its significance as well as enjoining us to be forgiving. She sees forgiveness as 'a process within the context of a triangular relationship, among the victim, the offender, and God', which is a peculiarly Christian obligation: 'it is an obligation to be generous as God is generous. Divine generosity meets the creature's imitative effort with miraculous aid, enabling the victim to forgive.'[25]

Yet can a practice and an understanding so decisively shaped by a specific faith be effective in the public sphere in a pluralist society? McCord Adams examines three thinkers who

---

[23] Haddon Willmer, 'Forgiveness and Politics', *Crucible* (July–Sept 1979), 100–5 (103–4).
[24] Marilyn McCord Adams, 'Forgiveness: A Christian Model', *Faith and Philosophy*, 8:3 (1991), 277–304 (290).
[25] *Ibid.*, 300.

suggest forgiveness must be thoroughly disentangled from the Christian soil in which it first took root if it is to be acceptable at all in secular discourse: Aurel Kolnai, P. Twambley, and Jeffrie Murphy.[26] McCord Adams persuasively shows that these attempts at transposition from a theological to a secular ethical context involve fairly drastic modification of the content of the notion of forgiveness, leaving a place for 'retributive hatred' (Murphy), either affirming that forgiveness must be deserved or earned, or suggesting that generosity is morally problematic.

Even if McCord Adams has shown that forgiveness is most at home in the Christian theological context, which initially shaped and constantly refreshes it, there is still the fact that if forgiveness is to be relevant in the public realm it has to some extent to be mediated through ethics and in constant dialogue with secular and alternative understandings. In his impressive recent book *Embodying Forgiveness: A Theological Analysis*, L. Gregory Jones explores these issues. He argues, like McCord Adams, that attempts to present a non-theological account of forgiveness have tended to diverge significantly at key points from what Christianity would wish to say, and that they have relied on ethical theories which are, from a Christian point of view, misleading. Like MacIntyre, he commends a broadly Aristotelian/Thomist approach, knowing that Aquinas introduced the notion of forgiveness into Aristotle's teaching and thereby radically modified the classical system of thought and action. The historical point is well taken, but the pressing need today is to press forward the contemporary dialogue about justice and forgiveness between theology and secular philosophies – a project to which McCord Adams's article and Gregory Jones's book are important contributions. And we must also welcome the seriousness with which some philosophers and criminologists such as Antony Duff quarry the Christian theological tradition for

---

[26] Aurel Kolnai, 'Forgiveness', *Proceedings of the Aristotelian Society*, 1973–4, 91–106; P. Twambley, Mercy and Forgiveness', *Analysis*, 36:2 (January 1976), 84–90; and Murphy and Hampton, *Forgiveness and Mercy*, and associated articles.

insights which may be relevant to the debate about justice in the public sphere.[27]

JUST COMMUNITY

Justice is essentially relational and can best be exemplified in a community of restored relationships and healed memories. Augustine constantly stressed the importance of justice. A state without justice becomes demonic; a decent state must express enough justice for human beings to flourish together in the commonwealth. The earthly city is fragmented and imperfect; it can do no more than aim at a partial, relative and provisional justice and peace arising out of curbing human selfishness and aggression and balancing out conflicting interests. This relative justice is a good necessary for healthy community life. It is, for Augustine, to be measured against the divine justice which is manifested in Jesus Christ, and it will be fully realised only in the coming City of God. Justice in its fullness is not and cannot be present in a broken, sinful world, but will be fundamental to the life of the City of God. As Augustine put it:

There is not any true justice in any commonwealth whatsoever, but in that whereof Christ is the founder and the ruler, if you please to call that a commonwealth which we cannot deny is the weal of the commonalty. But if this name, being elsewhere so common, seem too discrepant from our subject and phrase, truly then there is true justice but in that city whereof that holy scripture saith: 'Glorious things are spoken of thee, thou city of God'.[28]

Christians believe that they know something of the justice of the City of God because they have seen it exemplified in the life and relationships of Jesus, the Just One, in the community he gathered around him and in his teaching. Jesus enacted his teaching in his life and work.

The gospel traditions stress again and again that Jesus had friendly relations with, and even broke the rules by sharing meals with sinners, enacting what he taught in his parables –

---

[27] See especially Antony Duff, *Trials and Punishments*. Cambridge: Cambridge University Press, 1986.
[28] St Augustine, *The City of God*. II.21. London: Dent, 1945, vol. I, p. 64.

that the justice of the Kingdom of God involves breaking down rather than reinforcing and reflecting the barriers and divisions of the world in order to establish a new and just community.

The church is called to be a kind of anticipation of the life and the justice of the City of God, a colony of heaven, a preliminary and partial demonstration as it were of the justice of God. John Milbank, while recognising with Augustine that the world cannot yet live by the justice of the City of God, and that we must to some extent be resigned to this tragic necessity, argues that the church should seek to be an *asylum*, a place of refuge from the injustices of the world, and also a social space where a serious effort is made to pursue just practices, to demonstrate the justice of God.[29] This is also Stanley Hauerwas's point, that 'the church does not have a social ethics; the church *is* a social ethic . . . Put starkly, the first social ethical task of the church is to be the church – the servant community . . . What makes the church the church is its faithful manifestation of the peaceable kingdom in the world.'[30]

In Christian worship with the Eucharist at its heart, Christians perform 'the essential rituals of our politics',[31] which witness more clearly to the coming Kingdom and its righteousness. Indeed, worship is an anticipation of the Kingdom and its justice; it is a disturbance and a challenge, the proclamation of an alternative reality and a summons to the future.

How can we celebrate the Supper today amid the injustices of the world so that it challenges and transcends these injustices and points to the gracious justice of God? The question is more acute perhaps than we often recognise. Camilo Torres, the Colombian priest who died as a guerrilla, believed that in a society as profoundly unjust and divided as Colombia it was impossible for the Eucharist to be properly celebrated. Hence he said, 'I took off my cassock to be more fully a priest', and gave up celebrating mass.[32]

---

[29] John Milbank, *Theology and Social Theory: Beyond Secular Reason*. Oxford: Blackwell, 1990, p. 422.

[30] Stanley Hauerwas, *The Peaceable Kingdom: A Primer in Christian Ethics*. London: SCM, 1983, p. 99.

[31] *Ibid.*, p. 108.

[32] J. Gerassi (ed.), *Camilo Torres: Revolutionary Priest*. Harmondsworth: Penguin, 1979, p. 9.

The Spanish theologian José M. Castillo has declared, 'Where there is no justice, there is no Eucharist.'[33] 'Participation in the Eucharist . . . as it is celebrated today', declared Gustavo Gutierrez, 'appears to many to be an action which, for want of the support of an authentic community, becomes an exercise in make-believe.'[34] Even more sharply, Ulrich Duchrow asks whether a church which reflects the injustice of the world because it 'is divided among active thieves, passive profiteers, and deprived victims' is indeed the Body of Christ, capable of celebrating the Eucharist.[35]

Nevertheless, we need to recognise that the Eucharist is not the messianic banquet, but at best a foretaste. We are not yet in the Kingdom for the coming of which we pray. The Eucharist is nourishment for those seeking the Kingdom and its justice, and not the feast at the end of the journey. We need to recognise that injustice, hostility and division may well make our Eucharists questionable. And we need to recover ways in which the Eucharist may be a healing and effective sign and enactment of the divine justice. Our celebrations inevitably take place in a defective church and a deformed world, full of sin and suffering, injustice and oppression. But rightly used, the Eucharist can be an authentic anticipation of God's future, an appetiser for the coming Kingdom which nourishes expectation and hope for God's justice. As antepast the Eucharist is an *arrabon*: an earnest, a real, if partial, experience of the justice God has in store, a guarantee that it will come and an incentive to seek the justice of the Kingdom with pertinacity.[36]

---

[33] Cited in G. Wainwright, *Doxology*. London: Epworth, 1980, pp. 402, 568, n. 987.

[34] G. Gutierrez, *A Theology of Liberation*. London: SCM, 1974, p. 137.

[35] U. Duchrow, *Global Economy*. Geneva: WCC, 1987, p. 137.

[36] The last few paragraphs are adapted from my article, 'Ecclesiology and Ethics: A Reformed Perspective', *Ecumenical Review*, 47:2 (April 1995), 248–54.

CHAPTER II

The hope of justice

We have already encountered the importance of hope at various places and, in particular, in both our case studies. A prison regime that is not hopefully open to the future is destructive and demoralising for prisoners and staff alike. The May Committee sought a future-oriented element in prison regimes, and Professor Bottoms urged that statements of the aims of imprisonment should include 'some explicit dimension of hope'.[1] We also saw how poor people's lot was worse if deprived of hope, and how frequently a social hope was generated among the poor and the deprived, so that they became bearers of hope. Hope keeps open the horizon of the future and motivates to action; practice is enriched and strengthened if it is hopeful. Alan Paton, in a remarkable article on 'The Nature and Ground of Christian Hope Today', declared, 'I am a man of hope, . . . to me hope is inseparable from life'.[2] Yet hope hardly featured in the secular theories of justice which we examined; but it is hard to go far into the Judaeo-Christian understanding of justice without acknowledging the centrality of hope.

Hopes are, of course, of many kinds. Some are an escape from reality, pipe-dreams or expressions of alienation. Some are strictly individual and private. Other hopes of a political sort have shown during this century how hope as the search for utopia can become appalling tyranny. Other hopes have generated great and humane movements for reform and for

---

[1] Anthony Bottoms, 'The Aims of Imprisonment' in Garland, *Justice, Guilt and Forgiveness in the Penal System*, p. 8.

[2] Alan Paton, *Knocking at the Door*. New York: Scribners, 1975, p. 286.

liberation. Many, but not all, forms of hope are rooted, at least at their birth, in religious ground.

THE CHRISTIAN HOPE

Religion tends to generate 'a total hope', an orientation towards the future which is not partial or limited, but all-encompassing.[3] The Judaeo-Christian tradition especially appears to have had down the centuries a particularly close link with utopian hopes and an expectancy about the future. Indeed one can say that the linked themes of eschatology, promise and the future are central and indispensable elements in this tradition. Here, faith gives substance to hope, shapes and sustains hope; faith and hope are inseparably linked together.

This hope is at its heart and throughout social. The principal images used for the future are not those of the flight of the alone to the Alone, or the soul's ascent to God, but the powerful symbols of the Reign of God for the coming of which we pray, the City that believers seek whose builder and maker is God, the New Jerusalem, that comes down out of heaven from God. These images all suggest a coming just ordering of relationships; in hope we look forward to the future triumph of righteousness and justice. The hope also has judgement at its heart; there is here no evasion of the gravity of sin and offence, oppression and injustice. In the City, in the New Jerusalem, justice will be enthroned. In judgement the poor and the weak are to be vindicated and upheld. This hope challenges the existing orders of injustice, violence and brutality. The hope is good news to the poor and all who suffer.

Believers hope for something that will be given; they do not construct the City themselves. Blake's words, 'Till we have *built* Jerusalem', strike a distinctively modern and activist note. But we are enjoined to pray for the coming of the Reign of God, and to seek the Kingdom and its justice above all other things. We are to prepare for the coming of God's new order of which we already have a foretaste in the Jesus-event and in the life

---

[3] See Charles Davis, 'The Grounding of Religious Hope' in his *Religion and the Making of Society*. Cambridge: Cambridge University Press, 1994, pp. 198–9.

and worship of the church. And believers should also seek to discern the seeds of the Kingdom in the life of the world, and nurture them there.

Such social hopes are in practice forms of protest against the existing situation with its in-built injustice; they present, often in an elaborate code of imagery, an alternative reality; they refuse to make absolute present structures; they present an open future, full of possibilities; and thus they can motivate and sustain great movements of change. They can support people through times of oppression and suffering, and enable them to struggle for justice with pertinacity; but they can quickly degenerate into opiates, encouraging tranquil resignation to systemic evil and injustice.

Religious hope has down the ages generated countless movements of protest, revolution, or reform. Some of these involved the transposition into secular terms of religious language; some were naively utopian or escapist; others engaged directly with the power structures of society. Many forms of socialism and Marxism itself have been interpreted as secular transpositions of the Judaeo-Christian hope, new ways of seeking the City that has foundations, the Kingdom of God and its justice.

THE WITHERING OF PUBLIC HOPE

When Bishop Lesslie Newbigin returned to Britain after decades of ministry overseas, particularly in South India, he was often asked what was the greatest difficulty he faced in returning to Britain from India. His invariable answer was: 'The disappearance of hope.' 'Even in the most squalid slums of Madras,' he said, 'there was always the belief that things could be improved . . . In spite of all the disappointments since independence came in 1947, there was still the belief in a better future ahead.' In Britain, in contrast, the old hope, the steady confidence in a better future, appeared to have disintegrated. And this situation, Newbigin believed, poses vast problems both for western society and for Christian ministry in it.[4]

[4] Lesslie Newbigin, *The Other Side of 1984: Questions for the Churches*. London: British Council of Churches, 1983, pp. 3-4.

A few years later, Trevor Blackwell and Jeremy Seabrook explored 'the withering of public hope'. This erosion of hope they saw as corrosive both of healthy conviviality and of a personal sense of meaning and fulfilment:

Rage, helplessness, a sense of redundancy; a feeling of being in exile, of disappointment and dividedness; loathing, contempt and fear, a dread of being suffocated; a disabling self-doubt.

These are our feelings, living in Britain in the late 1980s. How different they are from anything we anticipated, as we were growing up in that changed world which our parents had won for us after 1945. The future at that time seemed expansive and filled with hope, not only personal hopes, but also the belief that the society in which we were to take our place was getting better, morally as well as materially. Modest though the lives of our families might have been, we felt that they were nevertheless bequeathing to us something of great worth: a vision of a better world that was in the process of being realised. They gave us to understand that this involved a decisive break with the punishing and destructive aspects of the life they had known; and we believed them. They were even slightly envious of us, for they felt that they might not live to see the furthest consequences of the changes they had helped to enact.[5]

Newbigin, Blackwell and Seabrook remind us that hope is a central component of any life that is worth living, and a healthy society needs some kind of shared social hope.

But hope is in crisis in our day. The traditional bearers of hope – utopian political movements, churches that sustain some kind of eschatological expectation, ideological systems that nourish an openness towards the future – all seem to be in decline and disarray. Is it possible in such a situation of hopelessness for hope to be reborn, for a resurrection of expectation to take place? What might this involve? And what are the responsibilities in this regard of Christians, of people who believe that the Judaeo-Christian tradition is not finally exhausted, of people who are convinced that political and social movements should nourish, explore and seek to implement a social hope which is at its heart a hope for justice?

The present situation is not without its ironies. That visionary

[5] Trevor Blackwell and Jeremy Seabrook, *The Politics of Hope: Britain at the End of the Twentieth Century*. London: Faber, 1988, pp. 3–4.

Marxist Ernst Bloch wrote his vast *Das Prinzip Hoffnung*, in which he saw Marxism as the heir of the biblical emphasis on hope, at a time when Marxist regimes and most Marxists had abandoned hope as a significant theme. He was, accordingly, treated as a heretic. Then, in the 1960s, Jürgen Moltmann took up Bloch's theme and sparked off an explosion of theological interest in the theme of hope. Once again, the owl of Minerva only takes flight when dark has fallen, for already in the sixties a mood of disillusion was beginning. And we have to attempt to understand why this was so, why there was so rapid a disenchantment with both the broad religious and metaphysical hopes and the more specific political hopes that had sustained people for so long.[6]

There was, first of all, a mounting sense of the bankruptcy of hopes that had failed. In the 1960s the young Alasdair MacIntyre declared that he remained a Marxist because he believed the Marxist project to be 'the only one we have for re-establishing hope as a social virtue'.[7] A similar Marxist hope flourished in the 1930s in the poverty-stricken Jewish community in the Glasgow Gorbals, in which Ralph Glasser grew up, and which he depicts so powerfully in his three-volume autobiography. One of their number returned with his family to the Russia they had left years before, in the belief that 'it was a new world in which the workers ruled, not the old despots who had ground the faces of the poor'. They were never heard of again.[8] Meanwhile the others met in the Gorbals to nourish their hope together:

---

[6] Ernst Bloch, *The Principle of Hope* [Das Prinzip Hoffnung]. 3 vols., Oxford: Blackwell, 1986; Jürgen Moltmann, *Theology of Hope: On the Ground and Implications of a Christian Eschatology* [Theologie der Hoffnung], tr. James W. Leitch. London: SCM, 1967; Rubem A. Alves, *A Theology of Human Hope*. London: SCM, 1972.

[7] Alasdair MacIntyre, *Marxism and Christianity*. Harmondsworth: Penguin, 1968, p. 88. Much of MacIntyre's complex intellectual pilgrimage and return to Christian faith might be interpreted as the search for a sure grounding for hope. This book is a rewriting of *Marxism – An Interpretation*. London: SCM, 1953, which MacIntyre wrote when he was still a Christian. In that book he wrote: 'If the Christian hope is to be realised in history, it must assume the form of a political hope; it must use the morally ambiguous means which are the only means to attain political ends. In other words, the religious content must be realised in political terms. But this is exactly what the young Marx did in his criticism of religion. Marxism is in essence a complete realisation of Christian eschatology' (p. 120).

[8] Ralph Glasser, *Growing Up in the Gorbals*. London: Pan, 1987, p. 6.

They sustained themselves with milkless tea and sometimes with black bread from the bakery. They talked with certainty and the passion of people who saw a bright deliverance within reach, convinced that they were in the van of those who would secure it. Listening to their throaty talk, so often punctuated by tubercular coughs and spitting, voices often raised in impatience with one another, it was possible to believe that at any moment they would compel the world to realise their dreams. Restless exiles, making a hard life in an alien environment, they nourished their souls by fixing their gaze on the far horizon, obstinately proclaiming the innocence of man and his necessary unity with all his kind. Theirs was a desperate optimism. Like storm-lost navigators they fed themselves with signs and portents.[9]

Disillusionment gradually impinged, as the awful reality of what was happening in the Stalinist utopia, the even more dreadful events in Nazi Germany, the Spanish Civil War and mounting hardship and unemployment at home percolated into people's consciousness. The 'profound resignation' that ensued among the older generation was alarming to the young: 'Did they want us to abandon hope before we had even started?', Glasser and his contemporaries asked.[10] Similar disillusion seems to have followed every modern flourishing of hope. The trenches of the Somme put paid for many to the sunny optimism of nineteenth-century liberal progressivism. The Spanish Civil War revealed for others the moral ambiguities of utopian expectations of the right and of the left. The Holocaust produced both despair and the Zionist determination to build in Palestine, the promised land, a new, secure Israel which claimed God's promises. The outburst of hope in post-war reconstruction which was embodied in the welfare state in course of time led to the depressing conviction that it was not fulfilling adequately, and perhaps could not fulfil at all, the immense expectations which had been invested in it.

THE END OF HISTORY?

Today it seems to many people that 'the winds have gone out of the sails of utopia'. Two writers may help us to understand

---

[9] *Ibid.*, p. 7.   [10] *Ibid.*, p. 47.

what is happening. Francis Fukuyama proclaims that we stand at 'the end of history'. This means that there is nothing left to hope for. We have arrived. The absolute moment is now. The triumph of liberal democracy means that there is nothing further to strive for, no possibility of fundamental criticism of our consumerist society. All that is left is to fine-tune heaven. 'Liberal democracy,' writes Fukuyama, 'is the only legitimate ideology left in the world.'[11] The hopes of the past have either turned sour or have shown themselves to be poisonous. We are better off without them. And so a New World Order is proclaimed to freeze and protect the absolute moment, the end of history, at which we have arrived. The other writer, John Kenneth Galbraith, sees the present moment as riddled with contradictions, injustices and inequalities. But because the majority of people in western liberal democracies are fairly prosperous, they have an investment in the maintenance of the status quo and live in 'the culture of contentment'. The contented are a majority of those who vote. They vote to protect their income and their status. They tolerate the hyper-rich for fear that any attempt to redistribute wealth might harm their own interests as well. They close their eyes to the fact that 'the comfort and economic well-being of the contented majority was being supported and enhanced by the presence in the modern economy of a large, highly useful, even essential class that does not share in the agreeable existence of the favoured community'.[12] Critics and reformers may be listened to with interest – but no action is taken. Any kind of utopianism is dismissed out of hand. Hope, they believe, has become redundant.

This is a comforting notion for the rich and strong. For them, the temptation is to believe that this is the best of all possible worlds. The present order they tend to see as part of the givenness of things. They are happy to believe that the search for utopia is the road to serfdom, that the benefits of their prosperity automatically trickle down to those less fortunate –

[11] Francis Fukuyama in *The Guardian*, 17 Sept. 1990. For a full development of the argument see Fukuyama, *The End of History and the Last Man*.
[12] Galbraith, *Culture of Contentment*, p. 29.

the theory that, in Galbraith's words: 'if one feeds the horse enough oats, some will pass through to the road for the sparrows'!

But the end of history and the erosion of hope is a dungeon for the poor and powerless. It was no misunderstanding that led Dante to put above the gateway into Hell the slogan, 'Abandon hope all ye who enter here!' In the culture of contentment the poor and the powerless are locked into their predicament without the possibility of radical change. They need a hope that strengthens and encourages them and a hope that holds up the possibility of a just society which is bound together by mutual accountability. Hopelessness for them is a state of resignation and despair. For others it is an essential part of the package of contentment; they are better off without hope, for hope makes people restless and critical of the situations and the systems in which they find themselves.

HOPE TRUE AND FALSE

In all this turmoil there was a sorting out of the authentic from the false. Some hopes were perverted or counterfeit, phoney hopes calculated to keep people passive and compliant, like our National Lottery, with its seductive promise of the heavenly finger bringing millions into the lucky winner's living room.

Religious hope can be, and often is, individualised and made so private that it has no obvious public bearing. When, in her 'Sermon on the Mound', Margaret Thatcher quoted from that strange chauvinist hymn, 'I vow to thee, my country', she concentrated on the verse about 'another country, I've heard of long ago' which grows 'soul by soul and silently' and whose 'ways are ways of gentleness and all her ways are peace'. It is for this other country, she suggested, that we should hope, and such hope has little bearing on what goes on in the earthly country, to which the singer vows 'the service of my love', 'the love that makes undaunted the final sacrifice'.

This position has, to be fair, a respectable theological ancestry, stretching back through Luther's Two-Kingdoms theory to a certain, very suspect, interpretation of St Augustine.

But whether it is indeed congruent with the biblical witness I would doubt, and whether it is capable of engaging effectively with false and diabolic hopes seems unlikely. Edwyn Bevan presented it in one of the preparatory volumes for the 1938 Oxford Conference on Church, Community and State. In the true Christian outlook, he wrote, there is no earthly goal in view. The human trajectory goes across the line of earthly history seeking a goal in the unseen world. This world is simply a platform to be crossed between birth and death, until people enter 'individual by individual', into the unseen world, the world always there beside the visible one. The creation of the Divine Community in that invisible world is the 'supreme hope', before which all earthly hopes pale into insignificance, as 'everything that happens on this temporal platform, now or in the future, is of minor importance'. 'Whenever the main stress is laid upon "building Jerusalem in England's green and pleasant land",' he concludes, 'the Christian attitude to the world is abandoned.'[13]

Accounts of the Christian hope can thus vary from the baptism of some secular political cause, so that no distinction is seen between the Nazareth manifesto of Jesus and the Internationale, to a private, escapist and alienating hope which has nothing to say to secular hopes except to deny their validity totally.

RELIGIOUS HOPE

Is it surprising that Charles Davis can declare that 'religious hope is an area of human experience and history riddled with deception', and call for 'a therapeutic critique to purify religious hope from neurotic and ideological elements'? Religious hope, he continues, has been used as a compensation to legitimate social oppression and injustice and as a way of avoiding facing the negativities of life and even the reality of death itself. We need therefore to struggle to find an authentic Christian hope, which in some sense is strongly validated from

[13] E. Bevan, *The Kingdom of God and History.* The Church, Community and State Series 3, London: Allen & Unwin, 1938, pp. 39–72 (56–7).

within the tradition, which itself has a tension between an other-worldly and a this-worldly interpretation of hope.[14]

It is universally acknowledged that the early church had close to the heart of its faith an eschatological expectation that the end was at hand, that the time of judgement was now, that a new and very different order was about to break in. This eschatology was expressed not in individualistic terms but by way of the great social and systemic images of the city, the new Jerusalem, and above all, of the Kingdom or Reign of God. The gospel was proclaimed as the good news of the Kingdom, which is not something we build, but a reality which will be graciously given to us by God. Meanwhile, the faithful are to seek the Kingdom and its justice, prefiguring that Kingdom and that justice in their common life, and judging the kingdoms of this world by the glimpses they have been given of the coming Kingdom and its characteristics. In the Letter to the Hebrews the life of faith is presented as a constant, lifelong seeking of the city whose builder and maker is God. Here it is faith that gives substance to hope and faith that sustains hope. 'Faith gives substance to our hopes and convinces us of realities we do not see.'[15]

Yet biblical scholars almost universally agree that even within the New Testament period, as the church became more confident, prosperous and established, the urgency of the expectation, the hope that the present order would be replaced, waned. And down the centuries, eschatology and hope have tended to decline in mainstream Christianity, and to be left to survive in millenarian sects and movements on the margins, whenever the church has become overly confident, secure, prosperous, powerful and respected. In the nineteenth century, for example, the Last Things became little more than an appendix in dogmatics textbooks rather than a living and central dimension of faith. The liberal belief in progress was something quite different from the Christian hope. It saw the building of the heavenly city as a cumulative human project, which was already well underway. If one had not already arrived at Jerusalem, at

---

[14] Davis, *Religion and the Making of Society*, pp. 199–200.   [15] Heb. 11.1.

least the foundations had been well and truly laid. The optimism about progress showed itself incapable of developing any serious critique of things as they were, because they were regarded as the necessary foundations of the future. Liberal theology served to endorse this sunny view of progress. Albert Schweitzer, in the afterglow of nineteenth-century liberalism, portrayed Jesus as a 'stranger' who was inaccessible to us precisely because he came from a context of eschatology, apocalyptic, hope which is totally different from ours.

Then came the First World War and the rise of Hitler, and the Holocaust. With these, liberal theology appeared to collapse, for a time at least, and theologians like Barth and Bultmann in their differing ways rediscovered eschatology and apocalyptic. It was as if themes and images which had lain more or less dormant for centuries suddenly sprang to life. People found that eschatology, and even the more lurid imagery of apocalyptic, was necessary if they were to understand what was going on around them; and hope was essential if they were to act faithfully, justly and wisely in a world that was full of evil and oppression. This is the process that Austin Farrer referred to as 'the rebirth of images' – ideas that most people thought were dead and buried still survive, submerged beneath the surface as it were, in the canon and in the tradition, particularly at the margins, and spring suddenly into life.

Sociologists like Norman Cohn and Vittorio Lanternari have famously argued that marginal sects and groupings of the oppressed have nurtured millenarian, apocalyptic and messianic forms of faith, most markedly in a Judaeo-Christian context. The early church was clearly such a community, reaching forward in hope to an alternative reality, an open future, God's gift rather than a human achievement. Bloch and Cohn in particular have shown how Judaeo-Christian eschatology not only provided themes and resources for messianic and apocalyptic sects (which were frequently persecuted by the official church) but also flowed into modern secular social and political movements of protest, reform and revolution.

But is it possible any longer for *religious* images to be reborn, for a religious account of hope to become once more influential? Can the Christian faith any longer sustain a living and relevant hope in cold times? The German philosopher Peter Sloterdijk doubts it. Both classical metaphysics and Christian theology, he argues, have outlived their public relevance: 'Both have undergone a historical process resembling mummification. Religion and fundamental philosophy have continued an existence in which they have outlived their usefulness over against the world and reality. They are scholastic ghost towns, uninhabitable and no longer plausible.'[16] He has a point. But is it possible that the image of a relevant and challenging hope can be reborn with the gospel as midwife? Can the expectancy which lies at the heart of the gospel, the refusal to regard the present as absolute or final, the belief in an open future and the confidence that grace will be given us in the future be purified and rekindled in the public realm? Can Christian faith regenerate the hope for justice? Can people again believe in promise? Is it possible in this age to spell out the relation between the hope of the Kingdom of God and the search for justice and peace in this world? Can the winds of utopia blow again in our age?

These must, I think, remain open questions. But there is also some evidence which suggests that religion is not in fact as 'mummified' as many people in the West believe. Even in cold times – perhaps especially when the atmosphere is icy – faith may still have the capacity to sustain and shape a social hope with clear political relevance. For St Paul, hope is like the pains of childbirth. The new is coming into being, and we await it with eager expectancy:

Up to the present, as we know, the whole created universe in all its parts groans as if in the pangs of childbirth. What is more, we also, to whom the Spirit is given as the firstfruits of the harvest to come, are groaning inwardly while we look forward eagerly to our adoption, our liberation from mortality. It was with this hope that we were saved. Now to see something is no longer to hope: why hope for what is already seen? But if we hope for something we do not yet see, then we look forward to it eagerly and with patience.[17]

---

[16] Cited in Jan Greven, 'The Failure of Utopian Expectations'. Typescript, 1990.
[17] Rom. 8.22–5.

This patient waiting is not at all acquiescence or resignation, but an active and confident seeking of the fulfilment of God's promises. It is the attitude that sustained Bonhoeffer both in his resistance to Hitler and in his martyrdom. He wrote just before his arrest:

There are people who regard it as frivolous, as some Christians think it impious for anyone to hope and prepare for a better earthly future. They think that the meaning of present events is chaos, disorder, and catastrophe; and in resignation or pious escapism they surrender all responsibility for reconstruction and for future generations. It may be that the day of judgement will dawn tomorrow; in that case, we shall gladly stop working for a better future, but not before.[18]

This kind of hope keeps people going when all around seems hopeless. In the South African theologian Denise Ackermann's words, 'it acts like a powerful alchemy enabling human beings to emerge from ghastly circumstances with their humanity intact . . . Hope is resistance. It actively resists the void of hopelessness.'[19]

HOPE AS VISION

Hope is inescapably a way of envisioning the future. Theology's concern with vision and with hope reminds us that it does not deal only with particular problems and policies and ethical conundrums, any more than it is concerned exclusively for the past or with the present. It is at least as concerned with the visions that provide the horizon of meaning within which a society exists, policies are formulated, and actions are taken. Vision is not theory, although most theories have an element of vision latent in them. Visions generate and sustain goals; they establish utopias, if you prefer that language. And as Rubem Alves has suggested, 'Where utopias are not imagined, ethics is reduced to solving problems within the established system.'[20] Or, even more sharply, in the words of the familiar

---

[18] Dietrich Bonhoeffer, *Letters and Papers from Prison*. London: SCM, 1971, pp. 15–16.
[19] Denise Ackermann, 'The Alchemy of Hope' in Dennis Brutus, *A Book of Hope*. Claremont, RSA: David Philip Publishers, 1992, pp. 28–9.
[20] Alves, *Theology of Human Hope*.

text, 'Where there is no vision the people perish.'[21] They perish because they are locked into the present, because they have given up seeking a better future, because in the absence of a sense of an open future, social life loses meaning and becomes an arena of unbridled selfishness. A society without vision is petty, selfish and cruel. But where there is vision and hope, in Alves's words, 'suffering loses its power to draw man to despair, and becomes the fertilising No from which the powers of bondage are destroyed for the sake of a new tomorrow.'[22]

I am not, of course, suggesting that all visions and hopes of a just order are equally good and desirable. There are competing visions, confusing visions and seductive visions in the world today, as in the past. The collapse of the East European dictatorships reminded us how a vision in many ways admirable led to dehumanising dictatorship and then decayed, eroded by its own inadequacies. Extraordinarily often, even in these secular days, social visions are couched in religious terms. I think of the vision of Martin Luther King: 'I have a dream . . . every valley shall be exalted, and every hill shall be made low . . . we will be free one day'.[23] And I also think of Margaret Thatcher's vision of the autonomous, responsible and generous individual, which she repeatedly rooted specifically in Christian conviction.

At such a time we have a responsibility to test visions and hopes, our own and others. This means for Christians that they constantly measure their vision against reality: does it help us to see the world as it is, and as it will be or might be, more clearly? Does it enable and encourage hopeful, courageous, just and loving behaviour? Does it help us to see evil, oppression and injustice for what they are, even if we benefit from them, and to respond to them with faithful steadfastness? Above all, does it challenge and enable us to do justice, and to love kindness and to walk humbly with our God?

---

[21] Prov. 29.18.   [22] Alves, *Hope*, p. 132.
[23] Martin Luther King, Speech in Washington (28 August 1963), *New York Times* (28 August 1963), 21.

Select bibliography

Ackerman, B. A. *Social Justice in the Liberal State*, New Haven: Yale University Press, c. 1980

American Friends Service Committee. *Struggle for Justice*, New York: Hill & Wang, 1971

Annas, Julia. *An Introduction to Plato's 'Republic'*, Oxford: Clarendon, 1981

Arendt, H. *The Human Condition*, Chicago: University of Chicago Press, 1958

Arens, Edmund. 'Towards a Theological Theory of Communicative Action', *Media Development*, 28:4 (1981), 12–16

Atherton, J. *Christianity and the Market*, London: SPCK, 1992

Avineri, S. and A. de-Shalit (eds.). *Communitarianism and Individualism*, Oxford: Oxford University Press, 1992

Barry, Brian. *The Liberal Theory of Justice: A Critical Examination of the Principal Doctrines in 'A Theory of Justice' by John Rawls*, Oxford: Clarendon, 1973
Liberty and Justice, Oxford: Clarendon, 1991
Justice as Impartiality, Oxford: Clarendon, 1995

Barry, N. P. *Hayek's Social and Economic Philosophy*, London: Macmillan, 1979

Barth, Karl. *Church and State [Rechtfertigung und Recht]*, London: SCM, 1939
Church Dogmatics, vol. I, *The Doctrine of the Word of God (Prolegomena to Church Dogmatics)*, Part 1, Edinburgh: T. & T. Clark, 1975

Barth, Markus. 'Jews and Gentiles: The Social Character of Justification in Paul', *Journal of Ecumenical Studies*, 5 (1968), 241–67

Bathory, Peter D. *Political Theory as Public Confession: The Social and Political Thought of St Augustine of Hippo*, New Brunswick: Transaction Books, 1981

Baynes, K. *The Normative Grounds of Social Criticism*, Albany: University of New York Press, 1992

Beckley, Harlan R. 'A Christian Affirmation of Rawls's Idea of Justice

as Fairness', Part 1, *The Journal of Religious Ethics*, 13:2 (1986), 210–42; Part II, *Journal of Religious Ethics*, 14:2 (1987), 229–46
Passion For Justice, Louisville: Westminster/John Knox Press, 1992
Benhabib, Seyla. 'The Methodological Illusions of Modern Political Theory: The Case of Rawls and Habermas', *Neue Hefte für Philosophie*, 21 (1982)
'The General and the Concrete Other: The Kohlberg-Gilligan Controversy and Feminist Theory', *Praxis International*, 5:4 (1986), 402–24
Situating the Self: Gender, Community and Postmodernism in Contemporary Ethics, New York: Routledge, 1992
Benhabib, Seyla and Drucilla Cornell (eds.). *Feminism as Critique: Essays on the Politics of Gender in Late Capitalist Societies*, Cambridge: Polity, 1987
Benne, Robert. *The Paradoxical Vision: A Public Theology for the Twenty-first Century*. Minneapolis: Fortress, 1995
Bonino, J. M. *Toward A Christian Political Ethics*, London: SCM, 1983
Browning, Don S. and Francis Schüssler Fiorenza (eds.). *Habermas, Modernity and Public Theology*, New York: Crossroad, 1992
Brueggemann, W. 'Justice – The Earthly Form of God's Holiness', *Reformed World*, 44 (1994), 13ff.
Burnside, Jonathan and Nicola Baker (eds.). *Relational Justice: Repairing the Breach*, Winchester: Waterside Press, 1994
Carter, Stephen L. *The Culture of Unbelief: How American Law and Politics Trivialize Religious Devotion*, New York: Doubleday, 1993
Cohen, Jean L. and Andrew Arato. *Civil Society and Political Theory*, Cambridge, Mass.: MIT, 1992
Commission On Social Justice. *The Justice Gap*, London: Institute of Public Policy Research, 1993
Social Justice In A Changing World, London: Institute of Public Policy Research, 1993
Social Justice: Strategies for National Renewal, London: Vintage, 1994
Daniels, Norman. (ed.). *Reading Rawls: Critical Studies on Rawls' 'A Theory of Justice'*, New York: Basic Books, 1978
Davies, J. (ed.). *God and the Marketplace*, London: Institute of Public Policy Research, 1993
Davis, Charles. *Theology and Political Society*, Cambridge: Cambridge University Press, 1980
Religion and the Making of Society, Cambridge: Cambridge University Press, 1994
Donnison, David. *A Radical Agenda: After the New Right and the Old Left*, London: Rivers Oram Press, 1991

Doppelt, Gerald. 'Rawls' Kantian Ideal and the Viability of Modern Liberalism', *Inquiry*, 31 (1988), 413–49
Dorrien, G. *Reconstructing The Common Good*, Maryknoll: Orbis, 1990
Duchrow, U. and G. Liedke. *Shalom – Biblical Perspectives on Creation, Justice and Peace*, Geneva: World Council of Churches, 1987
Dunn, J. D. G. 'The Justice of God: A Renewed Perspective on Justification by Faith', *Journal of Theological Studies*, 43:1 (1992), 1–22
Dunn, J. D. G. and A. M. Suggate. *The Justice of God*, Carlisle: Paternoster Press, 1993
Elliot, A. J. and I. Swanson (eds.). *The Renewal of Social Vision*, Occasional Papers, no. 17, Edinburgh: CTPI, 1989
Epsztein, L. *Social Justice In The Ancient Near East And The People Of The Bible*, London: SCM, 1986
Fern, Richard L. 'Religious Belief in a Rawlsian Society', *Journal of Religious Ethics*, 15:1 (1987), 34–58
'The Internal Logic of Justice,' *The Annual of the Society of Christian Ethics*, (1993), 23ff.
Forester, John. *Planning in the Face of Power*, Berkeley: University of California Press, 1989
Critical Theory, Public Policy and Planning Practice: Toward a Critical Pragmatism, Albany: State University of New York Press, 1993
Forester, John (ed.). *Critical Theory and Public Life*, Cambridge, Mass.: MIT, 1985
Forrester, D. B. *Theology and Politics*, Oxford: Blackwell, 1988
Beliefs, Values and Policies, Oxford: Clarendon, 1989
'Theological and Rational Bases for the Concept of Justice', *Societas Ethica Jahres Bericht* (1989), 9ff.
'Political Justice and Christian Theology', *Studies in Christian Ethics*, 3:1 (1990), 1–13
'Punishment and Prisons in a Morally Fragmented Society', *Studies in Christian Ethics*, 6:2 (1993), 15–30
Justice As Fairness And Justice As Generosity, Unpublished paper, 1994
Forrester, D. B. and D. Skene (eds.). *Just Sharing: A Christian Approach to the Distribution of Wealth, Income and Benefits*, London: Epworth, 1988
Friedrich, Carl J. *Transcendent Justice: The Religious Dimension of Constitutionalism*, Durham N.C.: Duke University Press, 1964
Fukuyama, Francis. *The End of History and the Last Man*. New York: Free Press, 1992
Galbraith, J. K. *The Culture of Contentment*, London: Sinclair and Stevenson, 1992

Galston, William A. *Justice and the Common Good*, Chicago: University of Chicago Press, 1980

Garcia, I. *Justice in Latin American Theology of Liberation*, Atlanta: John Knox Press, 1987

Garland, D. (ed.). *Justice, Guilt and Forgiveness in the Penal System*, Occasional Paper, no. 18, Edinburgh: CTPI, 1990

Gilligan, Carol. 'Do the Social Sciences have an Adequate Theory of Moral Development?', in R. Haan *et al.* (eds.), *Social Science as Moral Inquiry*, New York: Columbia University Press, 1982, pp. 33–51

In a Different Voice: Psychological Theory and Women's Development, 2nd edn., Cambridge, Mass.: Harvard University Press, 1993

Gray, J. *The Moral Foundations of Market Institutions*, London: Institute of Economic Affairs, 1992

Griffiths, Brian. *Morality and the Market Place*, London: Hodder & Stoughton, 1982

The Creation of Wealth, London: Hodder & Stoughton, 1984

Griggs, E. 'Hayek on Freedom and the Welfare State', *Politics*, 11:1 (1991), 37ff.

Gutierrez, G. *A Theology of Liberation*, London: SCM, 1974

The Power of the Poor in History, SCM Press, London, 1983

Habermas, Jürgen. *The Theory of Communicative Action*. 2 vols., tr. Thomas McCarthy, Boston: Beacon Press, 1984–7

'Justice and Solidarity: On the Discussion Concerning Stage 6', in Thomas E. Wren (ed.), *The Moral Domain: Essays in the Ongoing Discussion between Philosophy and the Social Sciences*, Cambridge, Mass.: MIT, 1990, pp. 224–52

Justification and Application: Remarks on Discourse Ethics, Cambridge, Mass.: MIT, 1993

Harris, Lord *et al.*, *The New Right and Christian Values*, Edinburgh: CTPI, 1985

Hauerwas, Stanley. *After Christendom?* Nashville: Abingdon, 1991

Haughey, J. C. 'Jesus as the Justice of God', in J. C. Haughey (ed.), *The Faith That Does Justice*, New York: Paulist Press, 1977, pp. 264–90

Hayek, F. A. *Law, Legislation and Liberty*, 3 vols. in 1, London: Routledge & Kegan Paul, 1982

New Studies in Philosophy, Politics, Economics and the History of Ideas, London: Routledge & Kegan Paul, 1982

Heller, A. *Beyond Justice*, Oxford: Blackwell, 1987

Hollenback, David. *Justice, Peace and Human Rights: American Catholic Social Ethics in a Pluralistic Context*, New York: Crossroad, 1988

Hoover, Kenneth and R. Plant. *Conservative Capitalism in Britain and the United States*, London: Routledge & Kegan Paul, 1989

Hughes, G. A. *et al. The Economics of Hard Choices: Justice and the Market*, Occasional Paper, no. 21, Edinburgh: CTPI, 1991

Ignatieff, M. *The Needs of Strangers*, London: Chatto & Windus, 1984

Jackson, Timothy P. 'To Bedlam and Part Way Back: John Rawls and Christian Justice', *Faith and Philosophy*, 8:4 (1991), pp. 423–47

'Liberalism and *Agape*', *The Annual of the Society of Christian Ethics*, (1993), 47ff.

Jantzen, G. 'Connection or Competition – Identity and Personhood in Feminist Ethics', *Studies in Christian Ethics*, 5:1 (1992), 1–20

Jones, L. Gregory. 'Should Christians Affirm Rawls' Justice as Fairness? A Response to Professor Beckley', *Journal of Religious Ethics*, 16:2 (1988), 251–71

Embodying Forgiveness: A Theological Analysis, Grand Rapids: Eerdmans, 1995

Joseph Rowntree Foundation. *Inquiry Into Income and Wealth*, 2 vols., York: Joseph Rowntree Foundation, 1995

Jubilee Policy Group. *Relational Justice*, Insight, no. 7, Cambridge: Jubilee Policy Group, 1994

Kairos Theologians. *Challenge To The Church*, London: British Council of Churches/Catholic Institute for International Relations, 1986

Kamenka, Eugene and Alice Erh-Soon Tay (eds.). *Justice*, London: Edward Arnold, 1979

Lamb, Matthew L. *Solidarity with Victims: Toward a Theology of Social Transformation*, New York: Crossroad, 1982

Lane, Robert E. 'Market Justice, Political Justice', *American Political Science Review*, 80:2 (June 1986), 383–402

Lebacqz, K. 'Justice, Economics And The Uncomfortable Kingdom', *Annual of the Society for Christian Ethics*, (1983), 27ff.

Six Theories of Justice, Minneapolis: Augsburg, 1986

The Three Rs of Justice, Oxford: Oxford Institute for Church and Society, 1986

Justice in an Unjust World, Minneapolis: Augsburg, 1987

Leonard, Stephen T. *Critical Theory in Political Practice*, Princeton: Princeton University Press, 1990

Lutheran World Federation. *Justification Today (Studies and Reports)*, Supplement to *Lutheran World*, 12:1 (1965)

MacIntyre, Alasdair. *After Virtue: A Study in Moral Theory*, London: Duckworth, 1981

Whose Justice? Which Rationality?, London: Duckworth, 1988

Macpherson, C. B. *The Political Theory of Possessive Individualism*, Oxford: Oxford University Press, 1962

May, William F. *The Physician's Covenant: Images of the Healer in Medical Ethics*, Philadelphia: Westminster Press, 1983
Mays, J. L. 'Justice – Perspectives from the Prophetic Tradition', *Interpretation*, (1983), 5ff.
McCarthy, Thomas. *The Critical Theory of Jürgen Habermas*, London: Hutchinson, 1978
McClendon, J. W. *Systematic Theology – Ethics*, Nashville: Abingdon, 1988
McDonald, J. I. H. *Biblical Interpretation And Christian Ethics*, Cambridge: Cambridge University Press, 1993
Meeks, M. D. *God The Economist*, Minneapolis: Fortress Press, 1989
Metz, Johannes Baptist. *Faith in History and Society: Toward a Practical Fundamental Theology*. Burns & Oates, 1980
Miller, David. *Social Justice*, Oxford: Clarendon, 1979
Miranda, José P. *Marx and the Bible: A Critique of the Philosophy of Oppression*, London: SCM, 1974
Mitchell, Joshua. *Not by Reason Alone: Religion, History and Identity in Early Modern Political Thought*, Chicago: University of Chicago Press, 1993
Moltmann, J. 'Justice for Victims and Perpetrators', *Reformed World*, 44 (1994), 2ff.
Moore, Barrington, Jnr. *Injustice: The Social Bases of Obedience and Revolt*, New York: M. E. Sharpe, 1978
Mortensen, V. (ed.). *Justice and Justification*, Geneva: Lutheran World Federation, 1992
Murphy, J. G. and J. Hampton. *Forgiveness and Mercy*, Cambridge: Cambridge University Press, 1988
Newbigin, L. 'Whose Justice?', *Ecumenical Review*, 44 (1992), 308–11
Niebuhr, Reinhold. *An Interpretation of Christian Ethics*, London: SCM, 1936
The Nature and Destiny of Man, 2 vols., London: Nisbet, 1941–3
Novak, D. 'Economics And Justice' in P. Berger (ed.), *The Capitalist Spirit*, San Francisco: ICS Press, 1990
Novak, M. *The Spirit of Democratic Capitalism*, New York: Simon & Schuster, 1982
Free Persons and the Common Good, Lanham, Md.: Madison Books, 1989
The Catholic Ethic and The Spirit of Capitalism, New York: Free Press, 1993
Nozick, R. *Anarchy, State and Utopia*, Oxford: Blackwell, 1974
O'Keefe, M. 'Authentic Relationships – Justice, Love and Spirituality', *New Blackfriars*, (1995), 30ff.
Okin, Susan M. *Justice, Gender and the Family*, New York: Basic Books, 1989

'Reason and Feeling in Thinking about Justice', *Ethics*, 99 (Jan. 1989), 229–49

Outhwaite, William. *Habermas: A Critical Introduction*, Stanford: Stanford University Press, 1994

Perelman, C. *The Idea of Justice and the Problem of Argument*, London: Routledge, 1963
Justice, Law and Argument, Dordrecht: D. Reidel, 1980

Pettit, Philip. 'Habermas on Truth and Justice' in G. H. R. Parkinson (ed.), *Marx and Marxisms*, Cambridge: Cambridge University Press, 1982, pp. 207–28

Peukert, H. *Science, Action and Fundamental Theology: Toward a Theology of Communicative Action*, Cambridge, Mass.: MIT, 1984

Phillips, D. *Towards a Just Social Order*, Princeton, Princeton University Press, 1986

Plant, R. *Social Justice, Labour and the New Right*, Fabian Pamphlet 556, London: Fabian Society, 1993

Plant, R. and N. Barry. *Citizenship and Rights in Thatcher's Britain*, London: Institute of Economic Affairs, 1990

Potter, Harry. *Hanging in Judgement: Religion and the Death Penalty in England*, London: SCM, 1993

Preston, R. *Religion and the Ambiguities of Capitalism*, London: SCM, 1991
Confusions in Christian Social Ethics, London: SCM, 1994

Raban, Jonathan. *God, Man and Mrs Thatcher*, London: Chatto & Windus, 1989

Raffel, Stanley. *Habermas, Lyotard and the Concept of Justice*, London: Macmillan, 1992

Rakowski, Eric. *Equal Justice*, Oxford: Clarendon, 1991

Raphael, D. D. *Justice and Liberty*, London: Athlone Press, 1980

Rawls, J. 'Justice as Fairness', *Philosophical Review*, 67:2 (April 1958), 164–94
A Theory of Justice, Oxford: Oxford University Press, 1972
'Kantian Constructivism in Moral Theory', *Journal of Philosophy*, 77:9 (Sept. 1980), 515–72
'Justice as Fairness: Political not Metaphysical', *Philosophy and Public Affairs*, 14:3 (Summer 1985), 223–51
'The Idea of an Overlapping Consensus', *Oxford Journal of Legal Studies*, 7 (1987)
'The Priority of Right and Ideas of the Good', *Philosophy and Public Affairs*, 17:4 (1988), 251–76
'The Domain of the Political and Overlapping Consensus', *New York University Law Review*, 64:2 (May 1989), 233–55
Political Liberalism, New York: Columbia University Press, 1993

Reventlow, H. G. and Y. Hoffman (eds.). *Justice and Righteousness*, Sheffield: Sheffield Academic Press, 1992

Ricoeur, Paul. *Oneself as Another*, Chicago: University of Chicago Press, 1992

Rifkind, M. *et al. Law and Order – Prospects for the Future*, Occasional Paper, no. 10, Edinburgh: CTPI, 1986

Runciman, W. G. *Relative Deprivation and Social Justice: A Study of Attitudes to Social Inequality in Twentieth-Century England*, Berkeley: University of California Press, 1966

Ryan, A. (ed.). *Justice*, Oxford: Oxford University Press, 1993

Sandel, Michael J. *Liberalism and the Limits of Justice*, Cambridge: Cambridge University Press, 1982

Schlosberg, David. 'Communicative Action in Practice: Intersubjectivity and New Social Movements', *Political Studies*, 43:2 (June 1995), 291–311

Schluter, Michael and David Lee. *The R-Factor*, London: Hodder & Stoughton, 1993

Schrey, W. *'Dike* etc', in G. Kittel and G. Friedrich (eds.). *Theological Dictionary of The New Testament*, Grand Rapids: Eerdmans, 1964–74

Shklar, Judith N. *The Faces of Injustice*, New Haven: Yale University Press, 1990

Siebert, Rudolph J. *The Critical Theory of Religion: The Frankfurt School*, Berlin: Mouton, 1985

Smit, Reynaud de la Bat. *The Justice of God and the Formation of Society*, Unpublished PhD thesis, University of Durham, 1993

Sterba, J. P. 'Recent Work on Alternative Conceptions of Justice', *American Philosophical Quarterly*, 23:1 (1986), 1ff.

Stout, Jeffrey. *Ethics after Babel*, Boston: Beacon, 1988

Talbott, T. 'Punishment, Forgiveness and Divine Justice', *Religious Studies*, 29 (1993), 151–68

Tanner, K. *The Politics Of God*, Minneapolis: Fortress Press, 1992

Thiemann, Ronald F. *Constructing a Public Theology: The Church in a Pluralistic Culture*, Louisville: Westminster/John Knox, 1991

Religion in American Public Life: A Dilemma for Democracy, forthcoming

Thompson, John B. and David Held (eds.). *Habermas: Critical Debates*, Cambridge, Mass.: MIT, 1982

Tillich, P. *Love, Power and Justice*, Oxford: Oxford University Press, 1954; New York: Oxford University Press, 1960

Unger, Roberto M. *Knowledge and Politics*, New York: Free Press, 1975

US Catholic Bishops. *Economic Justice for All: Catholic Social Teaching and the US Economy*, Washington: National Conference of Catholic Bishops, 1986

Vecchio, Georgio del. *Justice: An Historical and Philosophical Esssay*, Edinburgh: Edinburgh University Press, 1953

Walker, G. *The Ethics of F. A. Hayek*, Lanham, Md.: University Press of America, 1986

Weinreb, Lloyd L. *Natural Law and Justice*, Cambridge, Mass.: Harvard University Press, 1987

White, Stephen K. *The Recent Work of Jürgen Habermas: Reason, Justice and Modernity*, Cambridge: Cambridge University Press, 1988

Willmer, H. 'Forgiveness and Politics', *Crucible* (July–Sept 1979), 100–5 'The Politics of Forgiveness – A New Dynamic', *Furrow*, 30 (1979), 207

Wolff, R P. *Understanding Rawls*, Princeton: Princeton University Press, 1977

Wolterstorff, N. *Until Justice and Peace Embrace*, Grand Rapids: Eerdmans, 1983

Wood, C. *The End of Punishment: Christian Perspectives on the Crisis in Criminal Justice*, Edinburgh: CTPI/St Andrew Press, 1991

Woodhead, L. 'Love and Justice', in *Studies in Christian Ethics*, 5:1 (1992), 44–61

Wootton, B. *The Social Foundations of Wages Policy: A Study of Contemporary British Wage and Salary Structure*, London: Allen & Unwin, 1962

Woozley, A. D. 'Injustice', *American Philosophical Quarterly*, Monograph 7, Oxford: Blackwell, 1973, 109–22

Yoder, J H. *The Christian Witness to the State*, Newton: Faith & Life Press, 1964 *The Politics Of Jesus*, Grand Rapids: Eerdmans, 1972

Zorilla, H. *The Good News Of Justice*, Scottdale, Pa.: Herald Press, 1988

Subject index

References are to page numbers, and 'n' after a page number indicates that information may be found in a note on that page: 25n33 means note 33 on page 25.

Name index